Distributed by
Harvard University Press

MY HARVARD LIBRARY YEARS

1937–1955

A Sequel to
Random Recollections of an Anachronism

by

Keyes DeWitt Metcalf

Edited by Edwin E. Williams
with a Foreword by
Margaret Beckman

Harvard College Library
Cambridge, Massachusetts
1988

ISBN 0-674-59600-5

Preface

In July 1983, as soon as I had finished editing the manuscript of this volume, Keyes telephoned to Margaret Beckman, at the University of Guelph, asking her to write a Foreword. She agreed; I sent her a copy of the manuscript; and Keyes received her Foreword during August. He then discovered, however, that Readex Books, which had published *Random Recollections of an Anachronism*, covering the first 48 years of his life, would be unable to publish this volume. He was not well, and had made no arrangements for publication at the time of his death, on 3 November 1983. Fortunately the Harvard College Library has found it possible to take over the role of publisher.

In the Preface that he had prepared for this volume, Keyes wrote:

> This is the second volume, containing Part III, of my Random Recollections. It covers the years from 1937 to 1955, during which I was Director of the Harvard University Library and Librarian of Harvard College.
>
> When the first volume was published by Readex Books, a division of Readex Microprint Corporation, the President of the Corporation, William Boni, placed on the book-jacket a statement that I intended to go ahead with preparation of another volume to cover the period after I left the New York Public Library. This was described as a "calculated risk," because I was ninety-one when the first volume appeared. Volume 2 is now ready; but too many of us in our nineties, or even in our eighties, become verbose, and this volume will not cover the period after 1955.
>
> Consequently I am at work on Volume 3. It will cover a period during which my life was quite different from that of a library administrator, which I had been for fifty years. Since 1955 I have had more than 550 consulting assignments, mostly in academic libraries. There have not been 550 institutions, because in many cases I have been called back a number of times to the same place. Building planning has been my primary field of consultation, but many of the assignments have dealt with library problems of other kinds.
>
> The eighteen years at Harvard, as reported in this volume, include a constant struggle to improve the staff and to balance the budget during the difficult war period and the austere years that followed. This volume goes into some detail on the three new library buildings at Harvard for which I was responsible. Outside activities, including consultation for a variety of

libraries and work on behalf of library associations, are covered, as well as my preparations for retirement.

Mrs. Florence Pacl has patiently typed and re-typed draft after draft of the manuscript, as she did for much of the first volume. Ed Williams again edited the volume and prepared the index. Elinor, my wife, has for several more years had less attention from me than she should have had. To each of them, my heartfelt gratitude is given.

As he said in the third paragraph that has been quoted, Keyes had begun work on a third volume, covering the post-retirement years after 1955; but he had not progressed very far, and only he could write his recollections of more than 550 consulting assignments, plus teaching at Rutgers and Columbia and other activities of more than a quarter-century. There will be no third volume of recollections; but his architectural archives have been deposited at the School of Library and Information Studies of the Florida State University, Tallahassee, so material is available for research on these years.

I am indebted for editorial help to Kenneth E. Carpenter, Assistant Director for Research Resources in the Harvard University Library.

Edwin E. Williams

Cambridge, Massachusetts,
January 1988

Foreword

For those of us who came to academic librarianship after the second World War, "Keyes Metcalf" has been synonymous with "library buildings," and the definitive work, *Planning Academic and Research Library Buildings*, is a necessary touchstone for all manner of space problems or space planning, whether at library school or in administrative careers. This second volume of the Keyes DeWitt Metcalf autobiography is therefore most welcome, for it reveals what those who have been privileged to know or to work with him have always known: his concern for buildings has been neither primary nor independent. Here, in a fashion that is both subtle and wise, Mr. Metcalf reveals the essence of complete librarianship, providing examples, better than any case study could do, for librarians who want to understand the complexities of academic library administration.

I first saw Keyes Metcalf at the ALA Library Building Institute in Atlantic City in 1969, when a team from the University of Guelph was presenting its McLaughlin Library to the conference. Since some previously untested lighting and furniture concepts were included in the building, I watched for audience reaction as my architect colleague, Stephen Langmead, completed his part of the program. As slides of the movable bookstacks were flashed on the screen, I could not fail to notice an elderly gentleman slowly shaking his head in disagreement, and I whispered as Stephen took his seat on the platform: "Keyes Metcalf does not approve."

It was with some trepidation, therefore, that Stephen and I approached Mr. Metcalf two years later, at an IFLA Library Building Conference in Lausanne, Switzerland, and asked him to accept a copy of our new book on library design, based on the McLaughlin Library experience. Mr. Metcalf could not have been kinder, and, as part of a small group of English-speaking architects and librarians attending the Conference, we established a lasting friendship. Keyes — and it is impossible to call him Mr. Metcalf for very long — discussed the McLaughlin Library with interest and perception, and insisted that he come to the University of Guelph to view the building's controversial design features for himself when next in Canada. His visit the following September, during which he inspected and measured all aspects of the library building, also afforded the opportunity for discussions of the implications of library automation, and for comparisons between American and Canadian approaches to a variety of academic library concerns.

Since that time, I have attended other Library Building Institutes or ARL meetings with Keyes and have visited him and Mrs. Metcalf in their home in Belmont, Massachusetts. He has rushed me around libraries from Harvard to Rome, and we have discussed building planning, new technologies, catalogue codes, or librarians — good, bad, and indifferent — in hotels, airports, and in a growing correspondence. Always I have learned and have been the richer for his willingness to share his experiences, his successes and his mistakes.

Now that opportunity is available to everyone, as the former Director of the Harvard University Library and Librarian of Harvard College identifies the problems and describes the solutions he recommended during his tenure there from 1937 to 1955. The problems were many and varied but were really no different, albeit on a larger scale, from those any new university librarian might face. Mr. Metcalf placed immediate priority on securing a superior staff and explains how he carefully went about this task so that he would have a team he could depend on as he addressed the other important issues.

He analyzed the collections, their funding and selection methodologies, and set processes in motion to ensure broader discipline coverage as well as sounder financial support. No area of the Harvard library system escaped his attention, from catalogue card production to placement of the Widener circulation desk and to reserve book procedures. Encounters with the Duke of Windsor and Joe McCarthy, with recalcitrant faculty members and with difficult donors were also in his day's work, and his enjoyment of each and every aspect of librarianship is delightfully evident.

Finally, Mr. Metcalf turned to space, and in addition to planning the Houghton Library for rare books, the Lamont Library for undergraduates, and renovations to the Widener Library, he investigated improved and increased use of microfilm for newspaper storage and other space-saving ideas. His assessment of the costs of a cooperative storage library, including different shelving methodologies or space designs, is as valid today as when the New England Deposit Library was first launched in 1942.

In a foreword to the final library report which Keyes Metcalf wrote for Harvard University prior to his retirement, President Pusey noted: "Mr. Metcalf has set reasonable and realistic goals in his factual report on Harvard's problems. Even he, as one used to turning dissatisfaction into success, would be the first to wonder whether all could be achieved. But they are there to be sought as Mr. Metcalf has quietly and plainly indicated."

The "Harvard Years" of Keyes Metcalf's *Random Recollections* also sets forth goals and points directions, not just for Harvard but for all libraries and for all librarians. How fortunate we are to have the benefit of his wisdom and experience.

Margaret Beckman
University of Guelph, Canada
August 1983

MY HARVARD
LIBRARY YEARS

Contents

		Page
Introduction		*xv*
Chapter 1	Getting Acquainted at Harvard, September 1937 to August 1938	*1*
	The Office	
	Staff and Faculty	
	Libraries of the Graduate Professional Schools	
	Other Harvard Libraries	
	The Community	
	Death of Martha Gerrish Metcalf	
Chapter 2	First Year at Harvard: Staff Problems	*15*
Chapter 3	First Year at Harvard: Space Problems	*24*
Chapter 4	Special Projects of 1938–1941	*31*
	The International Documentation Institute	
	Foreign Newspapers	
	The Second Edition of the Union List of Serials	
	Experiment with a Photostat Machine	
	Duplication of Cards	
Chapter 5	Acquisitions	*41*
	The Howells Collection	
	The Trotsky Archives	
	Ruth Fischer	
	Israel Perlstein	
	Other Material from the USSR	
	The Theodore Roosevelt Collection	
	Hebraica and Judaica	
	Other College Library Collections	

Walter Lippmann
Disappointments

Chapter 6   Cooperative Storage Problems   56
             The New England Deposit Library
             The Midwest Inter-Library Center
             The Proposal for a Northeastern Regional
               Library

Chapter 7   The Houghton Library   71

Chapter 8   The Lamont Library   80

Chapter 9   Building Problems and Changes in Buildings   92
             Fire Protection
             Water Hazards
             Atmospheric Conditions
             Theft, Unauthorized Borrowing, and Van-
               dalism
             Lighting
             Other Building Changes

Chapter 10   James Bryant Conant   110

Chapter 11   The Library Staff After 1938   120
             Harvard Men Who Became Librarians
             Appointments of 1939–1942
             Appointments of the Later 1940s
             Appointments of the 1950s
             Reflections and Regrets

Chapter 12   The Council, the Faculty, and the Faculty Library
               Committee   136

Chapter 13   Libraries of Departments, Research Institutions,
               and Faculties Other Than Arts and Sciences   142
             The Law School Library
             The Business School: Baker Library
             The Medical School Library
             The Andover-Harvard Library of the Divinity
               School

The Graduate School of Education
The Graduate School of Design
Fine Arts
The Harvard-Yenching Institute
Other Harvard Libraries

Chapter 14   Service on *Ad Hoc* University Committees   151
              The War Defense Committee
              Directorship of the Fogg Museum
              The Harvard University Press

Chapter 15   Three Librarians of Congress   160
              Archibald MacLeish
              Luther Evans
              L. Quincy Mumford

Chapter 16   Department Libraries in Washington   181
              The Surgeon General's Library and Its Suc-
              cessors
              The Army and Navy Libraries
              Other Libraries in Washington

Chapter 17   Peru   191

Chapter 18   The Farmington Plan and the Library of Congress
              Mission   200
              Origins of the Farmington Plan
              The Library of Congress Mission
              The Beginning of Farmington Plan Opera-
              tions
              1950: My Farmington Plan Trip to Europe

Chapter 19   Library Association Assignments   221
              The American Library Association
              The Association of Research Libraries
              The Monticello Conference
              Senator Joseph McCarthy

Chapter 20   Miscellaneous Incidents, 1939–1955   230
              John Langdon Sibley
              Radcliffe College

The Installation of President Pusey in 1953
Local Residents
Three Proper Bostonians
Distinguished Visitors
Honors and Awards

Chapter 21   Assignments Resulting from My Position at Harvard   242
                   Boston Public Library Visiting Committee
                   Massachusetts State Library Trustee
                   Stockholder of the Harvard Cooperative
                      Society
                   The American Academy of Arts and Sciences
                      and the Linda Hall Library

Chapter 22   Other Consultation Assignments of the 1940s   252
                   The University of Illinois Library School
                   The Wisconsin State Historical Society and
                      the University of Wisconsin Library
                   The Columbia University Library
                   The University of Pennsylvania Library
                   The New York State Library at Albany
                   The University of Minnesota Library

Chapter 23   Preparation for Retirement and Selection of a Suc-
                   cessor   264
                   Selection of a Successor
                   Report on the Harvard University Library
                   Options After Retirement

Index   273

Introduction

In 1937, when I became Director of the Harvard University Library and Librarian of Harvard College, Harvard had the oldest, the largest and, I believe, the best university library in the United States. The institution that became Harvard College was founded in 1636. In 1638, a young clergyman named John Harvard, who had come to New England the year before, died at the age of 31, leaving his library of 400 volumes and half of his estate, worth approximately £800, to the new college, which later was named for him. During the following 126 years, with little money if any available for books or staff, the Library grew slowly. The collection consisted in large part of theological treatises and textbooks bequeathed by ministers who had graduated from the institution. There were some 14,000 volumes, a large library for that period, by 1764, when a fire destroyed Harvard Hall, which housed the Library as well as classrooms. Only about 400 books survived, including a single volume from John Harvard's bequest; these were on loan at the time of the fire. The Library still has a record of the books charged out then; in the late 1940s, when I had the pleasure of receiving one of these books from a distant descendant of the man who had borrowed it in 1764, I was able to find a record of the loan. The man who returned it said that he had found it in his father's library, which had come down through previous generations of his family. We did not ask him to pay a fine on the overdue volume.

Thomas Hollis, of Lincoln's Inn, continued to give the Library well-chosen books from time to time after the fire of 1764; he had many of them nicely bound, with a symbol on the binding of each book indicating its subject; an owl designated theology and, if Hollis disapproved of the author's views, he instructed his bookbinder to stamp the owl upside down. Hollis died in 1774, leaving a bequest of £500 to establish the Library's first endowed book fund, which is still providing income for current acquisitions.

A small group of Harvard graduates went to Germany for advanced study during the second decade of the nineteenth century. One of them was George Ticknor, who many years later was more responsible than anyone else for the founding of the Boston Public Library, our first large tax-supported library. Another was Joseph Green Cogswell, who persuaded a wealthy merchant, Israel Thorndike, to purchase for Harvard a great collection of books and maps relating to American history that had been assembled by a professor and librarian at Hamburg, Christoph Daniel Ebeling. Soon after Cogswell returned from Germany in 1820, President Kirkland asked him to become Librarian of Harvard College. He accepted and, two years later, reported to the President that he had reclassified and recatalogued the books for the last time. (Evidently he was not then an experienced librarian.) He also urged that Harvard build up a library collection similar in scale to the one at Göttingen, adequate to serve both undergraduate instruction and research. Kirkland was one of Harvard's better presidents, but he did not accept this recommendation, and Cogswell resigned.

At Northampton, Massachusetts, Cogswell was a teacher and administrator in the Round Hill School, which might be called the first progressive school in this country. Later he became acquainted with Samuel Ward, a New York banker who was the father of Julia Ward Howe. Ward introduced him to John Jacob Astor. After having been closely associated with Astor for a good many years, Cogswell persuaded him to provide money to start a reference library in New York City. When he died in 1848, Astor left a bequest for this purpose, and Cogswell organized the Astor Library, which was combined with the Lenox Library and the Tilden Foundation to form the New York Public Library in 1895.

The Harvard Library did not begin to collect all kinds of printed materials on a large scale until John Langdon Sibley became Librarian in 1856. Relatively little was purchased, because endowed book funds had not grown large enough to build a research library. Ransacking houses throughout the Boston area and soliciting gifts from Harvard graduates everywhere, Sibley built up a collection of books and pamphlets that made a good foundation for a university library. When he retired, the collection had quadrupled in size during his twenty-one-year administration, and endowment funds had increased to about $215,000.

Justin Winsor, who succeeded Sibley in 1877, had been Librarian of the Boston Public Library for ten years and was president of the American Library Association from its organization in 1876 until 1885; he was also a distinguished historian. He continued Sibley's work; endowment funds increased to more than $850,000 during his administration, and, when he died in 1897, Harvard's library was no longer insignificant compared to those of European universities. The next Librarian of Harvard College was William Coolidge Lane.

Even before Winsor's death, Archibald Cary Coolidge, a history professor at Harvard and one of the great builders of collections — in a class with Cogswell, John Shaw Billings, and Harry Lydenberg — had begun to use his own funds and those of his well-to-do friends to make large purchases, often of ready-made collections, chiefly in Europe, including Russia. Later, in cooperation with the New York Public Library and Northwestern University, he took the lead in one of the first cooperative acquisition enterprises, which was in Latin American history and literature. In 1910, he became the first Director of the Harvard University Library; one reason for the appointment was President Lowell's hope that Coolidge would be able to bring about better cooperation between the College Library and the many specialized libraries that had grown up independently throughout the University.

Following Coolidge's death in 1928, Robert Pierpont Blake became Director. William Coolidge Lane, disappointed at not receiving this appointment, retired the same year, and was succeeded as Librarian of Harvard College by Alfred Claghorn Potter, whose forty-year career in the Harvard Library was chiefly devoted to book selection from second-hand catalogs, filling many gaps in fields in which the Library was strong. Potter retired in 1936, and Blake wished to return to teaching and research. In 1937, consequently, I was the first person to be appointed both Director of the Harvard University Library and Librarian of Harvard College.

Chapter 1

Getting Acquainted at Harvard
September 1937 to August 1938

O N 1 SEPTEMBER 1937, when I came to my desk in Harvard's Widener Library, I began the most exciting year of my life since 1919, my first year in the Director's outer office at the New York Public Library. While my experience in practically all phases of library work at Oberlin and New York had been unusually broad, I had always worked under the immediate direction of someone else in the same building, except for the two periods at Oberlin when I was in charge but took no initiative and simply tried to do what I thought Professor Root would have done if he had been there. I had no direct relationship with the trustees at either Oberlin or New York. I had very little social life except for informal conversation with the younger men on the New York staff, sitting around a table in the staff cafeteria, or with senior members of the staff on weekend hikes, particularly those in the Catskills. (I had served as president of the local grade-school PTA in White Plains, and also as president of the New York Area Oberlin College Alumni Association Club.) I owned a dress suit, which I had worn only a very few times at library meetings and other formal events. I had never joined in the poker games that were enjoyed by some of my peers late in the evening at meetings of the American Library Association or Association of Research Libraries.

Cambridge provided a new and very different life for me and my family. My realization that this would be the case was one reason why I had hesitated to come to Harvard. Fortunately my fears were ill founded, and I think it is fair to say that Mart and I took to our new and different life "like ducks to water" (our two children were in college at Oberlin); but we avoided social involvements except for those connected with my library work.

THE OFFICE

Helen Powers, who continued as the Director's secretary, had been Coolidge's secretary during the last ten years of his administration and had been with Blake throughout his régime. As he had told me, and as experience was to demonstrate, she was an expert stenographer and typist, and could manage French and German as well as English. She worked very rapidly when speed was required. She seemed to know everyone connected with the University, and this was extremely valuable to me. The chief drawback, as far as I was concerned, was that she was a compulsive talker, and I found it difficult to dictate to her because she would so often break in with irrelevant remarks. Consequently, I resorted to a dictating machine throughout the eighteen years that followed, much to her disappointment. Her desk was in an outer office, but, with the door open, we could see each other and were within easy call. She was not the best of filers but almost always came up with what I requested. Still, I could understand why Paul Buck shifted her to another position after he succeeded me in 1955; with his long experience at Harvard, he did not need the store of information that was at her command.

When calling on Blake during each of the two previous academic years, I had seen the room that was to be my office. The equipment layout did not suit me for several reasons, but the room was large, with an agreeable outlook. A big window on the north looked out toward Memorial Church beyond the trees and grass of the Tercentenary Theatre, and there was another window to the west. (My office window in New York opened onto a paved court eighty feet square.) But the desk used by my predecessors at Harvard was not even a full-size executive desk, and had drawers on only one side of the kneehole. It did not take advantage of the view, but faced a door in one corner of the office, behind which there was a small room containing a wash-basin and some coat-hooks. Blake had left his personal collection of Georgian (Transcaucasian) books in dull bindings on shelves that filled the east wall except for the door that has been mentioned. These books were removed a year or two later.

I asked John Shea, the building superintendent, if a larger desk was available. He took me up to the Winsor Map Room on the top floor, where there was a desk so large that it had kneeholes on all four sides, with a row of drawers on each side of the narrower ends but only a shallow drawer for pencils and other small useful objects over the kneehole on each of the long sides. I decided to sit at one of the long sides so as not to be tempted to use the tier of drawers. Everything that was not in the hands of my secretary remained on top of the desk; I examined what was there at least once a day and kept it in a reasonably tidy condition. When I first saw it, the desk had a torn cloth top over oak. It was a little weak in the joints from sitting in the sunlight that came through a south window for many of its sixty years; but I used it for eighteen years after the maintenance staff had touched up the finish and put a new heavy cloth covering on top. (In more recent years it was used by Louis Martin, the Librarian of Harvard College, until he left in 1979 to become director of the Cornell University Library.) My pleasure in it was increased when Edward Gookin, the Library's Registrar, told me that he had started his library career more than forty years earlier when still in his teens as Justin Winsor's secretary, and that this had then been Winsor's desk. He added that Winsor had a superstructure on it for use when he was working with maps, one of his specialties. Gookin then pulled out a sliding shelf over one of the tiers of drawers, turned it over, and showed me where Winsor had written "Purchased in November, 1877," followed by his signature. Gookin went on to tell me that, as Winsor's secretary, he had been assigned the first typewriter used in the Library. He also pointed out Winsor's rule book, one of the few books then on the north wall of the office. It listed in chronological order the regulations which Winsor had promulgated. One of these, when the Library first installed a telephone, strictly forbade its use for personal business.

My predecessor had used what is known as a Harvard chair, a typical "Mother Hubbard" chair. It was comfortable and sturdy, but I did not want to use it because I knew I would be getting up and down many times a day, and this kind of chair would be hard to swing around. I ordered a swivel chair that would turn around easily, but first I tried the chair that Alfred Potter had used during his many years as Assistant Librarian in charge of the Order Department and later as Librarian of Harvard College. It had wheels on the two back legs that swivelled; he could swing around fairly easily, but the wheels changed the level of the seat, forcing him to lean forward over the desk, which I found uncomfortable. When I dictated I wanted to sit back and turn to look out the window and see the grass, trees, and Memorial Church. Clarence Walton suggested that a "Governor Winthrop" desk he had recently brought from Sarah Orne Jewett's house in Maine, long after her death, together with such books and furniture as the Library could use, would fit into the outside corner of the room, and this desk was placed there with the Potter chair next to it. In the same corner I hung on the wall pictures of those of my predecessors in whom I was particularly interested — Joseph Green Cogswell (he looked like a character depicted by Cruikshank for one of Dickens' novels), John Langdon Sibley, Justin Winsor, Archibald Cary Coolidge, and William Coolidge Lane. I then filled the vacant shelves with books about Harvard, including the historical works prepared by Samuel Eliot Morison for the Harvard Tercentenary, which had taken place the previous year, and a long file of Harvard class reports, containing autobiographical accounts by the alumni. To these I added copies of the Library's publications and other material relating to the Library and the University.

I found a small, wooden, two-shelf bookcase, put it beside my desk chair, and filled it with books that I knew I would want to consult again and again, including the latest *Who's Who in Library Service*, a small dictionary, and a Harvard catalog. I think that about half of my simple reference questions could be answered by the books on these two shelves, and half of the remainder from books shelved elsewhere in the office.

Walton suggested that he ask friends of Harvard to give us a large rug for the floor, but I said "no." We wanted books, manuscripts, and endowment funds, not furniture.

STAFF AND FACULTY

My next task was to become acquainted with members of the Widener staff, and I made it a point to talk to and remember the name of each one as I had done in New York. During the next few months I was able to talk at length with all those in supervisory positions about the persons reporting to them. I regularly made a daily visit to every part of the Library where there was a staff member, and spoke to each as I went past. I made it clear that all were welcome to come to see me individually or in groups, but that I would never make a decision affecting them without talking to the person to whom they reported. There were so many new names and faces that I was surprised at my ability to remember each of them. This is a talent that has been lost as I have grown older.

In my tours of the Widener building I followed my natural inclination, walking or running up and down stairs instead of taking one of the six widely scattered elevators. This, I later found, had been a mistake, because I did not learn at first hand of the inefficiency of the elevators and was not aware of it until there were complaints.

I knew that I ought to become acquainted with the senior faculty members and administrative officers of the University as rapidly as possible. The Faculty Club was only a few minutes' walk from Widener; I regularly went there for lunch and, unless I had a special appointment, sat at the long table frequented by those in administrative positions. This very useful practice continued until I retired. Professors and administrators talked freely, and I learned what they thought about what was happening in the University. This was a period of unrest because of slow promotion of untenured members of the faculty. Here, too, I heard for the first time about antibiotics when Alfred North Whitehead, in his eighties, rapidly recovered from an attack of pneumonia that would have been fatal a year earlier. Before it was reported in the newspapers, I learned about radar and how it served Britain during World War II. I learned why Cambridge's Fresh Pond Reservoir was kept far from full during periods of drought; by leaving more water in the city's pond in Waltham, pressure on the springs in Fresh Pond was reduced, making more water available. Many interesting and useful things could be learned at the long table.

LIBRARIES OF THE GRADUATE PROFESSIONAL SCHOOLS

I soon became concerned regarding the graduate-school libraries, that is, the libraries of faculties other than Arts and Sciences. I realized that my predecessors as Director had been expected to improve relations between these libraries and the College Library. This was not a question of physical consolidation, but of coordination of policies on book selection, staff salaries, and cataloging. Previous efforts had been relatively unsuccessful, to say the least. After visiting the chief librarians of the faculties in their own libraries, I arranged to have lunch with each of them.

I found that Blake had developed a more satisfactory relationship with the library of the Schools of Medicine and Public Health than with any of the others. He had regularly met with its library committee and had attended annual dinners with the deans and representatives of the Boston Medical Library. In 1929 they had tried to combine the latter with Harvard's medical library. A professional fund-raiser had been employed to seek money for construction of a building to house the two collections. Consolidation would have produced a medical collection surpassed in size and importance only by the Surgeon General's Library in Washington. Unfortunately, however, 1929 and 1930 were not good years for raising money, and the drive had been so unsuccessful that it had been difficult to pay even the campaign expenses. The representatives of both groups were unhappy and were inclined to be provoked with each other; but there were still hopes of consolidation. (This, unfortunately, was not to take place until some years after my retirement.) Sidney Burwell, the new dean of the Medical School, was very much interested and ready to help. Anna Holt, his librarian, was capable and easy to deal with; we became good friends, but I found that she did not get along well with James Ballard, the Boston Medical Library's elderly librarian, who had begun work there in 1892, and with the noted neurologist, Dr. Henry Viets, to whom he reported.

Harvard's Statutes made the Director of the University Library a member *ex officio* of the library committee of each of the graduate schools. I attended meetings of the Medical School's committee regularly with pleasure and profit, and was greatly impressed by a group that included Dean Burwell and George Minot, the discoverer of a cure for pernicious anemia. Not long before I came to Harvard, this committee had been able to combine almost all of the nearly twenty-five libraries of the Medical School; there had been a library for each department.

The Law School presented a different and more difficult problem. The librarian, Eldon James, was one of the great book collectors in law, as was his predecessor, John Himes Arnold. Encouraged by successive deans, Arnold and James had built up the largest and best law library in the country, with particular strength in international and in early English law. It was soon clear that, while James would be friendly, he would have nothing to do with me as Director of the Harvard University Library. He believed that in the future, as in the past, his library should be completely independent. (President Conant reports in his autobiography, *My Several Lives*, that he faced a similar attitude on the part of the Law School's dean.) James stated frankly that Coolidge had tried to give him instructions and make arrangements for purchases; he added that he had been deceived again and again by Coolidge. He said nothing about his library committee, though I knew that there was one. I became acquainted with its chairman and talked with him about his problems, but I was never notified of committee meetings, and thought it wiser to avoid an unnecessary confrontation as long as I had some influence on what was done about the library's chief problems. As will be recorded later, I had a major part in the selection of Arthur Pulling as librarian of the Law School after James left to head the Law Library at the Library of Congress. I was also able to help provide space needed by the Law Library and to arrange for better care of its wonderful rare-book collections.

The situation was still different at the library of the Graduate School of Business Administration. Dean Wallace Donham was very friendly. Arthur Cole, the Librarian, was about my age, and had been more responsible than anyone else for systematically building up its great collections. He was friendly, though Clarence Walton tried to persuade me that I would have trouble with him because Cole had been a candidate for my position as Director, had been greatly disappointed when he was not chosen, and was jealous of me. I am glad to say that there was never any trouble. Cole and I were good friends until his death only a few years ago, and he was of great value to the University Library as a whole for forty years, directing the acquisition program of Baker Library at the Business School, helping with book selection for the new Graduate School of Public Administration, and selecting additions to the economics and sociology collections in Widener Library. He helped to minimize unnecessary duplication by these libraries.

Here it should be added that, after Arthur Pulling became Librarian of the Law School in 1942, arrangements were made for regular checking of the Union Catalog in Widener by a member of the Law Library staff, and needless duplication among Harvard's four major libraries in the social sciences was further reduced. My later relations with the Business School Library will be reported in another chapter; but it should be noted here that I worked with Cole during my first year at Harvard, attending his library committee meetings and consulting with him on development of the Littauer Library at the new Graduate School of Public Administration. As explained in the last chapter of the previous volume, I had become involved in planning the building for this library during the summer before I arrived in Cambridge.

A fine scholar was librarian of the Divinity School, but personal difficulties caused him unhappiness, and he was a problem for his colleagues. Soon, fortunately, he was succeeded by Professor Henry Cadbury, who was assisted by Jannette Newhall, a very satisfactory librarian who years later became Librarian of the Boston University School of Theology and also taught there.

At the Graduate School of Education, Dean Henry W. Holmes was very much interested in the library. More than half of the education collection was in the Widener building because there was insufficient space at the School. Dean Holmes and I had many interesting and always friendly talks about the Education Library until his retirement in 1947.

The Graduate School of Design had two libraries, both in Robinson Hall but on different floors. Neither had enough space for its collections, and portions of both libraries were shelved in the Widener building until the construction of Gund Hall in the early 1970s. The College Library ordered and cataloged foreign books for these libraries. No problems arose in relations with them, and there were no special difficulties except shortage of space.

My work with the small library at Harvard's Dental School also went smoothly. It was later combined administratively with the library of the Schools of Medicine and Public Health.

An account of later developments in the libraries of the graduate professional schools will be given in Chapter 13.

OTHER HARVARD LIBRARIES

In 1937 there were nearly 1,800,000 volumes and pamphlets in the Harvard College Library, housed in the Widener building, and more than 1,215,000 in the eight libraries of graduate professional schools that have been mentioned above; in addition, there were some 860,000 in 67 other collections more or less closely connected with the Faculty of Arts and Sciences. As Librarian of Harvard College, I was directly responsible for the central collection in Widener, but the administrative status of the 67 other libraries was less clearly defined.

Only one of them, the Boylston Hall Library, a collection of reserved books for history, government, and economics, was fully attached to Widener administratively. Its librarian was John Gallen, who had been a member of the College Library staff since the early 1920s. He also watched over the Freshman Library in the Union and the seven house (dormitory) libraries. Gallen was a great asset during his nearly fifty years of service, which continued until his retirement quite a few years after mine. He had an uncanny ability to identify students who signed false names on call slips or interfered in other ways with the Library's service. I should add that he was also useful in making arrangements for the Senior Class activities at Commencement time, and was regarded by the University's administrative officers as one of the most valuable members of the College staff.

Among the 67 libraries, in addition to the undergraduate collections that have been mentioned, there were seminar collections shelved in Widener, libraries belonging to departments of the Faculty of Arts and Sciences, and six important collections belonging to research institutions. Only the Harvard College Library was supported by College Library funds; each of the other libraries depended on the unit of the University to which it belonged. Harvard's practice, going back to the time of President Eliot, had been for "each tub to stand on its own bottom." But all the libraries, including those of the graduate professional schools, were part of the University Library (*library*, not *libraries*) by provision of the Statutes. Except for the College Library, over which I presided, each of the libraries reported to a dean, faculty department, research institution, or other entity to which it was attached; but the Statutes required them to report also to me as Director, and stated that the Director should "visit and inspect" them.

Harvard institutions maintaining important research libraries in 1937 included the Arnold Arboretum, Astronomical Observatory, Grey Herbarium, Museum of Comparative Zoology, and Peabody Museum (anthropology). Another was the Harvard-Yenching Institute, and its library calls for attention here because I found it particularly interesting and became involved with it during my first years at Harvard. It was and is Harvard's major collection of materials in East Asian languages, chiefly Chinese, Japanese, and Korean; now (1983), with more than 600,000 volumes, it is the largest American university collection in its field.

In 1937 the Institute was presided over by Serge Elisséeff, a delightful gentleman and outstanding scholar who came from a Russian family that had been wealthy before the Revolution. He had spent much of his youth in China and Japan. His interest was primarily in the classical period rather than the twentieth century, and the library's collection reflected this. By 1937, however, a young man named John K. Fairbank was on the staff of the Institute, and he was joined a year later by Edwin Reischauer, who had been born in Japan while his father was a missionary there, and who had been graduated from Oberlin twenty years after my time. Fairbank and Reischauer were interested in the contemporary history and civilization of China and Japan, and they appealed to me for help in persuading Elisséeff to change his priorities to some extent. I eventually succeeded in doing this after I had enlisted the help of several trustees of the Institute with whom I was fortunate enough to become acquainted. I am glad to say that this did not affect my friendship with Elisséeff. It was a great delight to me to see the Harvard-Yenching Library increase in size and value, particularly when I realized that the basis for its support came from a bequest of Charles Martin Hall, the inventor of the process used for reducing aluminum from bauxite, of whom I have written in Part I, Chapter 3 of these Recollections.

Enough has been said to indicate that Harvard's decentralization presented problems that had not been solved in spite of efforts by

Presidents Lowell and Conant and by my predecessors in the University Library. As Director, I hope I made some contribution to coordination, but much more was accomplished under my successor, Paul Buck, and progress has continued since his administration. The situation did enable me, when I introduced President Conant as the speaker at a meeting of the Harvard Library Club, to suggest that one of our objectives in the Library was "coordinated decentralization." He liked the term, took it up, and began to use it to describe the administrative system of the University as a whole.

THE COMMUNITY

My efforts to become acquainted with Harvard professors and administrative officers have already been mentioned. There was also the Corporation, consisting of the President, five Fellows, and the Treasurer. Legally, as provided by the Charter, this body owns and operates the University; it approves annual budgets, but decisions involving a commitment for more than a year, such as appointments of professors, must also be approved by the Board of Overseers, on which the President and Treasurer serve with thirty members elected by the Alumni. It was understood that members of the Corporation should not be approached on official business except through the President. The other members were active in professions of their own; they contributed at least every other Monday to Harvard business, and should not be involved except as a group. University officers were sometimes asked to meet with the Corporation, particularly when plans affecting their own departments were under consideration.

I had not been in Cambridge long before the two out-of-town members of the Corporation came to spend Saturday afternoon in Widener Library and to talk with me. Soon, also, one of the members from the Boston area invited me to dinner at his home, and plied me with questions, beginning with, "Are you a pack rat?" He was one of the wisest men I have ever known, and I felt free to go to him for advice on library problems that did not directly concern Harvard. It was not long until I became acquainted, outside the Library, with the two other Fellows, and Henry Shattuck, the very capable Treasurer and one of the most influential men in Boston and Massachusetts politics, asked me to spend a Saturday afternoon with him in Widener. Very early in my career at Harvard I had come to know and greatly respect the members of the Corporation.

I was elected to membership in the Club of Odd Volumes, Boston's club for book collectors, similar to New York's Grolier Club, to which

I belonged, and to Cleveland's Rowfant Club, to which I also belonged for a good many years. The Club of Odd Volumes had monthly meetings at its house on Mt. Vernon Street in Boston, one of the old Bulfinch-type houses. Fifteen to twenty of its members lunched together regularly on Saturdays, among them George Lyman Kittredge; John Livingston Lowes; Carl Keller, the Cervantes collector; William King Richardson, a patent lawyer and ardent collector, of whom more will be said later; Augustus Peabody Loring, Sr.; and Stephen and Duncan Phillips. I made a point of going to the Saturday luncheons as well as to the monthly meetings, at each of which a member spoke on book-collecting or collecting of some other kind. This was a welcome opportunity for becoming acquainted with men in the Boston community who were interested in books, as well as for enjoying fine food and good table talk. Sooner or later many of the members generously added to the Harvard Library's special collections, particularly after Bill Jackson and Phil Hofer had joined the Library staff and the Club. The regular dessert at Saturday luncheons was a choice of two kinds of pie, and Kittredge, when asked which he preferred, would always say "both" and consume two pieces.

Harvard and Boston were noted for their dining clubs. One of the oldest at Harvard, the Shop Club, met once a month through the academic year. Its members, chosen to represent all departments of the University, have included a considerable number of Nobel Prize winners, among other great and interesting scholars, during my more than forty years of membership. Soon after I came to Harvard I was asked by Harlow Shapley if I would be interested in becoming a member. We met at the Faculty Club, and, at each meeting, one of the members spoke on a subject connected with his work. I was called on four times during my first twenty-five years. The Shop Club broadened my knowledge of what was going on in the University and the academic world.

Next came the Thursday Evening Club, which for many years met once a month, except during the summer, at the homes of those of its well-to-do Back Bay or Brookline members who were able to provide a fine dinner for fifty or more of us. Approximately half the members were Bostonians, many of them "proper Bostonians," and the other half were MIT or Harvard professors who provided the after-dinner talks. I remember my first meeting, which was at President Conant's residence in the Harvard Yard, not in Boston. Knowing nothing of the Club's customs, I came in a blue serge suit and found to my distress that I was the only one there who was not wearing a dinner jacket. Within a few years, I was asked to be the speaker, and told of the Library's collections

of letters written to William Dean Howells, including those from Mark
Twain, Nathaniel Hawthorne, Hamlin Garland, and Stephen Crane.
I quoted from these, and had the pleasure of being told later by Jerome
Greene and Ted Weeks, then editor of the *Atlantic Monthly*, that my
talk had been in the Boston tradition. (I confess that I do not know just
what that meant, and cannot be sure that it was a compliment.)

Unfortunately for me, the Shop Club and the Thursday Evening
Club met on the same evening month after month. As I became older,
the Shop Club gave up the use of dinner jackets, and it was easier to get
to the Faculty Club than to somewhere in Boston, so I did not go to the
Thursday Evening Club for several years. Finally, a few years ago, the
latter club had dinner at the Tavern Club in Boston. (Entertaining in
large private homes had been given up.) I decided to put on my "glad
rags," as I called them, and found upon my arrival that I was the only
person there who had dressed for the occasion. This seemed to be a
good time for me to resign. I could say that at my first meeting I had
been the only guest without a dinner jacket, while at my last I had been
the only member wearing one. Still, I resigned with regret.

During my first year at Harvard I found that there were other ven-
erable organizations which I was invited to join. One was the Massachusetts Historical Society, the oldest of the state historical societies.
Its membership was, and is, limited. Its great manuscript collections
are especially strong for Massachusetts, but are not restricted to that
state. I am still (1983) a member, and only two or three of the present
members were elected before I was. I have served as First Vice President
of the Society as well as on its Council and on various committees, and
I helped with planning the successful addition to its early-twentieth-
century building.

I was elected to membership in the American Antiquarian Society,
which was founded by Isaiah Thomas and has its headquarters in
Worcester rather than Boston because he thought it ought to be safe in
case of a British attack from the sea. This Society collects everything
printed in the United States before 1871; its library, the world's
strongest in this field, has flourished during my time under the direction
of Clarence Brigham, Ted Shipton, and Marcus McCorison. At present
its early American publications are being reproduced in microprint, a
project begun by Albert Boni and continued since his retirement by his
son, William. I served on the Society's Council for some twenty years,
and have also been First Vice President and Chairman of its Library
Committee. Several years ago I was also the consultant on the successful

addition to its building. At 88, I decided it was time to resign from the Council.

Before my first year at Harvard was over, I was invited to attend a meeting of the Colonial Society of Massachusetts, which theoretically, at least, elects as members only descendants of colonial Americans, but I was not invited to join. I believe that this was because its membership committee thought I was already a member. Naturally I did not complain; but many years later someone apparently discovered that I did not belong, and I was elected to honorary membership. Unlike the MHS and the AAS, the Colonial Society does not have a great library, but it has more money for publication than the others.

I joined two local library groups during my first year at Harvard. One was the Men's Library Club, with members including the top men (not women) in libraries and library-connected organizations throughout Massachusetts. Booksellers belonged to this club as well as academic, public, state, and special librarians. It gave me an opportunity to broaden still further my acquaintance with librarians of the area.

Finally, there was the Boston Chapter of the Special Libraries Association, with members from libraries of all kinds. I belonged to the national organization for many years, until the Association decided that its membership should be restricted to special librarians. Richard Hensley, Chief Librarian of the Reference Department of the Boston Public Library, who had previously worked at the Information Desk in the New York Public Library, invited me to a meeting of the Boston Chapter in the fall of 1937. I was seated next to Elinor Gregory, who was then President of the Boston Chapter, and first became acquainted with her then.

Because of all the groups that have been mentioned, as well as the Harvard Library Club and other evening meetings, life for Mart and me was quite different from what it had been during our New York days.

DEATH OF MARTHA GERRISH METCALF

During this year Mart made friends with neighbors in Belmont and people at Harvard. She enjoyed our new, larger, and more convenient house. Her health was better than at any time for many years. She had outgrown the migraine headaches that had afflicted her for thirty-five years. During the winter she had a severe attack of tonsilitis, followed by the removal of her tonsils, but recovery was easier than from any of her five previous operations.

We planned that our vacation in July would include a trip around the Gaspé Peninsula in Québec, following a stop at my Wellesley sister's summer residence at Pemaquid Point in Maine and continuing through Montréal, Toronto, and Niagara Falls. Our son, Gerry, was with us until we reached Buffalo, where he took a train back to Boston and then returned to Maine to visit friends. In Ashtabula, where she was visiting friends, we met our daughter, Margaret, and had lunch with her; she had just completed her Oberlin College requirements for graduation by going to summer school. We left her in Ashtabula, planning to pick her up there ten days later on our return trip, and went on to Oberlin, where Mart was to spend a week visiting her family while I was in Chicago, attending the University of Chicago Institute on Current Issues in Library Administration and delivering a talk on departmental organization in libraries.

We reached Oberlin on a Thursday afternoon, had a delightful dinner with Mart's family, and went to bed in the Oberlin Inn. Mart was awakened almost immediately with severe abdominal pains. Our old Oberlin doctor was on vacation. His substitute said that she ought to go to the hospital. She did not improve. Her illness had not been diagnosed, but it seemed best for me to go on to Chicago on Sunday, where I was to stay with my brother, Nelson, a professor and Director of Athletics at the University of Chicago. The conference began on Monday. My talk was scheduled for Tuesday. I telephoned to Oberlin each day. Mart was no better, and on Wednesday morning, 3 August, I returned to Oberlin, where I found her still in intense pain and growing weaker. I arranged for an expert surgeon to come down from Cleveland the next day to operate for intestinal blockage. The surgeon thought that the operation was successful; but her strength was gone, and she died the next morning. Mart was buried the following day in her family's Oberlin cemetery lot, and on Saturday Margaret and I left for Belmont.

My first year at Harvard, which had been so agreeable up to that time, ended on the saddest possible note. Even so, I was fortunate because Margaret, my daughter, would be with me and would attend the Katharine Gibbs business school in Boston. We found a capable woman to prepare our dinners for us five days a week and to keep the house in a livable condition.

Chapter 2

First Year at Harvard: Staff Problems

A S REPORTED in the last chapter of Part II, I knew before I came to Harvard that several senior staff members would retire in the near future. President Conant had assured me that he understood the situation. He also told me that he would be ready to approve the discharge of anyone on the staff whom I believed to be a trouble-maker; he had in mind a person whom he named. I had known the man before, and believed that he might be difficult, but decided, in view of the friends he had among members of the senior faculty, that it would be a mistake to ask the President to help me out in this way. Both the Library and I suffered a good deal for several years as a result of this decision; but, with the help of the United States government, what I hoped was careful handling on my part, and the man's own health problems, he was belatedly taken off my hands. At least I gained additional experience in an aspect of personnel work of which I had been ignorant in spite of twenty years of extensive work with staff problems at the New York Public Library.

President Conant told me that he would accept my recommendations on personnel matters, and that I should call on the Financial Vice President, Jack Lowes, when funds were required for changes or for new positions that I might wish to establish in order to provide better service.

The retirements that have been mentioned were three in number:

George Parker Winship, who had formerly been in charge of the rare-book collection but had not been in the Library for several years, had reached the retirement age on 31 August 1937, so his position was now vacant, and a replacement was desirable as soon as possible. I realized that the salary which had been paid, $5,000, was inadequate for the position.

Walter Briggs, who had been Assistant Librarian in charge of public services and then, during the academic year 1936–37, Acting Librarian

of Harvard College, was due to retire the day before I came; but he had
been asked to stay one more year in order to help me get acquainted,
which he did superbly. I was pleased, as many others were, when he
was given the honorary degree of Master of Arts at the Commencement
following his retirement, in spite of the fact that he had never attended
college.

T. Franklin Currier, who had been in the Library since 1894 and had
headed the Catalog Department since 1914, was to retire in two years.
(Although there were a number of fine catalogers on the staff, some
with administrative ability, several of them were also scheduled to retire
within a few years.) It was evident to me from my experience in trying
to fill a position similar to Currier's in New York, that a satisfactory
successor would be difficult to find. Currier had been a valuable member
of my American Library Association Committee on Cooperative Cataloguing in the 1930s, and one of the considerations that encouraged
me to come to Harvard was the knowledge that he was there. His great
Whittier bibliography had been published in 1937, and he continued,
after his retirement in 1939, to work in Widener on his bibliography of
Oliver Wendell Holmes, which was completed and published in 1953,
seven years after Currier's death.

In 1939 also, I was able to persuade his daughter, Margaret Currier,
who had gone to Library School at Michigan and was then working in
Yale's Sterling Library, to come to Harvard. Her career at Harvard,
first in Widener and later as Librarian of the Peabody Museum Library,
was notably successful.

I realized that there were positions to be filled in addition to those
left vacant by retirements. Construction was soon to start on the Littauer building of the new Graduate School of Public Administration;
while it would not be ready for occupancy until 1939, I believed that
a librarian ought to be appointed by the summer of 1938. I was asked
to select the person to fill this position and to determine the salary that
should be paid.

Improvement of public services in Widener was essential, I believed,
and personnel was not the only problem here; there were difficulties
arising from the building itself. The reference collection was in the
monumental reading room, and some of the shelves were more than 250
feet from the single, small reference desk, which was in an adjacent
room, next to the circulation desk. Reserved books as well as reference
works were shelved in the reading room; at the center of the long outside
wall on the north side of the room there was a large desk behind which
the most heavily used reserve books were kept. This was presided over

by a staff that, for a variety of reasons, was not popular with the students. Adjacent to the stack entrance was the shortest circulation desk I had ever seen in a large university library, but I soon realized that it would be adequate if the service were as good as it ought to be.

It was the reference service provided for students and faculty that bothered me most. Robert Haynes, a Bowdoin graduate who had completed two years of graduate study at Harvard and had been in charge of the circulation desk for some years, had succeeded Walter Briggs as Assistant Librarian for Public Services in 1936. One of his tasks was to assign the 250 stack carrels to graduate students and the more than 70 faculty studies to senior professors; there were not nearly enough carrels or studies to satisfy the demand. He also supervised the circulation desk, the reading room for current periodicals, the public catalog, service of the map room (which did not have an attendant) on the top floor, and a small, inadequate bibliography room, which supplemented the reference collection. In addition to all this, he was the only person available for giving reference assistance except for times when Alice Reynolds was not occupied with the Library's sizable interlibrary loan work.

It was evident that Harvard needed to catch up with the rest of the library world. I remembered how my librarian sister, who was graduated from Pratt Institute in 1902, had been the first reference librarian at Oberlin in 1904 and then, in 1910, the first person in a similar position at Wellesley. I realized also, from my experience at the New York Public Library, that there would be a tremendous demand for reference services at Harvard if they were available.

Haynes evidently had more than enough to do, and the circulation desk was not going as well under his direction as I thought it should. Consequently I decided that we should employ at least two new full-time reference assistants, although the reference desk was not manned during the evenings. In addition, I was prepared to suggest that there be a map-room librarian, because the fine collection that Justin Winsor had built up ought to be more accessible.

I thought also that the University Archives ought to be reorganized. They were shelved in a locked area of the bookstack, and supervised by a capable elderly woman (a member of the family of one of Harvard's nineteenth-century presidents), who was soon to retire. There was a fine collection of archives of the College, particularly during its first two hundred years, which had been of great interest to Lane and others, and had been used in preparing the volumes of John Langdon Sibley's biographies of Harvard graduates. (The volumes published up to this time covered only graduates from 1642 to 1700, but work on later years was continuing, financed by money that Sibley had bequeathed to the Massachusetts Historical Society; he had not given it to Harvard because the College had been unable to construct a new library building for him during his long administration as Librarian.) Most of the Archives collection, it seemed to me, consisted of books written by Harvard graduates. I thought that the valuable early material ought to be supplemented with official records of the past century, and I decided that the books by graduates should be removed and shelved in the main stack collection, classified by subject.

I talked with President Conant of all the personnel matters that have been mentioned. He approved a search for replacements for Winship and Currier, for a librarian for the School of Public Administration, and for two reference assistants in Widener. He suggested that we could wait for better map-room service until new funds became available and just the right person could be found to build up the collection and provide assistance to users. He warned against spending any considerable amount of money on the Archives, and said that I should talk with Lowes, the Financial Vice President, about any other new positions. With the latter's approval, I went to work on the selection problem.

I had known about the vacant rare-book position before I left New York, and Harry Lydenberg had told me of a young man named William A. Jackson who was cataloging Carl H. Pforzheimer's great collection of English literature. Lydenberg referred to Jackson as the only man in the rare-book field who could be spoken of in the same breath with Wilberforce Eames. Now, when I approached Jackson, I found to my pleasure and surprise that he would be interested in coming to Harvard. With the approval of Lowes, I proposed a salary larger than other assistant librarians received, and I talked with Jackson of his coming as Associate Professor of Bibliography as well as Assistant Librarian in Charge of the Rare Book Collection. He agreed to the salary I had suggested. He was a graduate of Williams College but had no advanced degree; this, fortunately, did not bother the University administration any more than my lack of advanced degrees had done.

It was after this that I first met with the Library Committee of the Board of Overseers. I reported on the personnel problems I was facing, and spoke particularly of Jackson, the only person I had as yet approached. The Chairman of the Committee was Charles Warren, a prominent Washington constitutional lawyer who, as I found later, was more than well-to-do. My report of the offer to Jackson prompted him to speak almost violently against spending library book funds for rare books, and he went on to say that I had no business to arrange a professorial appointment without the permission and approval of his Committee. This was something I had never heard of, and I feared that there would be trouble. However, with the help of Lowes, Jerome Greene (the Secretary of the Corporation), and President Conant, the appointment was approved, and Jackson began work on 1 September 1938.

Before he came to Harvard, Jackson told me that Philip Hofer, who had been Curator of the Spencer Collection at the New York Public Library from 1929 to 1934 and was then Assistant Librarian at the Morgan Library, was eager to leave the Morgan Library, would be very useful at Harvard as Curator of Printing and Graphic Arts, and would be ready to come at a nominal salary. I was delighted when Hofer agreed; he and Jackson joined the staff on the same day. These two appointments, my first at Harvard, may have been as important as any that I was to make during my eighteen years as Director. Thanks to Jackson's amazing ability, knowledge of book values and the book trade, and familiarity with collectors and their interests, as well as to Hofer's leadership in his field of graphic arts, Harvard's rare-book and manuscript collections much more than doubled during my administration, and their growth has continued through the years following my retirement.

In December 1937, I went out to the midwinter meeting of the American Library Association in Chicago, looking for persons to fill the other positions. On my way back, I stopped in Ann Arbor to visit the University of Michigan library school and talk with possible candidates. Andrew Osborn was teaching there; previously he had worked for ten years in the New York Public Library and had spent a year organizing the new library school at the University of Southern California. He agreed to come to Harvard as assistant to Currier, with the prospect, if all went well, of succeeding him in 1939.

I had also hoped to talk with Foster Palmer, the President of his library school class at Michigan. Osborn said he was the best prospect in the class, but I was unable to see him because he had just been quarantined with the mumps. I have always hesitated to employ anyone with whom I have not talked, but I decided to offer him the position. It was fortunate for me that he had the mumps because, when he reported for duty in September 1938, I found that he was painfully shy, and thought I had made a mistake. I am sure that I would not have offered him the position if I had talked with him first; but, as it turned out, I could not have made a better choice. He was to serve Harvard very successfully for forty years and, in my opinion, is one of the best reference librarians that our profession has produced. He also became skilled in automation, and was in charge of library automation efforts at Harvard for some years. Following an early retirement in 1975, he returned to work to serve as Acting Librarian at the Countway Library (containing both Harvard's medical collections and those of the Boston Medical Library) until a successor to Harold Bloomquist could be found. The search proved to be difficult, and Palmer administered the library for two years.

Homer Halvorson was my choice to head Widener reference services under Haynes. Halvorson had talked with me at the New York Public Library in 1937, just after receiving his Ph.D. from Harvard. I had offered him a reference position in New York, but he had not accepted it because he wanted to have a year of teaching experience before going into library work. He taught at William and Mary for a year and then came to Harvard in 1938 at the same time as Palmer.

A stop in Rochester followed my visit to Ann Arbor. There I talked with the head of one of the reference divisions of the Rochester Public Library about the Littauer position, and also had an opportunity to consult Charles Case, who was in charge of the Eastman Company's work with microfilm, about copying foreign newspapers on film. I found that I had to decide between the man at Rochester and Elmer Grieder, who was then at the Detroit Public Library but had worked at the New York Public Library for a short time while attending the library school at Columbia. I chose Grieder because I thought he could work better than the other man with the faculty. I knew that only an outgoing person could handle what I believed to be a difficult position in the new Graduate School of Public Administration.

This took care of my first priorities. Nothing was done about the map room at this time; later I was able to exploit Mrs. Kirk Bryan, the widow of a Harvard professor, who took charge and provided good service for several years.

The problem of the University Archives remained. Sometime during my first year at Harvard, Clarence Walton, the Assistant Librarian in charge of the Order Department, brought Clifford K. Shipton into my office, introduced him to me as "the reincarnation of John Langdon Sibley," and explained that he was working on the continuation of Sibley's Harvard graduates. I was impressed by Shipton and soon thereafter proposed that he come to the Library, starting in the summer of 1938, and reorganize the Archives while continuing to work part-time on Sibley. We were able to persuade the Secretary of the Corpo ration, Jerome Greene, to send Presidential and Corporation Archives from University Hall to the Library with the understanding that they could be used only with permission from him or from the President. During the next few years, Shipton was in touch with every department of the Faculty of Arts and Sciences, and he gathered together a tremendous quantity of archival material from them. By the time President Conant realized what was happening, his office had become the heaviest user of the Archives, and he never objected to what had been done. Greene, Shipton, and I drew up rules for use of all parts of the Archives; they were approved by the President and Corporation and, with minor amendments, are still in effect. By 1955, when I retired, Shipton had assembled a collection occupying as much space as 350,000 average volumes, but he found that approximately half of this material consisted of duplicates that could be discarded. The collections have continued to grow, and there has been difficulty in finding space for them as well as for staff and users; in 1976 the new Pusey Library finally provided quarters especially planned for the University Archives.

Shipton also encouraged the graduate professional schools to send their archives to Widener if they did not choose to set up their own archival collections. Law, Business, and Medicine retained their own records, but all three made better provision for their collections, the two latter with the help of Robert Lovett, whom Shipton had trained. Lovett, who had earned an M.A. in history at Harvard and a library degree from Columbia, worked under Shipton until 1953, when he became Head of the Manuscripts Division and Archivist at Baker Library of the Graduate School of Business Administration. For ten years, from 1957 to 1967, he also worked part time at the Medical School, organizing its archival holdings. He was the senior member of the University Library staff when he retired in 1979.

While building up the largest, best organized, and most useful university archives that I know of, Shipton was also employed as Librarian and subsequently Director of the American Antiquarian Society, succeeding Robert W. G. Vail in the former position and Clarence Brigham in the latter. He also continued his work on Sibley, nearly tripling the collection of biographies and bringing it down to graduates of 1775. At the Antiquarian Society he inaugurated and successfully continued, with Albert Boni's Readex Corporation, the project for microprinting all American publications from 1640 to 1801 that could be found in the Society's collections or elsewhere, revising and adding substantially to the Evans list. Ultimately the closing date will be 1820, and newspapers will also be included.

I am proud to be able to report that Jackson, Hofer, and Shipton, all of whom came to the staff at the end of my first year at Harvard, have been awarded honorary doctorates by the University for their accomplishments.

Thus far I have said little about those other than department heads who were on the staff in 1937. Except for two catalogers who were foreign-language experts, there were no library-school graduates on the Widener staff until the day I arrived; but this does not mean that there were no well qualified professional librarians there. I shall not attempt to mention all of them, but something must be said of those in key positions.

The Order Department depended on Gertrude Shaw and Gertrude Sullivan, both of whom had come to the Library before 1920. Miss Shaw was responsible for the routine work of book selection; she selected most of the English and American books herself, kept track of the recommendations of faculty members, checked them for duplication, and questioned suggestions that seemed to be unwise. She did all of this remarkably well. Later on, when I had more time than I could find at first, I had her bring all the faculty recommendations in to me every day, and I went over them with her. Gertrude Sullivan handled the financial part of the work, including payment of bills, and kept such close track of expenditures that I did not have to worry about overdrafts in the book-fund accounts. More will be said of the acquisition program in Chapter 5.

In the Catalog Department there were a half-dozen remarkably capable senior catalogers who had been in the Library for many years. Under Currier's guidance, Mildred Tucker, who had been the supervisor in the Department since 1913, had developed an unusually efficient method of cataloging with a relatively small staff. A group of experienced typists prepared typed cards for new acquisitions from the title-pages and order slips. In a large percentage of cases, the first cards were good enough to be used, occasionally with handwritten changes, for insertion in the catalog. In this way the routine part of the work was done with comparatively inexpensive help and, in the light of my experience with cataloging in the New York Public Library and the Library of Congress, I was very favorably impressed.

I have already mentioned Edward Gookin, the Registrar, who did the Library's accounting except for book purchases, prepared the payroll, and personally handed out the monthly checks to members of the staff, some of whom were in awe of him and some of whom were provoked by his seeming arrogance. Charles Grace, who had come to the Library in his teens, was Gookin's assistant and eventual successor; he was a joy to work with.

Mrs. Helen B. Allen, who had been acting head of the Rare Book Department in Winship's absence, resigned not long after Jackson and Hofer came; but her assistant, Carolyn Jakeman, stayed on for nearly forty years more, presiding over the reading room in the Houghton Library until her retirement. She worked well with both staff and readers, and also was the unofficial staff photographer who took pictures at all the special occasions.

I was not satisfied with the public service staff in the main Widener reading room and at the circulation desk, primarily because of two unsatisfactory appointments that had been made before I came, because reference service was inadequate as has already been explained, and because too many of the books requested for borrowing could not be found. We struggled for ten years with this latter problem until after the war, when an inventory could be taken of the stack. Meanwhile, changes in the charging system helped, as will be reported in Chapter 11.

These notes on the staff as it was in 1937 should not be concluded without mentioning that Susan Haskins, who had been in the Library for half a dozen years before going to the library school at Michigan, returned to Widener on the same day that I arrived. The number of library-school graduates on the Widener staff was doubled when she and I started work. Miss Haskins was eventually to succeed Osborn as head of the Catalog Department in 1956, the year following my retirement.

Chapter 3

First Year at Harvard:
Space Problems

I HAD MY FIRST talk with President Conant on space problems of the Harvard Library during my first month as Director. He told me that my predecessor, Blake, had convinced him that the Widener bookstacks would be full to capacity within three years, and that something must be done as soon as possible to solve this serious problem. Blake had suggested that the large, high-ceilinged main room in Memorial Hall (Harvard's Civil War memorial) might accommodate a multi-tiered bookstack holding as many as one million volumes. This room had served as the dining hall for the College in earlier years, but was now used only a few times a year for examinations, registration, etc. The part of the building that had once housed kitchens could provide space for readers.

President Conant suggested that I look into this. He went on to say that one of his reasons for asking me to come to Harvard was my familiarity with efforts to develop microfilm to replace printed material. (I had been chairman of the American Library Association committee in this field.) He wondered what Harvard could do along these lines. I replied that, while I believed that microcopying would eventually develop on a large scale, I did not think it a practicable solution to space problems. Film, unless published in sizable editions, could not replace books and periodicals in great numbers; we were certainly not ready for this at present, nor could we expect to be for years to come. To reproduce and then discard our present collections would cost more than to provide space for them, and students and professors would not accept microforms as a substitute until there were better reading machines than those now available. He was disappointed, but he agreed with me. Our talk ended after he had asked me to prepare a report within six months (that is, by March 1938) that would suggest plans for handling the library space problem through the rest of the twentieth century. No limitations were suggested except that costs must be kept in mind.

I struggled with the problem until March. Construction in Memorial Hall would be unwise, I believed. My first thought was that it might be possible to add to the Widener building; I remembered Gilmore Clarke's proposal for filling in the courts at the New York Public Library, as well as my own plans for an addition at the rear of that building. There were only two courts in Widener, and they were much smaller than those in New York. They were also irregular in shape, which would make them less useful and add to construction costs. Filling them would block many windows, including those of the Widener Memorial Rooms. I talked with Mrs. Allen, the acting head of the rare-book collection, and she said she had always hoped that her space problem could be solved in this way; but I soon learned that, in giving the building to Harvard, Mrs. Widener had specified that it was not to be added to in any way. It may be noted that, after my retirement and after most of my recommendations of March 1938 had been carried out, the idea of filling in the courts was revived. With at least tentative approval of the Widener heirs, plans were then made to fill in the courts, but it was found that assignable space gained in this way would cost several times as much per square foot as space in a new building.

I turned next to the possibility of replacing Widener completely with a new structure on a site large enough to provide space for it and for later additions, as I thought all sites ought to do. It was evident that there was only one place in the Harvard Yard where such a building might possibly be approved. This was in the southeast corner, where the Lamont Library now stands; but, even there, a new central library would have had to be a skyscraper, which many people would have thought undesirable. With the help of Henry Shepley, who was at work on the Littauer building, rough plans were prepared for a tall building there, with a base as large as the site would allow, and with a capacity for another twenty-five years if Widener remained in use. It was soon evident that a skyscraper in the Yard would not be a good idea and would not be permitted. South of the Yard, toward the Charles River, there was a large area where Quincy House was later built; but it seemed too far from the classrooms to the north as well as from the dormitories and the Radcliffe Yard. An area owned by the University was available north of the Law School and engineering buildings; it would have been adequate in size but was too far from the center of the College's educational facilities. (It is now used for the Graduate Center.)

I tried to figure out the gross square footage that would be required for the College Library's central unit by the end of the twentieth century, and estimated this at 700,000 square feet. In the light of my experience up to that time, I decided that I was not ready to recommend a new central building. It would have had to be so large that most of the new students and many of their elders would have been awed and confused by its internal arrangements, which inevitably would have been complicated. It would cost more than the University would be ready to consider. There was a further objection. The Widener building was the largest building ever given to Harvard up to that time, and it had been dedicated only twenty-two years ago. If Widener were discarded it would be difficult to persuade anyone to give a large sum for a new library building, and it would be expensive to adapt Widener for other purposes.

Giving up the idea of a new central building, I considered alternatives. Further decentralization was the only one that seemed practicable. I realized that Harvard's library, with seventy-six separate units, was already the most decentralized university library in the country. While I disliked the idea of going further in that direction, after long consideration I decided that it could be done without causing disintegration if it were handled carefully and if full attention were given to what I had called "coordinated decentralization." I believed that President Conant would agree, and I hoped that I could do something to pull the different parts of the University Library together, though my predecessors had tried with little success to do this.

How could coordination be increased while physical decentralization was increasing? I considered the functional situation in Widener. The rare-book collection was deteriorating because of unsatisfactory climate control and increasing atmospheric pollution in Cambridge. The situation was not as bad as at the University of Pennsylvania, which I had visited ten years before; there, in addition to the dryness at some times of year, dust and soot, much of it from the Pennsylvania Railroad a little to the north, was even more distressing. But the situation in Widener was not good. If a separate new building, preferably with an underground connection to Widener, could be provided for rare books and manuscripts, it would be easier to attract further gifts.

Service to undergraduates was unsatisfactory. Their reserve-book collection was in Widener's monumental reading room, supplemented by a reserve-book room for history, government, and economics in Boylston Hall next door, by the Freshman reading room in the Union across Quincy Street from the Yard, and by the seven dormitory libraries in undergraduate houses. Students, particularly under-classmen, had a difficult time using the public catalog in Widener with its millions of cards. I had heard of students who boasted that they had gone through their four years at Harvard and received their degrees without ever darkening the doors of Widener, and of others who had come in once or twice, tried unsuccessfully to find the books they wanted, given up in disgust, and never tried again.

The following incident may suggest the sort of thing that happened far too often. A student checked the catalog; after long effort, because there were thousands of cards under Shakespeare, he found a card for *Hamlet*, which he wanted, and turned in a call-slip for it. He had naturally selected the first copy of *Hamlet* listed; since all the cards were arranged by date of publication, the copy he requested was so valuable that it was kept in the rare-book collection and not ordinarily made available to undergraduates. He was told that the Library had other copies, and that he should look it up again and turn in another call-slip. This time he made his way to the last of cards for *Hamlet* and requested the most recent edition; this, of course, turned out to be in use by another student. It was then suggested that he go to the stack himself, and he was directed to the area devoted to Shakespeare. Instead of the catalog's thousands of cards for Shakespeare, he found scores of shelves of books, and decided that it was not worthwhile to search through them to find what he wanted. He left the building without being told that, if he had simply asked for a copy of *Hamlet*, one would undoubt-edly have been available.

I had already learned that little more than half of the volumes called for at the circulation desk were supplied to borrowers. As is usual in large university libraries, most of the circulation came from a small percentage of the collection. A large number of requests were for vol-umes suggested by instructors. Unless these were placed on reserve, most of the students requesting them were sure to be disappointed.

Graduate students, of course, were competing with undergraduates for many of these books. There were 250 stalls (as carrels were called) in Widener. These were assigned to graduate students, most of them to more than one student at a time, because there were not enough to go around. If a student found that the one assigned to him was occupied, he was free to sit in an adjacent stall, and it was unusual for all the stalls in any section of the stack to be in use at the same time. Each stall had a four-foot shelf on which books to be used day after day could be kept after the student had signed for them and placed a slip in each to show that it had been charged to him. John Shea or one of his assistants checked the stalls every day, looked for books that had not been charged, and returned these to the shelves. After a student had filled the four-foot shelf, he could ask to have a three-shelf bookcase installed behind his chair; since the stalls were 75 inches apart on centers there was plenty of room for these bookcases. The result was that some 40,000 of the volumes most in demand were charged to stalls, in addition to the thousands that were in circulation outside the building. There were also faculty studies, about 75 of them; most of these, each with ten to twelve sections of shelves, could house as many as 1,500 volumes. In order to insure themselves against inconvenient delays in their own work, the professors, of course, gathered everything that they expected to use during weeks and months ahead.

Still another problem had resulted from the economic depression; shelves in the stack had not been "read" to make sure that books were in their right places for a long time. Students using the stacks often were careless in replacing books, and mistakes were made by the staff who re-shelved volumes that had been borrowed. Special requests for books urgently needed were referred to John Shea, who had an uncanny talent, which I have never seen equalled, for finding misplaced books. This helped to take care of emergencies, but there were often long delays in providing books that were wanted.

Special attention had been given to sections of the stack that were most heavily used, but there had been no full inventory since early in the decade. No one knew, even approximately, how many of the books listed in the catalogs had been lost or stolen. Professors and graduate students were admitted to the stack, and books were checked only at exits from the building. As reported in Part II, Chapter 9, there had sometimes been serious losses.

To return to the problem of space and of improving services for undergraduates, I believed that service at Harvard was not as good as it had been at Oberlin thirty years earlier, and I knew of the special collection for undergraduates in Columbia University's Butler Library. I conceived the idea of a separate undergraduate library building with a good *college* library collection—about 100,000 volumes, I thought— selected to meet undergraduate needs. Books assigned for reading in courses would be reserved on closed shelves. Collateral reading would be on open shelves, together with a good "gentleman's library" much larger than the dormitory libraries or the collection in our Farnsworth (browsing) Room. A library of this sort ought to encourage undergraduate reading, which the great Widener stack did not seem to do. It would mean that the dormitory libraries, which were already filled almost to capacity though they had been established only a decade before, would not require more and more space; they could regularly weed their collections of books infrequently used. Still, an undergraduate library would reduce for only a short time the pressure for more space in Widener. It would enable us to provide better accommodations there for advanced scholars, but it was only a first, small step toward solving the space problem.

Before coming to Harvard, I had heard of President Eliot's proposal for a cooperative storage building, in which books would be shelved three deep and from which they would be made available to all the large libraries in the Boston area. Several of these libraries had been short of space in 1901 and 1902, when he made his proposal to the Massachusetts Library Association and the American Library Association; but it had been rejected by librarians and professors, who refused to admit that there were "dead" books, which is what Eliot called them. I did not approve of shelving the books three deep or of referring to them as "dead," but I thought his idea a good one in other respects. I suggested, therefore, that there be a storage building for "little-used books," placed on an inexpensive site and of plain, inexpensive construction. Almost anyone would admit that most large libraries have many books that are no longer frequently used; if these could be retrieved fairly promptly when requested, such a building could help to solve the space problem.

I now had three specific suggestions to make:

1) A rare-book library with climate control, connected to Widener with a tunnel and, if possible, a bridge. This would save space in the Widener stack and should attract gifts.

2) A library planned especially for undergraduates, which could satisfy most of their needs much better than Widener, where they filled the reading room and made it difficult to provide good service to professors and advanced students. This would relieve for only a year or two the problem of space for books.

3) A cooperative storage building for "less-used books" from all libraries in the area that could use such a facility to advantage.

Before submitting my report, I decided to include three additional suggestions:

1) Underground stacks might be provided adjacent to any of our present or future library buildings, particularly Widener. Further, when buildings for other purposes were constructed in the future, stacks might be provided beneath them if there were a large departmental library in the vicinity.

2) As opportunities arose, collections might be transferred from Widener to specialized libraries in theology, medicine, music, education, architecture, the fine arts, and the sciences. These would go to departmental and graduate professional school libraries where additional space would cost less than in a great new central building to replace Widener.

3) A large collection of school textbooks might be sent from Widener to the proposed storage library or to Teachers College at Columbia if our Graduate School of Education decided it did not need them; and materials of special interest to the Massachusetts Institute of Technology might be transferred to its library if our science departments approved.

My report of March 1938 included all of the foregoing suggestions. No recommendation was made as to the order in which the storage library, rare-book library, and undergraduate library should be provided; any one of them would provide relief for a limited period. President Conant took my report to the Corporation, which approved it in principle. When he told me of this, he indicated that, when any part of the University needed a new building, the head of the department in question was expected to do what he could to find the necessary money. I had not been prepared for this, though I knew that the College Library was expected to depend on its own endowment funds in building up its book collections.

A little later, Paul Sachs, Assistant Director of the Fogg Museum, invited me to dinner at his home. I found there the heads of University departments that had been particularly successful in obtaining new funds, and the evening was spent discussing how each had gone about this. The dinner, evidently, had been arranged for my edification. I was somewhat taken aback, since I had failed to realize that I was getting into this when I came to Harvard, but I absorbed as much of the good advice as I could. The major results of my efforts will be reported in Chapters 6, 7, and 8.

Chapter 4

Special Projects of 1938–1941

THE INTERNATIONAL DOCUMENTATION INSTITUTE

M Y FIRST YEAR at Harvard has been recorded as a very full and interesting one, with a tragic ending that left me almost in despair. Fortunately I did not have much time to think about this. Among the distractions that kept me busy, one was provided by the American Documentation Institute, with which I had been involved for several years. Within a month of my return from Oberlin, word came that the Rockefeller Foundation wanted me to go to England early in September as an American representative at the 1938 meeting of the International Documentation Institute. The conference was to meet first at Oxford and then in London. I was delighted to have the opportunity to go. I had never been abroad, except in Canada, and had never been on a ship, except on Lake Erie between Buffalo and Cleveland. September was a crowded month for ocean liners, and the only passages that I could reserve on short notice were on the Canadian *Empress of Britain* between Québec and Southampton both ways. I wanted to broaden my experience as much as I could, so I took a cabin to England, with the return in first class on the same ship some three weeks later.

Going over, I was seated for meals with three strange characters. One was a Canadian builder who was putting up cheap houses in the London suburbs. He told me that he could make good money by placing the water pipes to the houses above ground with no protection from the frost; people were not bright enough to realize that the pipes would probably freeze in severe weather. The second man, who was a Cockney, would say nothing about himself, and I decided that he was a spy of some sort. The third was a rather pompous, upper-class, but impecunious Englishman who was sure that a war with Germany was just over the horizon. He said that recent technological developments would insure British victory. I wonder if he knew about radar.

Before going to Oxford, I had two nights in London and stayed in a hotel that had been recommended by Charles McCombs of the New

York Public Library. It was near the British Museum. I awoke after my first night with the worst headache I have ever had; if I had not been so excited about seeing London, I would have stayed in bed. I was far from well and could eat no breakfast, but felt better as the day went on. I received my British Museum admission card from Arundel Esdaile, the Secretary, and was taken through the library. Esdaile was a very large man; I did not see him again until he came to the United States and stayed overnight with us, sleeping in the bed that had been lengthened to seven feet, two inches for the benefit of my son, Gerry.

I called on Henry John Brown of Stevens & Brown in his office nearby. He was now in his eighties; I had met him for the first time nineteen years earlier when I was in charge of the Order Division of the New York Public Library, and he had come over at the close of World War I to renew arrangements with us. I was exhausted when I returned to my hotel room but realized that there was an odor of gas in the room. I called the desk and was given another room; there was a bad leak in the pipe connected with the room's heater. If I had followed my inclination and remained in bed that first morning, I might well have died of gas poisoning.

At Oxford, I stayed in Lady Margaret College. John Marshall of the Rockefeller Foundation and Herman Fussler, who was then in charge of microfilm work at the University of Chicago Library, were the other American representatives. I had time to visit the bookstores and many of the colleges and their libraries, as well as to attend the Institute's dinner in Trinity Great Hall.

Following the advice of friends we had met at the Conference, Fussler and I went to the Cotswolds for the weekend, staying in a quiet village inn at Chipping Camden instead of in tourist-ridden Broadway a few miles away. We walked through the hills to Broadway, with fields of brussels sprouts stretching as far as the eye could see. There we rented bicycles, and the owner of the shop, much to my surprise, did not ask for a deposit. I had not ridden a bicycle since my graduation from Oberlin twenty-seven years earlier and was so occupied making sure I could manage one that I started down the road on the wrong side, forgetting that the British keep to the left. The shop owner rushed after me, shouting wildly, but I was able to reassure him that I understood the situation and would be all right. Fussler and I had two wonderful days seeing one of the most attractive parts of the world and then returned to London, where we stayed in an American-type hotel. I should have preferred the Bristol, where I stayed before, because I wanted to see as much as I could of the British way of life.

Our documentation meetings continued, with headquarters at the Victoria and Albert Museum, which was very much worth seeing. I met a librarian from Newcastle-upon-Tyne, Edwin F. Patterson, and talked with him about microfilm. He told me of his experience with strip (rather than reel) film and of its great advantages.

During the three or four days between the end of the meeting and my departure for Québec, I saw as much of London as I could. There were doubts about shipping because this was at the time of the Munich meeting between Chamberlain and Hitler, and there was a war scare. Fussler, who had spent the summer in France working on microfilm problems for his chief at Chicago, M. Llewellyn Raney, was naturally upset at the possibility that he might be unable to get back to his family. Under the circumstances, he was less interested than I was in seeing the city. With Mart's death still much on my mind, I was restless; the political crisis made me feel ready for anything, and I did not worry about being delayed in returning to my work at Harvard.

Ralph Brown of Stevens & Brown took me in tow, and we spent one full day walking from one end of central London to the other. I hunted up my British brother-in-law, whom I had not seen since just after my father's death more than forty years earlier. His wife, my sister Ethel, had died in 1897, and he had later become a missionary to the Indians in Venezuela, where he barely escaped being murdered. After his return to England, he had remarried and was now living in Wimbledon, near the tennis courts. He was seventy and had shrunk from the six feet, four inches and 250 pounds that I remembered; he now seemed to be about my size, not the largest man I had ever known. To my delight when I was seven or eight, he used to hold his arms out in front of him and, when I grasped his great thumbs, swing me up and down.

Fussler's boat finally went off on schedule, and mine followed. I was looking forward to the trip in first class. The route was from Southampton to Cherbourg, and thence to Québec. I was seated in the dining room at a table with the First Mate and a delightful suburban Chicago couple and their married daughter, who was eager to get home to her husband. I found that they knew Archibald MacLeish, who had come to Harvard as Curator of the Nieman Foundation, and whom I had met for the first time just before I left Cambridge. We had hardly left Cherbourg when we ran into one of the severest gales that our Captain had ever experienced, according to the Chief Mate at our table. For the first and, thus far, only time in my life I suffered from seasickness and, much to my disappointment, had to spend two days in my room. I recovered and enjoyed the rest of my trip with my companions.

I drank my first champagne and must confess that I liked it, but saw one of my table mates (not one of those mentioned above) continue to drink until he became difficult. I played my first and only game of beano. We saw icebergs off the coast of Labrador and went on through the Strait of Belle Isle to Québec.

I knew that New England's first very severe hurricane in a century had taken place before I left England and was naturally worried about my daughter. I telephoned to her from Québec to say that I hoped to get home the next evening. I could hear Margaret give a little gasp and realized that for some reason she was upset. She then admitted that she was scheduled to go to the first party to which she had been invited since coming to Massachusetts two months earlier. I told her not to wait for my arrival but to go to the party. There she met Maxwell Small, an MIT student who had been graduated from Bowdoin and then decided to take a year off before going to Edinburgh to study for his doctorate in philosophy. He had shipped around the world as an able seaman and came back with the decision that he would take naval architecture and marine engineering at MIT instead of going on with philosophy. He and Margaret met at the party, apparently fell in love at first sight, and were married almost exactly two years later.

Max then had a successful and interesting experience with the United States Steel Company, building ships during the war at the Kearney Shipyard in Newark. This made it impossible for him to be released for military service. After the war he was advisor to small industrial firms in Worcester, Massachusetts, where he was employed by the Chamber of Commerce; this gave him the broadest of engineering experience. He then joined the Brookhaven National Laboratories of the Associated Universities Incorporated, near Bellport, Long Island. He became the Chief Engineer, was in charge of building their two atom-smashers and, later on, the sophisticated radio-astronomy tele-scope at Greenbank, West Virginia. Back at Bellport, he served at one time or another as Chief Planning Officer, and temporarily as Treasurer after his predecessor in that position got into trouble. Later he became interested in sewage disposal and pollution control on Long Island and is spending his retirement working on that serious problem.

Urging Margaret to go to her party was one of the most important decisions of my life; it led to a happy marriage and to two upstanding grandsons, each with a very satisfactory wife and each with two of my great-grandchildren. I should add that Margaret, before her marriage to Max in September 1940, completed her year at the Katharine Gibbs

Secretarial School and then became secretary to the *Harvard Law Review*
for an extremely interesting and amusing year.

Foreign Newspapers

I had become acquainted at least to some extent with Harvard's
library collections during my first year in Cambridge. What I observed
there, like what I had learned at the New York Public Library, led me
to believe that American libraries had not acquired foreign newspapers
on a satisfactory scale. Very few of these papers were to be found in
our great historical collections. I realized that this was because newspapers presented three serious problems for libraries. They occupied
a tremendous amount of space. The cost of binding them was very
large. Finally, because the wood-pulp paper on which they were printed
deteriorated very rapidly, it did not seem worthwhile to acquire or keep
them. I remembered that we had tried in New York to preserve newspapers by pasting Japanese tissue on both sides of each sheet and that
we had later substituted microfilm copies for the originals of New York
City papers.

Harvard, I was convinced, ought to acquire a much larger selection
of foreign newspapers than any American library had done in the past,
and these acquisitions should not be limited to papers of England,
France, and Germany. I decided that it would be desirable to get at
least one newspaper from each of the major countries, to make a master
film negative and perhaps a positive copy for Harvard, and to offer
positive copies for sale at a reasonable price to other libraries. This
would cost much less than to acquire, bind, and provide space for
newspapers in their original form. It was evident that the acquisitions
budget then possible at Harvard was inadequate for this purpose. Fortunately I had reached this conclusion only a few weeks before President
Conant asked me for suggestions on use of the Nieman Fund. As
reported in Chapter 10, he approved my proposal that some of the
income from this fund be used for foreign newspapers.

I then decided to seek a grant from the Rockefeller Foundation to
support a cooperative project. In New York I saw David Stevens,
Director of the Foundation's Division of the Humanities, with whom
I had worked on cooperative cataloging and other problems before I
came to Harvard. I requested $6,000 for a revolving fund to enable
Harvard to acquire foreign newspapers selected by the University's
History Department. It was understood that at least one paper from
each of the major countries of the world would be included, beginning

with the *Manchester Guardian*, the *Times* of London, *Le Temps* from Paris, the *Frankfurter Zeitung*, *Pravda* and *Izvestiia* from the Soviet Union, and so on through the rest of the world, including China, Japan, India, Australia, New Zealand, South America, Africa, and Canada. The grant was obtained, Harvard made arrangements for receiving the papers and having them filmed, and copies were offered for sale. With $5,000 from the Nieman Fund we could buy a positive copy of each film for Harvard. The price for a positive copy was one third of the cost of acquiring the original newspaper, making the master negative, and producing two positives.

Everything worked out well from the start. The newspapers were asked to provide a current subscription free of charge because inclusion in the project would make them better known in the United States. Somewhat to my surprise, almost all of them agreed. The work of microfilming was divided between the Recordak Corporation, a subsidiary of the Eastman Company in Rochester, with which I had worked closely ever since my first experience with microfilm in the early 1930s, and the Graphic Microfilm Service, which had its headquarters in the Boston area and was headed by two men whom I had encouraged to enter the field and with whom I could talk at any time about problems that might arise.

The plan went into effect in the summer of 1938, a year before World War II began. During the war, inevitably, we had trouble in obtaining newspapers from countries directly involved in hostilities. As a result, the revolving fund of $6,000 was used up, and we just escaped a deficit. After the war, however, most of the missing files were obtained, and more libraries subscribed than I had anticipated. Despite post-war inflation, we began to accumulate a surplus without increasing charges.

By 1953, fifteen years after the project began, we had $15,000 in the bank and master microfilms worth $75,000. We were adding to both of these figures annually. By this time inflation had made it necessary to increase the appropriation that supported the Nieman fellowships, so we could no longer use income from the Nieman fund for acquisitions; but the $15,000 took care of the cost of Harvard's copies until other funds could be obtained. A regular profit from an enterprise of this kind might have involved the University with the Internal Revenue Service. With the approval of the Rockefeller Foundation, Harvard University, and the Association of Research Libraries, we turned over the accumulated master films to the Midwest Inter-Library Center (now the Center for Research Libraries), which was delighted to include them in its program. If I am not mistaken, the Center is now filming more than 150 foreign newspapers instead of the 40 with which we started. Libraries belonging to the Center can borrow film copies on interlibrary loan if they do not choose to purchase positives for their collections.

It was fortunate that the project started just before the war, and that afterward we received copies of papers from France, Germany, Italy, Scandinavia, and the Low Countries that could not be sent across the Atlantic at the time they were published. I look back on the whole foreign newspaper project as one of the most worthwhile undertakings in which I have been involved.

THE SECOND EDITION OF THE UNION LIST OF SERIALS

As related in the preceding chapters, I was busy during my first year at Harvard becoming acquainted with a new and complex situation, dealing with personnel problems, including the replacement of senior members of the staff who were about to retire, and working on plans for providing the space that would soon be needed. There were still other matters that required attention. They involved expenditures not provided for in the budget, but I was convinced that means ought to be found for dealing with them.

One of these matters was the need for foreign newspapers. The response to this has been reported immediately above. The second was to obtain funds for the storage library I had proposed. This became the New England Deposit Library and will be the subject of the first part of Chapter 6.

The third objective was to improve Harvard's Union Catalog, in which books throughout the University Library were listed. In April 1938 the Carnegie Corporation of New York approved a grant to the Library of $10,000 a year for three years; this was to be used for coordination. It enabled us to establish a messenger service and to coordinate the Library's exchange program; but most of the funds were used to fill gaps in the Union Catalog's record of holdings of the Arnold Arboretum and libraries of the Business, Divinity, and Law schools.

Finally, funds were needed to enable the Library to contribute a record of its holdings for inclusion in the second edition of the *Union List of Serials*. Winifred Gregory, with headquarters at the Library of Congress, was already at work on this with James Thayer Gerould, retired Librarian of Princeton University whom she later married. In Part II, Chapter 15, I have written of her work on cooperative cataloging.

During the 1920s, Miss Gregory's headquarters as editor of the first edition of the *Union List* had been in the New York Public Library, and

I had worked closely with her there. I knew that she had been unhappy about Harvard's contribution to the first edition. In spite of — or perhaps because of — his great interest in building up Harvard's collections, Archibald Cary Coolidge thought it unnecessary if not undesirable for Harvard to participate. I knew that he wished to spend all the money he could in buying serials for Harvard; it would be expensive to prepare a record for inclusion, and listing would inevitably attract requests for interlibrary lending, which would also mean additional expense for the Library. Apparently he had planned to do nothing about the *Union List*. Harry Lydenberg, a loyal Harvard graduate who was on the committee in charge of preparing the first edition, felt that Harvard ought to be included and found funds to make this possible. Even so, I regret to say, Harvard had not been very much interested; it had accepted the money, but I am not sure that it put its heart into the work. The listing for Harvard was incomplete and, in some cases, inaccurate.

I felt that we ought to do better for the second edition and put part of the serials staff to work on the task. I also appealed to Dr. Keppel of the Carnegie Corporation for funds, and the grant that has been mentioned above was helpful; as soon as I learned that it would be made, I employed Reuben Peiss. When he started work in the summer of 1938, I could pay him only $75 per month, which was painfully low even at that time; but soon thereafter, I am glad to say, the salary could be greatly increased.

Peiss had been graduated from Trinity College, Hartford, in 1933, had earned his M.A. at Harvard the next year, and then, while teaching at Trinity for three years, had completed his work for the doctorate except for his dissertation. Realizing, however, that there was little opportunity for him to obtain a college teaching position (perhaps because he was Jewish), he had attended the library school at the University of Michigan, where Andrew Osborn was teaching, in 1937–38. Osborn recommended him to me. He immediately took charge; the results were excellent, and work on the project was nearly completed before he joined the Office of Strategic Services during the war.

His work for the OSS kept Peiss in Europe throughout the war, most of the time in Switzerland and Portugal. He did so well that, as recorded below in Chapter 18, Luther Evans put him in charge of the Library of Congress Mission to Europe in 1946. The Mission acquired and distributed to 113 American research libraries more than 800,000 volumes published in Germany, France, and Italy during the war years.

Peiss then became a member of the faculty of the School of Librarianship at the University of California, Berkeley, where he was teaching in 1950 when the Scarecrow Press published his translation of Alfred Hessel's *Geschichte der Bibliotheken*. Brought up to date, twice the length of the German original, this was entitled *A History of Libraries*. He sent me an inscribed copy, which I have prized; but I was in Europe working on the Farmington Plan, and the volume did not reach me until after Reuben's untimely death. I have always regretted that I was unable to thank him for it.

EXPERIMENT WITH A PHOTOSTAT MACHINE

My predecessor as Director, Robert Blake, came into my office one day to say that he had found (I think in the archives of the American Board of Commissioners for Foreign Missions, which had been deposited at Harvard) a very early Georgian manuscript — apparently an eighth-century text of chapters of the New Testament. The manuscript had evidently been soaked in water, and the ink had run; it was almost completely illegible. I was asked if there were anything that could be done. As has been recorded in Part II, Chapter 2, I was put in charge of photostat work at the New York Public Library in 1913, and I have been interested in copying machines ever since. I asked the photostat operator in Widener to make an overexposed copy of a sheet of the manuscript, and then to copy that with underexposure. The overexposed copy brought out the blurring effect of the water as well as the original lines; but the second copy presented a very light text with practically no blurring. Much to his pleasure, Blake was able to read the manuscript.

DUPLICATION OF CARDS

During my early years at Harvard, Robert F. Fiske, the son of an admiral in the United States Navy, was in charge of the bindery at Harvard. He was a very ingenious young man, and we often talked about mechanical problems of various kinds in which the Library was involved. As a result of Currier's work from the beginning of the century, we were cataloging our acquisitions less expensively than any of the other large libraries. Still, when cards for a book were not available from the Library of Congress, there was a good deal of what seemed to be unnecessary duplication of effort in typing additional cards for entry under titles, subjects, etc.

Fiske, Osborn, and I thought that if we could team up six typewriters, each with a long strip of card stock, a single operator might be able to produce as many as six cards at once.

IBM was interested; the machines were provided and, sometime during 1941, it seemed to me that our problem was solved except for perfecting the gadget that would move the strips of card stock exactly 7.5 cm. so that 7.5 x 12.5 cards could be cut from them with a special knife in the bindery. Just at this moment, however, the government told IBM that it must give up all research and development work that was not connected with defense efforts. We were left "holding the bag." By the time the war was over, better and simpler methods of card duplication had been found, so it may have been just as well that we had to abandon our invention.

Chapter 5

Acquisitions

THE FIRST MONTHS of the academic year 1938–39 were as busy as those of my first year at Harvard. Jackson and Hofer were in the rare-book room. Halvorson and Palmer were at the reference desk, Shipton was in the Archives, and Osborn was with Currier in the Catalog Department. Grieder was at work organizing the Littauer Library of the Graduate School of Public Administration. Peiss was hard at work on Harvard's contribution to the second edition of the *Union List of Serials*. Work on the foreign newspaper project was beginning, and I was much more content with the public services we were giving. I had also brought Fred Kilgour into the office to serve as my general assistant.

I was now prepared to devote more time to Widener acquisition problems. During the previous year I had been able to persuade the Faculty Library Council to give up, at least for the time being, the practice of devoting most of its attention to dividing up and allocating by department the income from book endowment funds. This had been one of its chief occupations in the past, but I am glad to report that there was no return to the earlier practice during my eighteen years at Harvard. It should be added that allocation of fund income was not a simple matter because there were numerous funds and most of them were restricted by terms of gifts to use for specific subjects.

Fortunately the complicated bookkeeping that was required was handled by Gertrude Sullivan, who had been in the library since 1913. She kept the records so well that we never ran embarrassing deficits and always had small balances left over for the next year. As soon as I thought I could give more time to book selection, I personally checked all recommendations for purchases that came from members of the faculty, with interesting but not unexpected results. The examples that follow are indicative of the problems I encountered.

Professor Clarence Haring was a distinguished scholar; he kept track of publications on Latin American history, checking the comparatively few Latin American second-hand catalogs as well as lists and book reviews in current periodicals. In my opinion, however, he was too selective, rarely recommending a purchase unless he knew something about the author and was convinced that the work was important. At the other extreme was Taylor Starck, who selected the books in the area of Teutonic languages and literatures — German, Scandinavian, Dutch, Afrikaans, and Pennsylvania Dutch. He wished to purchase practically everything that he found listed, and I had to turn down a large share of his recommendations.

As I had done in the New York Public Library, I began to check the book reviews in the *American Historical Review*, the *Geographical Review*, *Foreign Affairs*, the *Times* of London, the *New York Times*, and similar publications, and to suggest for purchase titles that I thought we ought to have if we were to build up satisfactory collections. I think I was able to persuade Professor Haring that you cannot build up a great collection if you acquire only the outstanding books, and I did my best to make Professor Starck understand that we could not buy everything that was available. This work, of course, put me in touch with the professors who represented other departments of the College and had been assigned responsibilities for book selection.

Meanwhile I found that we could rely on Gertrude Shaw, who had served in the Order Department under Potter and his successors since 1918 and was doing wonderfully well in selecting current British and American publications, going as far as possible with the funds available. She was the person to whom members of the faculty brought their recommendations, and, one might say, she kept them in line. I could not have found more capable persons for these important positions, and I was fortunate that Gertrude Sullivan and Gertrude Shaw stayed on in the Library until after my retirement.

Clarence Walton, who had been Assistant Librarian in charge of the Order Department since 1931, told me that one of the rules — or policies, at least — under Coolidge and Blake had been that duplicates were in no circumstances to be purchased from the Library's endowed book funds. The History, Government, and Economics departments provided funds of their own for purchase of reserve books in their fields, and some duplicates were purchased — not from College Library funds — for the Freshman Library in the Union. It took some time to change the system, but eventually we began to spend $10,000 a year for duplicate reserve books. We found that by doing this we could save more than that sum on staff salaries that had been paid in an attempt to provide satisfactory service without badly needed duplicate copies. The earlier practice had also aggravated other problems, including mutilation and unauthorized borrowing.

The Howells Collection

A change of policy on the purchase of manuscripts should also be recorded. Walton insisted that the Library never bought manuscripts, though we had, of course, accepted many as gifts. Fairly early during my first year at Harvard, I found that Goodspeed's was offering for sale a large collection of letters that William Dean Howells had received from his literary friends all over the world between 1860 and 1910. The price seemed to be reasonable. If I am not mistaken, this purchase made it evident for the first time that Harvard was interested in manuscripts, and I believe that this helped to attract many valuable gifts of manuscripts thereafter.

The Howells letters had to be arranged, listed, and calendared in order to make them readily available for use. They were turned over to Arthur Hamlin, who had been graduated from Harvard in 1934 and had worked in the Library as a student assistant throughout his undergraduate years. Before I came, he had been appointed Curator of the poetry collection, with the task of organizing and building up the Woodberry Poetry Room; this had been established in 1931 with an endowment by Harry Harkness Flagler, and acquisitions were supported in part by income from the Morris Gray Fund. In addition to modern poetry, the collection included phonograph records of poets reading their own verse. Professor Fredcrick Packard was particularly helpful in developing this collection of recordings; it has grown to be large and valuable, and copies of many of the records have been made available to other libraries.

Hamlin arranged the Howells letters alphabetically by the names of their authors, and I made them the subject of talks I gave during the next few years at the Shop Club, the Club of Odd Volumes, the Thursday Evening Club, and Wellesley College. There were letters from Hawthorne, Emerson, Longfellow, and others, beginning with the first visit to Boston by Howells more than 130 years ago. A large number of letters from Mark Twain were particularly interesting; these were published years later by the Harvard University Press with the permission of the Clemens heirs. A letter from Hamlin Garland said that his whole literary career had been changed because Howells had encouraged him to write about his own past life instead of writing second-rate novels. I remembered reading Garland's *Boy Life on the*

Prairie in my youth, as well as Howells' *A Boy's Town*, telling of his youth in Ohio, which brought back to me my experiences as a boy in the same state fifty years later. The letters included one from Stephen Crane saying that *The Red Badge of Courage* was a result of Howells' encouragement. Most of the leading American authors of the half-century following 1860 are represented, as well as many Europeans.

The purchase led to my acquaintance with Howells' daughter, Mildred, and his son, John Mead Howells, a successful architect. Their mother was a sister of W. R. Mead; his firm, McKim, Mead, and White, planned the Boston Public Library, which was erected in the 1890s. William W. Howells, the son of John Mead Howells, was a professor of anthropology at Harvard later on, and we became friends. Mildred Howells was interested in the collection and over the years added to it many more manuscripts of her father's and first editions of his works. She spent her summers in Peterborough, New Hampshire, and her winters in Tryon, North Carolina, where I recovered my health during the winter of 1903–04. During the fall and spring she used to spend some time at the Women's College Club on Commonwealth Avenue in Boston, where Elinor and I met with her occasionally. I might add that she gave us a copy of her father's *Their Wedding Journey* as a wedding present.

THE TROTSKY ARCHIVES

Another important manuscript acquisition came in 1940. We learned that it might be possible to obtain the archives of Leon Trotsky, who had lost out in the struggle with Stalin for supremacy in the USSR and, after several years in Turkey, France, and Norway, had settled in Mexico City, hoping to escape assassination. His representative there wrote to Harvard and at least two other American libraries, indicating that, because he was short of money and wished to insure their preservation, he was prepared to sell his archival collection covering the years through 1936. We immediately expressed interest, and a generous friend of the Library, John W. Blodgett, Jr., promised to provide the funds that would be needed.

Arrangements were made to have William Langer, who had been a protégé of Coolidge, and was now a professor of history at Harvard and a member of the Library Council, go to Mexico City. He talked with Trotsky, and an agreement was reached for purchase of the papers by the Harvard Library. They were to be transported by ship from Vera Cruz to Boston. On 20 August 1940, shortly after the shipment had been made, Trotsky was assassinated. Jean van Heijenoort, who had been Trotsky's secretary, translator, and bodyguard from 1932 to 1939, told me that Stalin's agents had been on the ship with him, apparently hoping to throw him and the archives overboard. (The foregoing was written two days before van Heijenoort, then Professor of Philosophy, *Emeritus*, at Brandeis University, was to speak at the Houghton Library on the history of the Trotsky papers. His talk was published in the July 1980 issue of the *Harvard Library Bulletin*.)

Immediately after the assassination, Trotsky's widow deposited the rest of his papers in the Harvard Library; these were not formally purchased until 1946. The benefactor, once more, was Jack Blodgett.

Trotsky had stipulated that his correspondence be closed for forty years, and the Harvard Corporation approved this restriction; it was feared that the lives of some persons involved would be endangered if the material were available for consultation. The talk by Professor van Heijenoort on 2 January 1980 marked the opening of the archive.

Ruth Fischer

This seems an appropriate place to record the Library's dealings with Ruth Fischer, who became a good friend of the Library not long after she fled from Paris at the time of the German occupation in 1940. She was a remarkable woman. Her maiden name was Eisler, and her brother, Gerhart Eisler, had been one of the chief Communist propagandists in this country before he was deported. Her husband was assassinated, apparently by Stalinists, while in a telephone booth in Havana. She had been listed as the First Communist in Austria following World War I. She had gone to Berlin and there became a secretary of Rosa Luxemburg, the Communist leader of the Spartacus League whose body was thrown into the river in Berlin after her assassination. After having become the leader of the Communist Party in the German Reichstag during the early 1920s, Mrs. Fischer went to Russia and was a member of the Politburo. She was a supporter of Trotsky, and, after his defeat by Stalin, she was arrested and sent to prison, probably to be executed. (I understand that she was the only defender of Trotsky in the Politburo who survived.) Apparently she bribed the jailor; in any event, she escaped and fled to Paris, having made up her mind to spend the rest of her life fighting Stalin. She did not dare to return to Germany, but was able to visit Switzerland from time to time and to travel widely in Asia. Just before the Germans entered Paris in 1940, she managed to escape and come to New York.

Mrs. Fischer was called to my attention by Clemens Heller, an Oberlin graduate who had gone to the Western Reserve University Library School and had worked, not successfully, for the libraries of Ohio State University and the University of Pennsylvania. He was recommended to me by Oscar Jaszi, a prominent Hungarian statistician and author who had become a professor of political science at Oberlin. Heller was useful to the Harvard Library for several years in development of its Central European collections. Later he went to Paris, where he taught at the Sorbonne and directed the Maison des Sciences de l'Homme. He suggested that we get in touch with Mrs. Fischer because we had the Trotsky papers. Sidney Fay, a senior history professor at Harvard whose special field was Central European history and the origins of World War I, and I arranged to have her speak to one of his classes. We were favorably impressed, and, after I had consulted the Office of Strategic Services to make sure that the Government knew and approved what we were doing, I went to work to find funds to help support her. Assistance was volunteered by John W. Blodgett, Jr., one of the loyalest of Harvard alumni and perhaps one of the most conservative politically; he had enabled us to buy the Trotsky papers, and he now helped to finance her work on them. She was occupied with this and with lectures for classes at Harvard until a few years later, when the Office of Strategic Services took over her support. Some of the results of her work were published by the Harvard University Press.

Ruth, as we came to know her, visited our home in Belmont from time to time, and on one occasion gave us an ivory Buddha that she had brought back from India, where she had gone to meet with the leader of the Indian Communist party. She wrote an article for *Foreign Affairs* on Ho Chi Minh, President of the North Vietnam Republic, which was the first account of him that I read. In New York she had an apartment on Central Park West where I called and saw her large collection of Communist materials, which she agreed to leave to Harvard.

(A parenthetic personal note: As a result of our interest in Mrs. Fischer, Sidney Fay and I became good friends, and he arranged to have the royalties from his books turned over to the Library to be used as I proposed. I remember one evening when he and his wife had come out to dinner with us in Belmont, and he remarked that he had looked me up in *Who's Who in America* and had found that we had the same birthday; he had been born exactly thirteen years before I was. When Elinor then said that her birthday was eight days before mine, Mrs. Fay announced that we were double twins, since her birthday was the same as Elinor's.)

Mrs. Fischer moved back to Paris, taking her library with her, after my retirement. As she had promised, it was left to Harvard on her death. Douglas Bryant went to France and made arrangements for its shipment to Cambridge. Harvard's position as one of the great centers for Slavic studies is supported by this collection as well as by the Trotsky Archives, the Russian materials collected by Archibald Cary Coolidge, those that I was able to acquire, chiefly through Israel Perlstein, and those that have been collected by the Slavic Department of the College Library and by the Russian Research Center since that time.

ISRAEL PERLSTEIN

Reference to Perlstein in the preceding paragraph reminded me of our connection with him and the third Vollbehr incunabula collection. (The story of Vollbehr's first and second collections is told in Part II, Chapter 6.) The first included a copy of the Gutenberg Bible, and was acquired by the Library of Congress. The second was purchased by the Huntington Library in Pasadena. It turned out that there was a third collection, though originally it had been supposed that everything Vollbehr gathered had gone to the Library of Congress, and then it was believed that the Huntington Library had acquired everything else. But there was a third; Vollbehr, for some unknown reason, had become very short of funds and was trying desperately to sell it. He had borrowed some $125,000 from the Bank of America in San Francisco, using the collection as security; the bank was to be repaid at a certain time and was to take over the collection if not repaid. Finally Vollbehr called Perlstein and asked him to come to San Francisco to meet with him. He hoped that Perlstein, who had become well known as a second-hand dealer, would be willing to lend him enough to release the collection from the bank, with the understanding that, if the books could not be sold for the sum he expected to receive, they would be turned over to Perlstein. The two met in San Francisco, stayed in the same hotel, and were assigned adjacent rooms with a very thin wall between them. Sometime during the evening Perlstein overheard a conversation between Vollbehr and someone else; it disclosed the following points:

Vollbehr had asked a University of Chicago professor who had a reputation as an authority on incunabula to appraise his collection. This man had come up with the figure of $750,000 and was now attempting to persuade Lessing Rosenwald, a great book collector and a member of the Board of Trustees of the University of Chicago, to buy the collection for that amount and give it to the University. Rosenwald, he said, was seriously considering the purchase; if he turned it down, Vollbehr hoped that Perlstein would lend him $125,000 to get it out of the hands of the Bank of America. Perlstein also learned that Vollbehr was in the United States as a Nazi representative in charge of propaganda and had overspent the funds sent him by the Hitler government.

Perlstein was Jewish, and was naturally very much incensed; soon after he had returned to New York he telephoned to me one evening to tell his story and to say that he hoped I could get in touch with Rosenwald and prevent him from paying $750,000 to buy the collection for Chicago. I remember that we talked that evening for the better part of an hour; by the end of the conversation I was lying on the floor with the receiver pressed against my ear until the ear was sore. I agreed to approach Rosenwald and see what I could do to prevent the sale. Rosenwald and I met in New York at his luncheon club on Wall Street. After I had told my story, he turned down the Vollbehr purchase.

Perlstein, meanwhile, had received a complete list of the incunabula and a description of their condition. At my suggestion, he gave it to the Chief of the Acquisition Division of the New York Public Library, Robert Lingel, whom I had taken on there as Carl Cannon's assistant in the 1920s. Before coming to the New York Public Library, Lingel had been in charge of the dispersal of the George D. Smith rare-book collection after Smith's death and W. N. C. Carlton's return to library work; he knew as much about prices of incunabula as anyone I could recommend. He appraised the collection at $115,000. Perlstein had decided to advance somewhat more than that for it, which Vollbehr was unable to repay. Efforts to sell it as a collection for a price that would give Perlstein a reasonable profit were unsuccessful; he finally turned it over to Gimbel Brothers' Department Store in New York, where it was sold at retail on commission, and Perlstein came out just about even.

Not long after this, Vollbehr left the country with another man's wife and got back to Germany just before our communications with that country were cut off by the war. I have heard nothing more of him since.

Harvard continued to deal with Perlstein for Slavic publications, as the New York Public Library had done during my years there. Problems arose after World War II, when relations between the United States and the USSR were strained. As time went on, Perlstein was no longer able to acquire books from Moscow but was able to make arrangements through Warsaw. When this channel was cut off, he dealt through Prague; still later, he turned to Belgrade.

OTHER MATERIAL FROM THE USSR

Perlstein was not, of course, our only source for Russian publications. Something should be said of our acquisitions of Soviet publications from an establishment called the Four Continents Bookshop, which was on Fifth Avenue across from the New York Public Library. This shop had a large collection of Slavic books for sale, and there were regular additions to its stock. The proprietor told me that he had been informed by our government that he could not sell books for delivery outside of Manhattan Island, not even across the bridges to Brooklyn or Queensboro. For some time, consequently, Harvard representatives made a trip to New York almost every week to select and buy Russian books and bring them back to Cambridge.

I soon learned that Four Continents was buying new American publications on a large scale and sending them to the USSR. Neither Perlstein nor Four Continents was able to supply copies of the Russian weekly that listed new publications of the Soviet Union as the *Publishers' Weekly* listed ours. Somewhat later, we also learned that United States Customs had quite regularly been dumping overboard into the harbors Soviet publications arriving in New York or San Francisco.

Thanks to Archibald MacLeish's connections with the administration in Washington, I was enabled to meet with representatives of the State Department, the proprietor of the Four Continents shop, and others, including Stephen and Laurence Duggan, who were working on our relations with Russia. As a result we were assured that, theoretically at least, the problem of obtaining Soviet publications in this country had been solved.

THE THEODORE ROOSEVELT COLLECTION

An acquisition that delighted me was the Theodore Roosevelt collection. I had been very much interested in Roosevelt since 1900, when his candidacy for Vice President on the ticket with McKinley brought him to Elyria, Ohio, my boyhood home, to speak in the County Courthouse Square. I was eleven years old and not tall for my age; the crowd was large. In order to see him, I climbed a tree and, to my amazement, he came and stood under that tree while he made his campaign speech. My first vote in a presidential election was cast for him in 1912, when he was the candidate of the Progressive "Bull Moose" Party. In 1919, only a few weeks before his death, I saw him for the second time as I was rushing to the Lexington Avenue subway at Grand Central station in New York; as I turned the corner of Forty-Second Street and Madison

Avenue, I saw him walking toward me with his hand outstretched to greet an old friend, saying "Dee-lighted."

After his death, his friends established the Roosevelt Memorial Association, with a museum and library collection occupying quarters in the house at 28 East Twentieth Street, New York, where he was born. R. W. G. Vail, who had attended the library school of the New York Public Library and had worked at the Library's reference desk, was in charge of collecting material. (He was a great collector.) Nora Cordingley, who had been a classmate of mine in the first year of library school, was in charge of the Association's library. The basic collection had been assembled by 1928, and Vail came back to the New York Public Library; he later became Librarian of the American Antiquarian Society.

By the 1940s, members of the Memorial Association who had been friends of T.R. were getting along in years and realized that it was time to prepare for the future when they would no longer be active. The Association decided that it could keep up the museum in the Roosevelt House but that the library ought to be turned over to an institution that could build on it and make it available for historical research on the Theodore Roosevelt years. Hermann Hagedorn was President of the Association at this time, and he talked with the librarians of the New York Public Library, Columbia University, and Harvard about what should be done with it. There were not a great number of manuscripts in the library, but there was a fine collection of books, pamphlets, photographs, clippings, and other ephemera that would be useful to historians working on the period from the 1880s to Roosevelt's death.

The New York Public Library was interested and offered to house the collection in a room on its top floor. Columbia, likewise, offered a room in its Low Library and agreed to employ a curator. I suggested that the collection would be used more if it were placed in the Widener bookstack at Harvard with the American history collection, kept as a unit but shelved adjacent to Harvard's other books on the same period. I proposed that the Association provide a small grant each year, $250, to help us add to the collection, and that Nora Cordingley, who was still with the Association's library, be made a member of the Harvard Library staff, where she could catalog additions and see to it that the material was cared for properly. Rare or irreplaceable items would be separated from the main collection and deposited in our rare-book library, where they could readily be consulted by scholars.

I went down to New York one evening to meet with the Trustees. I remember particularly Hermann Hagedorn, two great federal court judges, Augustus Noble Hand and Learned Hand, and one of President Garfield's sons (if I remember correctly, the one who had been president of Williams College). This was one of the most interesting meetings I have attended, and at its conclusion the group voted, much to my pleasure, to turn the library over to Harvard.

Since that time there has been a great amount of research of T.R., and his reputation has risen. There had been a decline in interest earlier; but many scholarly works, including editions of his letters and several biographies — at least two during the preparation of this volume — have restored him to his earlier status, and I believe that he is now generally regarded as one of our great presidents. Interest in the collection has continued; when the Pusey Library was opened in the early 1970s, a special exhibition area for it was provided there. The one sad event in the story came in 1951, when Nora Cordingley dropped dead while at work in the public catalog room in Widener.

HEBRAICA AND JUDAICA

When I came to Harvard I found that we had reasonably good Hebraica and Judaica collections. A great scholar in the field, Professor Harry Wolfson, did much to build them up, and Abraham A. Roback deserves to be remembered for his contributions to our holdings in Yiddish.

One day I was asked to speak in an auditorium near Brattle Square in Cambridge about Jewish collections in American universities, particularly those at Harvard. I was somewhat reluctant but tried to prepare myself with help from Fanny Goldstein, a member of the staff of the Boston Public Library; I also drew upon my knowledge of the Jewish Division of the New York Public Library. The speaker was expected to dress, and I went in my dinner jacket. I was given an elaborate introduction. Then, as I left my chair to go to the podium, and before I took from my pocket the copy of the paper I was going to read, I pushed down my jacket on both sides, and both hands encountered the remains of chewing gum on which I had been sitting. It was difficult to dispose of the gum, but from then on the talk went off without any further problems. Though it was published in the *Journal of Jewish Bibliography*, I have to confess that it was not a good one. Re-reading it, however, has reminded me of how much was added during my period at Harvard to our Hebraica and Judaica collections, in large part through the generosity of Lee M. Friedman, whose many gifts during his lifetime were followed by a substantial bequest. During recent years the Judaica

Department of the College Library, headed by Charles Berlin, whose title is Lee M. Friedman Bibliographer in Judaica, has attracted more than two hundred endowed book funds, and Harvard's collections in this field are believed to be stronger than those of any other university library.

OTHER COLLEGE LIBRARY COLLECTIONS

In the foregoing pages I have mentioned only a few of the major collections that came to Widener from 1937 to 1955; my annual reports for those years list many more. Likewise, for rare-book and manuscript acquisitions of those years, the separate reports of the Houghton Library by William A. Jackson should be consulted; I shall touch here upon only a few collections with which I was particularly involved.

From the time he came to Harvard in 1938, and even more successfully after the Houghton Library was opened in 1942, Jackson was able to attract gifts of collections, as well as money with which to purchase rare books and manuscripts, from numerous friends of the library. Philip Hofer, in his field of printing and graphic arts, was equally active, and he purchased a great deal for the Library from his own funds. After Jackson's untimely death in 1964, his successor, William H. Bond, ably carried on, and Hofer, though he officially retired in 1968, is still, in 1983, as interested as ever in building up the Department of Printing and Graphic Arts.

The Emily Dickinson collection, which occupies a special room in the Houghton Library, includes many manuscripts of her poems, letters, the family library, and furniture and pictures from the Dickinson home in Amherst. It was given in 1950 by Gilbert H. Montague; we nearly came to grief in connection with it, and I remember all too well the hurried trip that James Barr Ames and I made to Mount Desert Island to see him, only two days after I had returned from my long trip to Europe to make arrangements for the Farmington Plan. It all came out happily, and many millions of dollars were eventually bequeathed to Harvard by the donor.

Another room in Houghton houses the William King Richardson collection, consisting of early printed books in fine bindings, most of them related to Greek and Roman civilization. Richardson, an active member of the Club of Odd Volumes, had regularly obtained advice from George Parker Winship and later from Jackson and Hofer. I remember that once, when Jackson was out of town, Hofer and I visited Richardson's Beacon Street home at his request, and he agreed to finance the room that would hold his collection, with the understanding that it would be designed to resemble as closely as possible the one on Beacon Street in which his books were shelved.

I was fortunate also to have a part in acquisition of the Edward Sheldon collection. Sheldon was a Harvard graduate of 1907 and a nephew of the Edward Sheldon who, during much of my time in New York, was treasurer of the New York Public Library and chairman of the Bank of the United States Trust Company of New York. The nephew was perhaps the most successful American playwright of the 1910s and 1920s; he died prematurely after having been crippled for years with arthritis. His mother donated funds for an exhibition room and quarters for his manuscripts in Houghton.

Carl Keller, whose great collection of Cervantes came to us over a period of years, followed by a bequest that now amounts to more than a million dollars, was one of the members of the Club of Odd Volumes with whom Jackson, Hofer, and I became well acquainted at the Saturday luncheons.

Two donors of buildings will also be remembered always for important collections that they gave the Library. Thomas W. Lamont gave us his fine Masefield collection as well as a large endowment fund for needs of the Library other than acquisitions. The Keats collection presented by Arthur A. Houghton, Jr., combined with Amy Lowell's bequest of 1925 and other gifts, has made Houghton Library's Keats Room a world center for research on the life and works of John Keats.

Early in the 1940s, William Inglis Morse, a retired Anglican clergyman living in the house at the corner of Brattle Street and Fresh Pond Parkway in Cambridge that had been built for President Eliot after his retirement, began to give the Library manuscripts and printed books from his remarkable collection of Canadiana. His gifts over the years greatly increased the strength of our Canadian collections. Gifts from his daughter, Susan Morse Hilles, and her husband later enabled Radcliffe College to construct the Susan Morse and Frederick Whiley Hilles Library, which was opened in 1966 and became an administrative unit of the Harvard College Library in 1971.

WALTER LIPPMANN

Walter Lippmann, a member of the Harvard Class of 1910 who was graduated in 1909, was for many years considered to be one of our greatest political savants.

More than thirty-five years later I have learned that it was Wilmarth S. Lewis (of whom I shall have occasion to write elsewhere in this volume) who talked with him about presenting his archives to Yale. Soon afterward he came to Harvard to receive an honorary degree. Apparently his conscience troubled him because he had negotiated with Yale without first having talked with Harvard. President Conant referred him to me, and I suggested that I go down to his Georgetown house in Washington to look over the collection.

I spent the better part of a day with him there. The house was packed full with his papers, correspondence from prominent persons almost everywhere in the world, and other relevant manuscript material. It was a wonderful collection. I made a quick estimate of the cost of putting it into shape for use by scholars. There were perhaps forty tons of material, and the collection would increase; Lippmann was, in fact, active for another thirty years, and I remember well the occasion in the early 1970s when he came to a meeting of the Massachusetts Historical Society, talked about the political situation, and answered questions.

It would cost $100,000, I thought in 1944, to deal with the collection. This was during World War II, and I did not think it proper to acquire something and then put it away, untouched and unusable, for years. Regretfully, I decided that Harvard ought not to accept the collection, and told him that, if he had to decide then, it should go to Yale. This may well have been one of the major mistakes that I made during my Harvard years, and I have been wondering ever since how bad a one it was.

DISAPPOINTMENTS

I remember with regret two other important collections that were offered to Harvard but not acquired; in both cases, however, there were understandable reasons for the outcome.

One was a fine collection of German publications, which was shelved for a number of years in the Germanic Museum (now the Busch-Reisinger Museum), where it had been deposited by a German scholar, Curt von Faber du Faur. After a long period during which Harvard had made the collection available for use by scholars, its owner indicated that, if he could receive an appointment to the faculty, he would be glad to present his books to the University. The policy of the Library and the University administration had always been to refuse gifts with strings attached unless there were some exceptional reason, and we were unwilling to make an exception in this case. The collection then went to Yale with its owner.

There was a similar opportunity to acquire the Arctic collection of Vihjalmur Stefansson, the explorer. He had worked at Harvard for several years early in the century. He had always been interested in the literature of Arctic exploration, had gathered a tremendous collection, and was living in New York City, where the cost of housing and caring for his collection was growing to be too much for him. He offered it to Harvard if we would employ him as curator or custodian. While the collection would have been good to have, it was in a field that we had not emphasized. Bowdoin and Dartmouth were interested, and, when we decided not to accept it on the conditions under which it was offered, it went to Dartmouth. Stefansson moved there and continued to work with it as long as he lived.

Chapter 6

Cooperative Storage Problems

THE NEW ENGLAND DEPOSIT LIBRARY

THE NEW ENGLAND Deposit Library was ready for use early in 1942. As has been stated in Chapter 2, it was an indirect result of a proposal made by President Eliot of Harvard to the Massachusetts Library Association at its meeting late in 1901 and repeated by him at the annual conference of the American Library Association, held at Magnolia, Massachusetts, in June 1902. I was encouraged to revive President Eliot's proposal, because we had learned in New York during the 1930s that we could inexpensively house a large section of our infrequently used material in a storage warehouse, provided that any volume needed could be brought back for use at Forty-Second Street within twenty-four hours or could be made available in a storage place to which a reader could go without too much trouble. The material stored in New York, because of the large size of many of the volumes, took the space of some 200,000 regular books; it was used very little, but it was not "dead." We found that one attendant could take care of this collection without seriously reducing the effectiveness of our service. Materials in New York's warehouse have greatly increased in bulk since storage there began in the early 1930s.

Four questions, it seemed to me, needed to be considered if there were to be a cooperative storage library for the Boston area:

1) Was I right in believing that, because quite a number of the larger libraries in the vicinity were short of space as well as of funds to provide additional space, they could be persuaded to cooperate?

2) Could the cooperative organization be financed?

3) How should the books for storage be selected?

4) How could we launch the proposal and provide a building?

I took up the fourth problem first because I hoped I could make progress on it independently. If we were to persuade the other libraries to join Harvard, I was convinced that the building must be in Boston, and I looked into the possibility of finding a warehouse there that might be acquired at a reasonable price. Fortunately I was able to go to William H. Claflin, Jr., who had recently become Harvard's Treasurer. I told him about the warehouse in New York and asked if he could suggest a suitable one in Boston that might be available. (It should be remembered that the Harvard Corporation had agreed in principle to the proposal in the spring of 1938, as reported in Chapter 3.) Claflin was interested at once, and he obtained a list of vacant or partially vacant warehouses in Boston that might be considered. It should be kept in mind that the country was still in the throes of the Great Depression and that buildings could be purchased for considerably less than would have been the case in the 1920s.

We visited a number of warehouses in Boston's North End, near North Station and the bridges to Charlestown, as well as others on Commonwealth Avenue in the area that Boston University later used to advantage. Not far from the Boston Garden we found a warehouse with floors that would hold the weight required for book storage; it could be purchased for what seemed an absurdly low price. Claflin obtained an estimate of the cost of putting it in shape for library use. However, he called attention to the traffic congestion that could be expected in the vicinity once the economy recovered. He suggested that Harvard had land back of the Business School on the Boston side of the Charles River and that the University might make this available free of charge. He thought it would be possible to build an inexpensive, functional building there, where we would not have to worry about access or parking. The building could be enlarged if need be, and would be less than a mile from Widener. It could be reached from Boston libraries as easily as a downtown site.

The next step was for me to suggest a plan for the building. I drew up a sketch for an oblong structure with an entrance in the center of one of the long sides, and with space on the first floor for reader accommodations, catalog, staff, and a shipping and receiving room. The remainder of that floor, as well as the basement and the floors above, would be filled with shelving. I had worked closely with Henry Shepley on details of the plan for Littauer Center and felt free to ask him to look at my proposal. He spent about a half hour on it; when he left, we had revised my plan, proposing a six-story rectangle as the main part of the building. In front of the short side facing the street, he suggested a two-level (basement and entrance) cross-bar, making a T on those floors, with the reading room, which would also house the catalog, on one side, and a work-room in the basement below it. On the other side there would be toilet facilities and a shipping room, with the furnace room below them. The space between these two sides would provide a small entrance lobby, beyond which stairs on one side and an elevator on the other would go up to all floors.

Next came the stack, with a broad central aisle nearly one hundred feet long. This aisle would be entered directly from the front door after the elevator and stairs had been passed. There would be only two windows on each stack floor, one at each end of the central aisle. On each side of the central aisles there would be stack ranges thirty feet long, extending to the outside walls, which would mean that the aisles between ranges could be entered only from the central aisle. Ranges for books would have ten double-faced sections; they would be three feet, eight inches apart on centers, with two deep structural columns, thirty-plus inches long by eighteen inches deep, in every third range. Each of these columns, which would be in pairs, one on each side of the central aisle, would occupy the space of one double-faced book section. They were to be placed so as to provide modules twenty-two by eleven feet in size, with six ranges in each bay.

The ranges for newspapers and oversized books were placed five feet, six inches apart on centers, so there were four of them in each bay. These ranges were thirty inches deep, instead of eighteen, with twelve sections, each thirty inches wide, per range; it would have been wasteful to shelve newspapers flat on standard thirty-six-inch sections.

There would be adequate incandescent lights in the center aisle, but only one light bulb in each of the stack aisles on either side of it. Each bulb, at the end of a long cord, would be protected by a grating, resembling those with which I had been familiar at Oberlin nearly forty years earlier. This would make the cost for lighting very low.

The stack temperature was to be kept at a much lower than normal figure, since the stacks would not be open to the public, and staff members, who would not visit them very frequently or remain in them long, would be physically active while there.

The reading room was to have a higher temperature. The furnace was to be constructed so that it could be used for either coal or oil, whichever proved to be cheaper at the time, and could be shifted from one to the other without great difficulty or expense.

Thanks to Shepley's planning, the building would not look like a factory. It could be placed on the lot so that an additional stack unit with the same dimensions could be placed on either side of the first, tripling the capacity. If three more were to be added back of the first three, the capacity would be multiplied by six.

Planning the building cost practically nothing. The capacity of the original unit was to be approximately one million standard volumes, if they were shelved by size. We estimated the cost at $250,000. To get ahead of my story, when we were ready to proceed with construction, it was built by the Harvard maintenance staff.

One serious difficulty arose during construction. This was just before the United States entered the war. We had ordered inexpensive commercial steel stacks with shelves that could be adjusted by removing screws at each corner of each shelf. There were holes for the screws at one-inch intervals in the uprights; shelves, therefore, could be moved if necessary, and the design seemed appropriate since they would probably not often have to be shifted. We were able to obtain enough steel for two levels of stack, but, during the construction period (the last half of 1941), the shelving for the rest of the building was taken away by the government; it was inevitable, even if some of us had not realized it, that preparedness would create an enormous demand for steel. We needed to install most of the shelving because space had been rented to the cooperating libraries by this time. Harvard's Superintendent of Buildings and Grounds suggested that the shelves be made of wood, and he "tooled up" in order to construct them on a production line at a cost considerably less than we had paid for the steel shelving. This brought the total cost of the building down to $225,000.

Construction and its problems were preceded, of course, by work on organization and financing. Once I had a fairly definite plan for a building on a satisfactory site, I was ready to find out if other librarians in the Boston area could be interested in the proposal. I talked informally with the librarians of the Massachusetts State Library, Boston Public Library, Boston College, Boston University, Tufts, MIT, the Boston Athenaeum, and Wellesley. Northeastern University had not yet reached a stage of development at which participation would be desirable. All the librarians with whom I talked proved to be interested except Wellesley's, who was hoping to have a new building soon. At a luncheon in the Bellevue Hotel on Beacon Street, the group decided to try to go ahead with the proposal.

We organized, electing Dennis Dooley, Librarian of the Massachusetts State Library, as President. We felt that he could help us politically, and he was very much interested because his library was seriously overcrowded. (It still is, more than forty years later.) A state charter would be needed if we were to avoid taxation. Ammi Cutter, who later became Associate Justice of the Supreme Judicial Court of Massachusetts, was retained to deal with our legal problems. (He was a great-nephew of Charles Ammi Cutter, once Librarian of the Boston Athenaeum, third president of the American Library Association, and author of catalog rules, the Cutter classification, and Cutter book-numbers.)

Ammi Cutter went to work and a charter was approved by the General Court of Massachusetts within a reasonable time; we had agreed to call our institution the New England Deposit Library, since it seemed possible that membership would someday extend beyond the Boston area. Cutter was asked to continue as our legal counsel but had to give up the assignment from 1942 to 1946 while serving in the Army. His place was taken by another member of his firm, Harold Stearns Davis, whom I was glad to meet; his brother was the Oberlin history professor who had been very good to me during my first two years in college and had recommended me to his successor, who almost persuaded me to come to Harvard and study for a Ph.D. in history. I remembered calling on Professor Davis at his home in Pittsfield, Massachusetts, during the summer of 1909 when I worked on a farm in the Berkshires.

With a state charter and an approved plan for the building, we were ready for construction as soon as money could be obtained. I was assigned the task of finding the funds and proposing budgets. I had gone down to New York in the spring of 1938 to call on Frederick Keppel, the president of the Carnegie Corporation. He had approved proposals that I had presented to him before I came to Harvard, and I could talk with him easily. As I have told in Chapter 4, he approved grants to Harvard for 1938 and ensuing years to make the Library's union catalog more nearly complete and enable Harvard to report its holdings for the second edition of the *Union List of Serials*. Now, however, when I asked for $250,000 to construct a cooperative storage building for the New England Deposit Library, he said that he would consider it carefully and suggested that I walk with him to Grand Central Station, where he would catch his train for Croton-on-Hudson. I remember very well how, just before he reached his car on the train, he turned to me and said, "Your storage library proposal is a good one and ought to be carried out, but I know enough about librarians to know that they will not cooperate, and I'm not going to burn my fingers on the proposal."

I was naturally upset and unhappy about Keppel's decision. Later, however, I went to Harvard's Treasurer, William H. Claflin, who, as has already been related, had taken a real interest in the storage library. I told him my story. He was favorably impressed, and said, "Let me see what I can do about it." He then asked the Harvard Corporation to lend $250,000 to the New England Deposit Library; there was to be a thirty-year mortgage with interest at two-and-one-half percent. This, of course, was a much lower rate than Harvard was then receiving on its investments and represented a great bargain for our enterprise.

I am glad to be able to report that the building was completed well under the estimated cost of $250,000, that the mortgage was paid off in little more than fifteen years instead of thirty, and that, soon after I retired, the New England Deposit Library had a surplus that could have been used for construction of a second unit. During this time it had not raised rates for rent on the space used by the cooperating libraries. This had been fixed at $200 a year for each double-faced, ten-unit range for regular-size books (where there were three ranges to a bay), and $300 for the newspaper ranges, which were two to a bay. This came to less than $1.50 per square foot of floor space, which was much less than we might have expected. It was enough to cover the cost of operating the new library, including salaries of the staff, heating and lighting, and messenger service between the building and cooperating libraries; it also covered interest and amortization of the mortgage.

We were able to rent four of the six floors to libraries immediately. Charges for these floors would have balanced the proposed budget but would not have helped to pay off the mortgage. But the United States was at war by this time; a federally supported agency at Harvard was working on a special camera for use on aircraft and was looking for space. It found that the New England Deposit Library was of sturdier construction than any other building available at the time. This would prevent undesirable jarring. We rented two floors to this agency until the end of the war. This put us far ahead financially and enabled us to make payments on the mortgage immediately.

I might add here that, even before the new library began to operate successfully, Keppel, who had turned down my application for a grant by the Carnegie Corporation to construct the building, was in Cambridge one day to visit his son, Frank, who was then President Conant's assistant. He came to my office in Widener and apologized for having said that librarians would not cooperate. This was one of the highlights of my seventy-five years in library work. But I am still inclined to think that his earlier statement had a rather firm foundation. I say this on the basis of my experience both before and after the Deposit Library was established.

During the war, the Victory Book Campaign, which was collecting reading matter for members of the armed forces, used space in the library that had been rented but not yet occupied. Books collected by the Campaign were arranged by author, and those regarded as suitable were shipped to the camps. The others were turned over to Harvard; they included a large quantity of American fiction published after 1875. With minor exceptions, Harvard had collected little of this up to that time, but the English Department was now interested in it.

Apropos of the Victory Book Campaign, I cannot resist the temptation to tell of a request that was made to me to give a talk on the radio appealing for books for the soldiers. I prepared a five-minute talk; but, when I went to the broadcasting station, I found that a speech had been prepared for me on the assumption that those conducting the campaign knew more than I about what should be said. Fortunately there were a few minutes before I went on the air, and I was able to glance through the text. I found in it a story about a soldier with a European background who had previously done very little reading in English but who now reported that, thanks to his use of books provided by the Victory Book Campaign, he had learned to read and speak English "profusely." I caught this in time to change the wording slightly.

At the time when the Board of Directors of the New England Deposit Library authorized me to go ahead with construction and financial planning, Elinor Gregory, Librarian of the Boston Athenaeum, was appointed as the new organization's representative to see to it that I proceeded as I should. It was not long after this that she agreed to our marriage. I reported this to the trustees at the next meeting of the Board, and Elinor presented her resignation from the assignment as my overseer. Father Keating, the Librarian of Boston College, agreed; since we were now to become one in the eyes of the Church, he could not see how she could continue to check on my actions.

The final question to be decided before the building was occupied was how to select the books to be deposited in it. It was left to each of the libraries to use its own discretion, but an author card bearing a union catalog location symbol was to be provided for each work. This would facilitate retrieval by the depositing library as well as borrowing by the others. Anything in the building was to be available to patrons from any of the cooperating institutions.

In order to save space, Harvard decided to shelve its books by size, and they were classified accordingly. Within each size-group they were arranged by number in the order of their assignment to the Deposit Library. Each shelf was filled to capacity. The ceilings were higher than is normal in bookstacks, and shelving by size made it possible to get as many as a dozen shelves into some single-faced sections, each of which could then hold as many as 400 of the smaller volumes. This greatly increased the total book capacity. Cards for the Harvard books were filed in both the Harvard and Deposit Library catalogs, with class-marks preceded by "K," a letter that had not previously been used in the Harvard classification. The "K" was followed by a symbol indicating the size-group of the book, and then by its serial number in that group.

This was a relatively easy decision; it was harder to decide how to select the books. Some of the bound newspapers were obvious candidates. There was no need to keep the *New York Times* in Widener now that the Library had acquired a microfilm copy. We knew that some of the old files of Boston newspapers were rarely used, so these could be sent. One of the senior catalogers went through the Widener stack looking for multi-volume works of which the Library had many editions, few of them in demand. An example was Gibbon's *Decline and Fall of the Roman Empire*. If I remember correctly, there were more than sixty editions of this in Widener, including only a few that were of current interest. There were sets of old encyclopedias such as the *Britannica*, which needed to be preserved but were seldom used. There was a tremendous collection of primary, elementary, and secondary-school textbooks, which was not used heavily after the retirement of Dean Holmes of the Graduate School of Education.

Altogether, we found that nearly one fifth of the bulk of the Widener collections could be sent to storage without causing very much inconvenience. The cost of the work came to about fifty cents per volume, including selection, changing the class-marks, and, I might add, the cost of constructing space for the volume in the Deposit Library. At 1940 prices, stack space in Widener would have cost at least one dollar per volume. Today it would be perhaps four times that amount; but construction cost per volume in the Deposit Library came to only twenty-five cents.

Two special groups of material that were sent to the Deposit Library by Harvard may be worth particular mention here. Early in the 1950s, when we were still struggling with the problem of selection, we turned to James E. Walsh, a cataloger in the Houghton Library, who had done graduate work in the classics and was highly regarded by members of the Classics Department. He was asked to make selections in that field, and he found a large part of the collection that, in his opinion, was so little in demand that it could safely be sent to storage. The books that he selected were segregated, and members of the Classics faculty were asked to examine them and pick out anything that they wanted to have kept in Widener. Out of several thousand volumes they found fewer than a dozen.

In 1946, as reported in Chapter 18, Harvard received more than 58,000 volumes from the Library of Congress Mission. Andrew Osborn selected volumes from this collection for storage in the Deposit Library. There were quite a few German books published during the Nazi régime that ought to have been kept in Widener in the opinion of one or more professors. Whenever a member of the faculty disagreed with Osborn's selections, he was asked to report to me, and, to avoid difficulties, the books in question were immediately returned to Widener. This prevented a campaign against our practice. Considering the amount of material now in the Deposit Library, I think it fair to say that there have been amazingly few difficulties. This has apparently been true also in the case of the other participating libraries, which, incidentally, did not shelve their books by size.

Sometime in the late 1940s, a study was made of the number of calls for books that Harvard had sent to the Deposit Library, and we found that the average volume there was requested less than one percent as often as the average volume in the Widener stacks. Even so, many of the volumes in storage may well have been books held by no other American library, and we should have been unwilling to discard them.

Messenger service, charged to the Deposit Library, was arranged by Harvard; a station wagon made the rounds every day, visiting each of the libraries that wanted to borrow books, deposit them, or return them.

Something should be said here of the later history of the New England Deposit Library. It has had in some ways a checkered career. It has continued to provide space for storage of approximately one million average-size volumes. It enables the cooperating institutions to house infrequently-used books outside their own buildings at a very reasonable cost. It has enabled each of them (except Boston College, which became a member of the group but did not use any space) to avoid, at least temporarily, the necessity for providing space in a new building or an addition to an old one. It has not seemed to inconvenience anyone seriously.

It should be added that Tufts University, MIT, Boston University, and Harvard have each, since the opening of the Deposit library, built one or more new libraries or added to their old ones during the boom periods of the 1950s and 1960s.

In other ways the Library has been a disappointment. Thus far, at least, there has not been a demand strong enough to justify construction of an additional stack unit. Some of the space for possible additional units is still available, though construction of two of them would no longer be convenient because of the adjacent WGBH broadcasting station and, it might be added, Jimmy Crockett's Victory Garden.

A greater disappointment, in my opinion, stems from my failure to realize that, because of the diversity of the libraries participating, there would be few duplicates among the books deposited. I had hoped that storage space could be saved because some duplicates could be sold to advantage and others discarded. Harvard uses nearly half the building; between them, the Boston Public Library and the Massachusetts State Library use approximately one third. These three libraries have very different acquisition programs, and the demands made on them are so different that, even if their collections contain copies of many of the same books, the books that any one of them sends to storage are rarely duplicates of those sent by either of the others. Boston-area newspapers are an exception; but duplicates of these have been kept in the hope that, in spite of deterioration, a usable copy will survive until microfilms become available.

Another disappointment, also caused by the fact that acquisition policies of the cooperating libraries differ greatly, is that it has seemed impracticable to try to promote a program for periodical acquisition by the Deposit Library. Under a plan of this sort, when it seemed that a single copy of a periodical would be sufficient to meet the needs of the group, this copy would be kept at the Deposit Library. But, though only one copy may be needed in the area, that copy usually seems to be so useful at the library subscribing to it that keeping it there is preferable to having it in the Deposit Library. The situation would have been different if cooperating libraries had been more alike in character, as were those in the Midwest Inter-Library Center (now the Center for Research Libraries) of Chicago.

Experience soon revealed the most serious mistake that had been made in planning the building. When the first truckload of books arrived, the truck was too high to back into the covered loading dock, despite the fact that the opening was large enough to accommodate the largest trucks then being used by Harvard. On the other hand, experience has demonstrated that we were wise to provide a heating unit that could be changed from coal-burning to oil-burning or *vice versa* with a minimum of expense.

The staff required has been minimal. The first librarian, Robert L. Work, was a professional who gave the library a good start before he left for military service. He was replaced by Maisie E. Parsons, who had worked in the Widener Catalog Department. When she left to become Librarian of the Harvard Dental School, she was succeeded by

Edward L. Gookin, the College Library's Registrar, who had reached the Harvard retirement age of 66 after more than 45 years in the Library. He, in turn, has been succeeded by non-professional employees, who have been able to provide the necessary service. Little additional help has been needed for paging and shelving since the early days when additions to the collection were coming in rapidly.

As has been noted, the opulent 1950s and 1960s produced new library buildings for four of the participating libraries, thereby reducing the demand for additional space in the New England Deposit Library. I venture to say, however, that Harvard could make good use of all the present building if the other participants were to withdraw. I still believe that it was worthwhile in the early 1940s to establish the first regional cooperative storage library and that we should continue to develop various kinds of interlibrary cooperation, including storage. I want the Library of Congress, as the national library, to do a great deal for us, but there are limits to what it can do and should attempt to do. My involvement in other cooperative storage efforts is recorded in the following sections of this chapter.

THE MIDWEST INTER-LIBRARY CENTER

The New England Deposit Library began to operate smoothly early in 1942, and I continued my interest in it as Vice-President of the Corporation and Operating Manager until my retirement from Harvard. I was convinced that it should not be the only one of its kind. I soon became involved in a somewhat similar venture that, some years later, became the Midwest Inter-Library Center, now the Center for Research Libraries, occupying a large building adjacent to the University of Chicago campus. Our New England Deposit Library is clearly an ancestor of the Center; I understand that President Robert Hutchins of the University of Chicago, when he heard about our plans, decided that a similar organization would be desirable for major research libraries of a large area in the Middle West.

Bob Hutchins had been in my brother Nelson's Sunday-school class at Oberlin; many years later, Nelson was brought to the University of Chicago to succeed Amos Alonzo Stagg as Director of Athletics and Professor of Physical Education. Bob's father, William J. Hutchins, gave the required course in the Bible that I took as a freshman in 1907-08, and my sister Marion corrected student papers for him, beginning the following year and continuing until he left Oberlin to become president of Berea College. He was one of the most eloquent preachers

I have known; his sermons, each one a gem, were always held to twenty minutes in length.

I am sure that early Oberlin connections had nothing to do with Nelson's going to Chicago, and I do not suppose that they prompted President Hutchins to write to me as he did soon after arrangements for the New England Deposit Library had been completed. He explained that presidents of eleven mid-western universities and heads of two independent research libraries were considering something along similar lines; he hoped that I would come to Chicago to meet with them and that I would then look into the desirability of a storage-library project centered in Chicago. I was glad to attend the meeting, at which the John Crerar Library, the Newberry Library, the University of Chicago, Northwestern University, and nine state universities were represented. I told them of my experience with the New England Deposit Library and of the difficulties we faced in organizing and beginning operations. They asked me if I would go to each of the thirteen institutions to discuss the possibility of cooperative storage in the Middle West. I was so busy with my work at Harvard, including the Houghton and Deposit Library buildings, as well as with the Association of Research Libraries and the American Library Association, that I did not dare to accept an assignment that would take as much time as this would; but I offered to find someone who would do it under my direction and would make a report. This was approved by the group.

I was able to persuade John Fall of the New York Public Library, with whom I had worked before I came to Harvard, to visit the thirteen libraries and do the field work. He proved to be a very satisfactory person for the task. He had been supervisor of the main reading room in the New York Public Library and later was Chief of the Economics and Documents Division and Editor of the *Public Affairs Information Service*. (Still later, as will be reported in Chapter 18, he carried out another assignment at my request.) He found that, while twelve of the thirteen presidents approved of the project, twelve of the thirteen librarians opposed it.

I reported to President Hutchins and the group that, to my regret, I thought it would be unwise to go ahead at the time. We were in the midst of problems arising from World War II. In any case, a new enterprise of this kind would have little chance of succeeding unless those participating were enthusiastic about it.

The project was revived during the late 1940s, and the same thirteen institutions were asked to reconsider it. Twelve of the thirteen presidents had retired or moved to other positions during the intervening years, but their successors agreed with them, and the vote of presidents was still twelve to one in ,favor of the project. Twelve of the thirteen librarians had also been replaced during the interim; but the vote of librarians was now twelve to one in favor. The new librarians, for the most part, had been trained between the 1920s and the early 1940s in the library schools of Columbia or the University of Chicago, and some of them had worked at these universities.

In view of the change in attitude of the librarians, it seemed evident that the time had come to go ahead. The Rockefeller Foundation and the Carnegie Corporation provided funds for the building on a site made available by the University of Chicago. I was pleased by the Carnegie Corporation's changed attitude, but not surprised, remembering what Keppel had said when he visited my office in Widener.

The Midwest Inter-Library Center was planned and built. Angus Macdonald of the Snead Stack Corporation was the contractor for the stacks. For the purpose, he designed hinged shelving, put together in such a way that each range had books six deep instead of two deep. As I understand it, he was asked to deliver the stacks with so little time for detailed planning that he did not have an opportunity to do it as precisely as he would have liked. When the attached shelving was swung around, there was a little difficulty with the wheels supporting it. On the whole, however, it worked out well. It was less expensive than some of the newer types of compact shelving but did not save as much space.

I was asked to speak at the dedication of the Midwest Inter-Library Center building, and I found it very gratifying to see what had been done and to feel that I had been at least indirectly connected with the enterprise. I was particularly impressed by the attitude of the new generation of librarians. Still, while they approved of the plan, not all the librarians were ready to give it whole-hearted support. Jealousies, perhaps, were inevitable.

Ralph Esterquest, the first librarian of the Midwest Center, had headed the Pacific Northwest Bibliographical Center, and an excellent start was made during his administration. Some ten years after I retired, he became Librarian of the Countway Library, in which collections of Harvard's Medical School and the Boston Medical Library were brought together. He was succeeded in Chicago by Gordon Williams, who managed a difficult situation superbly.

The organization has now become the Center for Research Libraries, and Harvard is among the members from all over the country that have joined. The building has been enlarged, a sound acquisitions program has been developed, and clearly the Center is one of the great successes in library cooperation. Incidentally, the Foreign Newspaper Project, which was transferred to the Center from Harvard more than a quarter of a century ago, is still going well. Gordon Williams has recently retired, but I see no reason why the Center should not continue to prosper.

The Proposal for a Northeastern Regional Library

To my great regret, I was not successful toward the end of the 1940s in establishing a Northeast library center. I am inclined to think that giving up the effort was one of my major mistakes. At the time I believed that at least four regional cooperative storage centers ought to be set up. There should be, in addition to the one then already operating in Chicago, one in the West, one in the South, and one in the Northeast. Each of the four would receive duplicates that could be sold to advantage, and each should develop a cooperative acquisition plan for its area.

With the improved transportation and electronic transmission systems that we have today, and with a central lending library like the one in the United Kingdom, perhaps we would not need four regional centers if we had a larger number of cooperative storage systems for smaller areas, such as those served by the New England Deposit Library, the Hampshire Interlibrary Center, and the cooperative plans in Washington, D.C., and North Carolina. Only time will tell. I still believe that it would have been worthwhile to establish a Northeast regional center in which the New York Public Library and the libraries of the University of Pennsylvania, Cornell, Yale, Brown, Harvard, and MIT would have deposited copies of many of the same books, making it possible to eliminate a great deal of needless duplication.

The most difficult question seemed to be the location. After talking with the librarian of each of the institutions, I made a rather definite proposal that space for the library be acquired to the north of Stamford, Connecticut, near the New York state line, in an area then being considered as a location for headquarters of the United Nations. This would be near the highway from Washington to Boston. It was approximately half way between Boston and Philadelphia. Land and construction costs would be lower than in New York City, where the New York Public Library and Columbia very naturally thought the new library ought to be placed. At a critical time, after I had made the proposal and the New York institutions had opposed it, I was scheduled to go to Europe for the Farmington Plan and to be away for several months. At any rate, the proposal was turned down, although I believe that arrangements could have been made to go ahead if I had been willing to accept a location in New York City. Soon thereafter, the trustees of the various institutions called in a very capable research group to study the problem. A report was made, and the idea was dropped. Perhaps it ought to be revived.

In this connection, I recall the proposal made in Congress for four additional copyright-deposit libraries, placed in the four regions proposed above, to receive all publications that are copyrighted. Nothing came of this. As time goes on, I am inclined to think that more and more libraries will decide that they cannot continue to shelve and circulate more millions of infrequently used books, many of which are printed on paper that is disintegrating. With four regional libraries, it would be easier to arrange for economical micro-reproduction or reprinting of material that should not disappear from the face of the earth.

Chapter 7

The Houghton Library

P ROPOSALS FOR solving the Library's space problem, as listed in my report of March 1938 to President Conant, included a rare-book and manuscript library, near the Widener building and connected with it, with air-conditioning to control temperature and humidity and to minimize pollution. Satisfactory air-conditioning had been installed in very few libraries at that time and was lacking in Widener and other Harvard library buildings. The rare books in Widener, except those in the Widener Memorial Rooms, were housed on the ground floor and part of a stack adjacent to the rare-book reading room on the first floor, not far from the Director's office. During my first years in Widener, when it was evident that these books were deteriorating because of dryness, we installed a very fine spray in the rare-book stack aisles; this kept the humidity up during the winter months, but we soon found to our dismay that it left a layer of residual dust on the books.

The Harry Elkins Widener collection, made up largely of English literature, was in the center of the building on an intermediate level between the first and second floors. It was (and is) entered from a landing on the monumental stairs leading up from the first floor.

Like other rare books, the Widener collection needed a controlled atmosphere. Fortunately, it was in an area that could be closed off, and we were able in time to install in the basement, two levels directly below, air-conditioning equipment to keep the humidity up and provide some temperature control in the Widener Rooms. Our problem then was with the four large windows, two on each side of the rooms, which frosted up because of the higher humidity during cold weather. Water from the frost melted and ran down into the exhibition cases immediately beneath the windows. Installation of double windows some distance outside the old ones took care of this.

It was necessary to keep the Widener collection in these rooms because of the terms of gift of the building, and Harry Widener's

brother and sister financed the air-conditioning. In the 1940s the
Wideners turned over to the Library the Gutenberg Bible that Harry's
father had purchased for him at the Hoe sale while Harry was abroad
on the trip from which he did not return because of the sinking of the
Titanic in April 1912.

As illustrations of what may happen to rare books, I should like to
digress here to record two serious episodes involving the Widener collection, one just a few months before I came to Harvard, and the other
some time after I retired. In the spring of 1937, a man dressed as a
priest came to the Widener Room and asked to use three books. He
signed for them, of course, and, strange as it may seem, used the name
of R. W. G. Vail, who had worked in the New York Public Library
with me on two different occasions and was then the Librarian of the
American Antiquarian Society. Neither of the attendants in the room
recognized the name, and they thought the man was a legitimate reader.
After he had worked with the books for a considerable period, he said
he would return shortly, and it was assumed that he was going to the
men's room or perhaps to lunch. It appeared that he had left the three
books in the solander cases that had been made for them. He failed to
return, however, and the cases were found to be empty.

I was told about the theft soon after I reported for duty at Harvard
in September 1937, and I immediately asked Clarence Walton, the
Assistant Librarian in charge of the Order Department, to write to
several of our English rare-book dealers, asking, without explaining
why we were interested, if they had copies of the books for sale. Maggs,
a prominent London bookseller, reported that the most valuable of the
three was available. We wrote back, asking the dealer to look for our
secret mark. This was found, and the book was returned to us; we
refunded the comparatively small sum that had been paid for it, and
George Widener reimbursed us.

The other untoward event occurred long after my retirement. A man
who evidently knew nothing about books — or, at least about selling
them — except that the Gutenberg Bible was valuable, having managed
to get onto the Widener roof one day, stayed there until the Library
closed. He then let himself down by a rope anchored to the roof,
reached one of the double windows of the Widener room, broke through
the window, entered the room, broke the glass of the case that held the
two large volumes of the Bible, placed them in a knapsack, and then
tried to pull himself hand over hand up the rope to the roof. He lost his
hold somewhere on the way and, with the volumes in the sack on his
back, fell to the concrete floor of the light court, which must have been

at least fifty feet below him. He was badly injured, and eventually his groans were heard by the night-watchman. The police were called. The man was taken to the hospital, where he recovered remarkably soon; he was then released on bail until his trial. After consultation with lawyers and psychiatrists, the judge found "no probable cause for prosecution" when the man agreed to commit himself to a mental hospital. I understand that he had been there only a month or two when the doctors declared him sufficiently recovered from his mental illness to be released. There was no explanation of what he expected to do with the Bible.

The two volumes in the sack suffered little damage except to their bindings, which were skilfully repaired by experts from Macdonald's Bindery in New York. They were returned to the exhibition case, in which non-shatterable glass had been installed. The incident is reported here simply to indicate one of the problems faced by a library with rare books, in the hope that it will help to prevent a similar occurrence elsewhere in the future.

More could be said about the Harry Elkins Widener collection or about crime, but the subject of this chapter is the separate library for rare books that I proposed in March 1938. When Bill Jackson began work six months later as Assistant Librarian in charge of the Rare Book Department and Associate Professor of Bibliography in the Faculty of Arts and Sciences, I told him about the meeting of the Overseers' Library Visiting Committee at which Charles Warren had objected to his appointment and to the purchase of rare books. Soon afterward, Jackson suggested that Arthur Houghton be invited to serve on the Visiting Committee, and this was approved. Houghton, a member of the Harvard Class of 1929, had become greatly interested in book-collecting during his undergraduate years, and had specialized in John Keats. By 1938 he had brought together the greatest collection of books and manuscripts by Keats or relating to him to be found anywhere; it exceeded even the collection in the Keats House at Hampstead, in Greater London.

Warren continued as chairman of the Visiting Committee for 1938–39. I was able to arrange to have Jackson attend the dinner, which was at the Harvard Club in Boston. As I expected and feared, Warren again brought up the question of buying rare books and manuscripts. He vigorously repeated his objections to spending money for them, and cross-examined Jackson about his plans. As could have been expected, Jackson defended what he was doing very well and made a better case for rare books and manuscripts than I had been able to do the year before.

Houghton was sitting at the table near us, and it was evident that he was unhappy about the situation, though he said very little. The session ended after I had completed my report on the Library, including my suggestions for additional space and the fact that the Corporation had approved in principle my proposal for a separate rare-book library. Warren made no objection, though he was obviously unenthusiastic and continued to oppose the purchase of rare materials. I should add that I believe he was simply trying to prevent the Library from buying rare books at the expense of other books and journals needed by faculty and students. This interpretation of his attitude was confirmed nearly fifteen years later when his will included bequests from his residual estate of some $10,000,000 to Harvard, with sizable portions of it for the libraries. This bequest, divided between the Faculty of Arts and Sciences and at least three of the graduate professional schools, was to support work in American history; there is now a Charles Warren Center for Studies in American History, and Nathaniel Bunker, who is in charge of selecting American publications for the College Library, has the title, Charles Warren Bibliographer of American History.

The meeting in question, however, was in 1939. On the following day, Houghton came to see Jackson and me, saying that he strongly disagreed with Warren. He realized our great need for suitable quarters to house the rare-book and manuscript collections and was prepared to provide funds to construct a separate rare-book library. He did this with stock of the Corning Glass Company, which up to this time had been a family-held enterprise. The stock was not to be sold for some years to come, and I am glad to be able to report that the University lost no money in the transaction, though the building that resulted from the gift cost more than had originally been expected.

Houghton wanted William Graves Perry, head of the Boston architectural firm of Perry, Shaw, and Hepburn, to do the work. Perry had planned Houghton's home on the Eastern Shore of Maryland and had gained a national reputation with his work on the reconstruction of Colonial Williamsburg. The Corporation approved his selection as architect.

A satisfactory site was chosen. This was some thirty feet east of Widener on the brow of the hill where it had been proposed early in the century to erect a building that would have replaced or added to Gore Hall, which housed the College Library before Widener was built.

(I have seen the plans for this structure, which was to have been round, resembling a circus tent in shape. Fortunately, it was never built.)

The Houghton Library, as it was eventually to be called, was to have an underground connection with Widener. Moreover, despite terms of gift providing that the Widener building was not to be added to, the Widener heirs approved construction of a bridge between the two buildings, provided only that it should not resemble either building in color, and that the brick used for the new building should have a different pattern from the brick in Widener. This was approved by the University's lawyers.

The covered bridge connecting the buildings was sheathed with metal, painted gray; naturally enough, it aroused some criticism, but it has greatly facilitated communications between the two libraries. Its width was important. For little more than a bridge of minimal width would have cost, it was made wide enough to house the catalog for the rare-book collection at a location readily accessible from either library. (Houghton books are represented in the public and official catalogs in Widener, but are analyzed in greater detail in the bridge catalog. The sole catalog of the manuscript collections is also on the bridge.) The Widener end of the bridge is on the level of the building's first floor and what is called level 1 of the stack. At the other end of the bridge there is a door to the Houghton reading room.

Houghton quite properly wished to go over the plans with the architect, with Jackson, with me, and, on occasion, with Hofer; he did so without causing trouble for any of us. He could not have been more helpful, and there were no difficulties of the kind that arise with too many donors. He was particularly interested in having the building fit into the Harvard Yard. We agreed that it should be called the Houghton Library. He gave us his great Keats collection and offered to make an annual donation sufficient to hire a curator who would also serve as Secretary of the Keats-Shelley Association of America. We did not hesitate to make an exception to our rule against accepting gifts with strings attached and kept his collection together in the Keats Room, with a small adjoining room for its curator.

Two other exceptions to this rule were made during the planning. One of these has been mentioned already; it was the Richardson Room for the collection of finely bound, printed, and illustrated books, as well as important mediaeval manuscripts, assembled by William King Richardson, a Harvard graduate of the Class of 1880. He agreed to bequeath this to Harvard and provided a room for it at his own expense, reproducing, insofar as possible, the library in his home on Beacon Street.

The other special room installed at the outset was the Amy Lowell Room. Miss Lowell was a poet, a sister of President Lowell of Harvard, and a lifelong collector of "association books" and of Keats, whose biography she wrote. (Perhaps it should be explained that association books are books noteworthy for their past ownership.) The collection was left to Harvard by Miss Lowell, who died in 1925, with the understanding that it would be kept in a special room. The income from her residual estate was to come to Harvard after the death of a close friend who was still living in the 1940s. President Lowell had accepted the gift, but had told the Library not to worry about a special room for the collection. When I came to Harvard in 1937, I found that minimal housing was being provided for it in a Widener closet opening out of the newly established Woodberry Poetry Room. Jackson and I felt an obligation to provide an Amy Lowell Room in Houghton with the collection in locked cases where it could be seen by visitors. The room assigned to it was reached through the Keats Room, and the Keats curator was near at hand to supervise it and answer questions.

The Amy Lowell story did not end here. The income from her residual estate, to be used for purchasing additions to her collection, began to come to Harvard in the 1950s. At first it came to about $30,000 a year, and that figure, thanks to the wise investment of her trust, has greatly increased. Year after year it has enabled the Library to acquire treasures such as Tennyson's working notebooks. The collection, of course, has increased in size; in 1977, when previously unused space on Houghton's second floor was opened, it was possible to provide a larger room with additional exhibition facilities for the Amy Lowell collection.

There were several crises (if that is the proper term) during the planning and construction of the Houghton Library. The architect had assured us that it would be possible to have three levels of bookstacks below the ground floor of the building, with the lowest stack level higher than the bottom floor of Widener; consequently, if we ever had trouble with water in Hougton, it would flow through the connecting tunnel to Widener, where there would be a sump pump. We had counted on this, but, to Perry's dismay and mine, it proved to be impossible. Air conditioning, with which he had had little previous experience, required thicker floors than he had realized. Jackson, Hofer, and I had to accept this, knowing that, if the collection grew as rapidly as we anticipated, the Houghton stacks would be overcrowded within ten years. They were. Fortunately, as will be explained in the next chapter, additional space could be provided in time.

There was a disagreement regarding the colors to be used in the exhibition room just off the entrance lobby on the first floor. Locked shelving on the walls was to house the incunabula collection. Perry proposed that, while the shelves would be walnut in color, the walls should be what was called Williamsburg blue, which he had used in his reconstruction of Colonial Williamsburg. I believed that the walls should be white, because I thought we would tire of the Williamsburg blue in time. I had just sense enough to give in, and I think none of us have regretted the Williamsburg blue during the past forty years. It should be added that floor cases in the room house changing exhibits and that the room is used also for meetings, social events for staff and friends of the Library, and chamber-music concerts.

While I now think I was mistaken in advocating white walls in the main exhibition room, I can report that the combination of walnut shelves and white walls has proved to be satisfactory in the smaller exhibition room used for Hofer's collection of printing and graphic art.

Several interesting innovations in Houghton may be worth reporting. Cold cathode lighting was used in the exhibition cases, for the first time in a library, I believe. This made it possible to install the tubes in (and not over) the cases, which were ventilated so well that, with lights on all day, the temperature and relative humidity in the cases did not change as much as one degree. The insulation throughout the building was so effective that temperature and relative humidity, except in extremely hot or cold weather, did not change over weekends when the building was closed, even if ventilation and lights were turned off. Continuous records of the temperature and relative humidity were kept for the bookstack during the thirteen years before my retirement. As far as I can remember, the temperature never dropped more than two degrees below the planned level of 68 or rose more than two degrees above it, even in the most extreme weather. The relative humidity remained equally close to 50 percent.

There was one mistake in planning that I failed to recognize for several years. The circular stairway from the first to the second floor turned to the left going up; consequently, when anyone goes down the stairs and keeps to the right, he uses the narrow side of the treads. Here, as in many other buildings, falls have resulted from time to time, and a senior member of the College Library staff once broke his arm. I have checked circular stairs in all parts of the world and have found that, in countries where traffic keeps to the left, stairs turn in the opposite direction from those in the United States. It is my opinion that they turn the wrong way in both cases.

Two additional features of the Houghton building should be mentioned. It seemed to us that there was little danger of fire. We placed fire extinguishers throughout the building, but we did not want to do what was later done in the Beinecke Library at Yale, where there is an installation to flood the whole building with carbon dioxide within a very short period after a fire starts. This, of course, was before the advent of halon, which extinguishes fire but is not toxic.

We were more afraid of water than of fire. Aprons were installed under all horizontal water pipes of any kind, including roof drains, plumbing, heating, and ventilating pipes. If any pipe were to break or leak, the water would come down to one of the lower floors into a basin and provide an alarm. There were about a dozen water cocks above the basin, and, by turning them one by one, it would be possible to determine immediately where the leak was. The walls were so constructed that it would be easy to get at and repair any pipe. During the forty years since the building was opened, I understand that there has been only one leak, which was discovered and repaired before it did any damage.

A feature of the building is its oval entrance lobby surrounded with locked and glazed exhibition cases, each containing a representative selection of books from one of the Library's great collections. It is obvious to anyone entering the building that it is a library.

There are exhibition areas on the second floor, and we had expected that some of our elderly friends would need an elevator more readily accessible than the staff elevator, which is behind locked doors. Space for a second shaft was provided, but it was found that the staff elevator could easily be made available on the relatively few occasions when a visitor was unable to climb stairs. Eventually the unused shaft provided part of the space on the second floor in which the Emily Dickinson collection, which includes a replica of her room in Amherst with her own furniture, was housed for some years. On the first floor, the area reserved for the shaft has been used as a small room in which Library publications are displayed; these can be purchased from the Department of Printing and Graphic Arts.

The Houghton Library was so attractive and functional that the remarkably competent senior members of the staff, Jackson, Hofer, Bond later on, and their associates, have succeeded in greatly increasing the collection in size, importance, and value. Most of this has been made possible by gifts of books and manuscripts, by money given for acquisition of items called to the attention of donors by the Houghton librarians, and by the income of endowed book funds designated for the purchase of rare books and manuscripts. It is many years since any unrestricted income has been used for such purchases.

In the 1970s gifts by Mrs. Donald F. Hyde and Arthur Houghton provided for finishing space previously unfinished and unused on the second floor. This made space available for the Amy Lowell collection that has been mentioned above and for a suite of rooms in memory of Donald Hyde, including a new seminar room and areas for shelving and display of the Library's great collection of eighteenth-century English literature. It should be noted also that a great deal of additional space for the Library's collections was provided beneath the Lamont Library in 1948 and in the Pusey Library, which opened in 1977.

Rare-book collections, both at Harvard and elsewhere, grow for two reasons. Material that had not previously been regarded as rare becomes rare because of its age or scarcity when it attracts the attention of collectors and when its historical importance becomes increasingly evident. Moreover, members of the present generation seem to be more inclined than their elders were to remove books from open stacks without authorization. It is inevitable that more and more books in a library as old as Harvard's must be transferred to protected facilities like the Houghton Library.

Some professors and librarians go further and urge an abandonment of the open-shelf policy that has proved to be so useful to scholars; they advocate a return to the system that was prevalent a century ago. Perhaps this statement simply proves that, in my nineties, I am an anachronism, as indicated in the title of these Recollections. But I still agree with Paul Buck, my successor as Director of the Harvard University Library, that Harvard's open-shelf policy is of prime importance for the University's educational program, and I hope it can be continued. At the same time, I am pleased that the University was able, during my years there, to construct and occupy the first separate facility for a university collection requiring special care, support, and service of the kind that the Houghton Library has been able to provide.

Chapter 8

The Lamont Library

T HE TWO PRECEDING chapters have told what was done about two of the recommendations in my report of March 1938. A third recommendation in that report called for a separate building designed for undergraduate library service. While use of this building and its collections should not be restricted to undergraduates, it ought to house the printed materials of particular interest to them, including assigned and collateral reading for courses, as well as a collection for general and recreational reading larger than those to be found in the dormitory (house) libraries or the Farnsworth Room, Harvard's specially endowed collection for browsing. The collection of the undergraduate library, except for books in greatest demand for assigned reading, should be on open shelves, more readily available than the vast collection on ten levels of stack running around three sides of the Widener building.

My recommendations had been approved in principle by the Corporation. After work had begun on the New England Deposit Library and the Houghton Library, arrangements were made for me to present the undergraduate library proposal in more detail to deans and department heads of Harvard College. Having been encouraged by their response, I started looking for a building site and prepared rough plans that would be useful, I hoped, when funds for construction became available. It had been indicated that it was up to me to do what I could to find those funds.

I had a definite notion regarding the site. If possible, it ought to be in the College Yard, near Widener and preferably connected to Widener by bridge, tunnel, or both. These connections were not needed for the convenience of students, but to facilitate the transfer of books and movement of library staff between the two buildings. With these considerations in mind, I wanted to build on the space north of the Wigglesworth dormitories and west of Widener, where Boylston Hall stood (and stands). Boylston was then occupied by reserve-book collections for history, government, and economics, and by the Harvard-Yenching Institute, with its Chinese-Japanese Library, which was rapidly outgrowing its quarters. The building was made of granite and was seventy years old. In my ignorance, I thought it should be considered expendable because there was relatively little assignable space in it, considering its total square footage and the cost of operation and maintenance.

I talked with Henry Shepley about this. He agreed with me that Boylston could not be regarded as an efficient or effective building, with its high ceilings, large central court, and stairwells that wasted space. I then showed him my rough plan for the undergraduate library. There was one public entrance with a charging and control desk adjacent to it; there were three stories and a basement. A small central bookstack on each floor was surrounded on all sides, except on the entrance level, by reading areas and individual carrels along the outside walls, a plan which has been used at Harvard and elsewhere during later years. We found to our regret that the site was not large enough to house the number of volumes and seating accommodations that I proposed. I learned later than many persons wanted to preserve Boylston Hall because it was where Theodore Richards, the first American winner of the Nobel Prize for chemistry, had done his work on atomic weights, and the building in which President Conant had started his scientific career. Boylston Hall was later gutted, the floor levels were changed, and the large central court and monumental stairs were cut down in size. New space would have cost almost as much as renovation, but the building was kept as an architectural monument.

Giving up the Boylston Hall site caused me to realize how many square feet of floor space I wanted, and Shepley gave me an estimate of the cost. We then looked elsewhere for a site. He made two suggestions. One was the south end of the block now used by Holyoke Center. He knew that this block, though then occupied by commercial enterprises for the most part, belonged to the University and would probably be used sooner or later for a Harvard building. His second suggestion was the block that was then available but is now occupied by Quincy House, which was built after World War II. I was not happy about either of these proposed sites, although they were possibilities. Shepley sketched in plans for the undergraduate library on both locations.

There seemed to be only one available space in the Yard now that the Houghton Library was being planned to go just east of Widener. This was the southeast corner of the Yard. We thought it ought to be used for an addition to Widener, with a bookstack for several million volumes, additional library services for graduate students, and a more suitable shipping and receiving room than Widener could accommodate. A tunnel would connect it to Widener.

Shepley produced plans for a tall building with as many as fourteen stack levels. I believed that even this space would ultimately be filled and asked him, "What next?" He made two suggestions. The Freshman Union was just across Quincy Street; he thought it expendable because its maintenance costs were high for the use it received. His second suggestion was to use the west side of Quincy Street, including the space then occupied by the President's House. Since the building was only thirty years old, the site seemed both impossible and undesirable to me. He replied, "It doesn't belong in the Yard and it can be moved across the street to the space between the Faculty Club and the Fogg Museum." (This is the site now occupied by the Carpenter Creative Arts Center, the only building in the United States designed by Le Corbusier.) We quickly came to realize that neither of these solutions to the library space problem was practicable at that time. The Yard should not have a skyscraper, and we were not ready to move the President's House across the street.

We began to think of an underground structure in the area now occupied by the Pusey Library, and we dropped further planning until funds should become available. Meanwhile the Graduate School of Design arranged to have the senior class of its School of Architecture use the design of an undergraduate library as the project for its senior thesis. A dozen or more proposals resulted in the spring of 1942, and I spent two days discussing the plans with faculty and students.

If I have correctly deciphered the almost illegible Phillips Brooks House calendar kept by Helen Powers, it was on 22 March 1939 that I went to New York, had luncheon on Wall Street with Franklin Parker, and dined at the New York Harvard Club with a group of Harvard graduates who were known by Jackson and Hofer to be interested in the Harvard Library. I was seated between Thomas W. Lamont and Henry S. Morgan, both members of the Morgan firm on Wall Street. As soon as we were seated, Lamont leaned in front of me and said to Morgan, "I'm going to have to leave for another appointment immediately after dinner and so, with your permission, I am going to talk to Mr. Metcalf through dinner, and you will have to leave him to me for that time." He then turned to me and said, "What do you consider the greatest need for Harvard's library today?" I was somewhat taken aback but recovered enough to say that, since the staff situation had been taken care of reasonably well and progress had been made toward providing a storage library and a rare-book library, the greatest need was a library for undergraduates. He asked me about my reasons for this opinion, and I gave those that have been reported in Chapter 3. He seemed to be very much interested and asked for more details. I did my best to explain the background of my proposal. He then asked, "If $500,000 could be found for the construction, would that take care of it?"

Fortunately I had been prepared by my talks with Henry Shepley to answer this question. I said I was sorry to have to say that this would not be enough; it would take $1,000,000. Lamont replied that this was more than he thought could be provided at that time, but that he was very much interested. He suggested that I come to see him at the Morgan company's offices on Wall Street in about a year. He did not indicate whether he thought he could provide the funds himself or would try to raise the money. I was encouraged when I returned to Cambridge, but realized that the problem was far from solved.

Following his suggestion, I arranged for appointments with Lamont annually during the next five years. Within a year after our first conversation, the war situation had become critical and, understandably, he said that this was not the time to do anything about the library; but he was still interested and asked me to keep in touch with him.

A committee appointed by President Conant published the report entitled *General Education in a Free Society* (commonly referred to as "the red book") at the end of July 1945. Paul Buck was the chairman of the committee, and I understand that much of the report was written by John Finley. A copy was sent to Mr. Lamont at his summer home in North Haven, Maine. Early in August I had a letter from him saying, "I received the General Education report on Friday and read it over the weekend. It is evident that if its recommendations are to be carried out successfully, as I believe they should be, the undergraduate library, which we have been talking about for a number of years, will be needed even more than it has been in the past. I suggest that you get in touch with my secretary and make arrangements to come and see me in my office the week after Labor Day to talk to me about it."

I called the secretary immediately and was given an appointment. Lamont greeted me cordially, as he had done before, and started out with, "You told me in 1939 that the building you wanted could be constructed for $1,000,000. I think that could be provided. Have you anything further to say?"

I replied, "I'm sorry. It could have been built for $1,000,000 in 1939. I think it will cost at least $1,500,000 today." Lamont seemed disappointed, and said, "You know, I am on the board at Exeter Academy, and I feel I should give as much there as to Harvard, and $3,000,000 in all is more than I can swing. But I will see what I can do."

I went back to Cambridge disappointed, but not in despair. Early the next month President Conant called me and gave me the good news that Lamont was prepared to give the $1,500,000 that I had suggested. He asked me to get in touch with the Treasurer, William H. Claflin (whom I had come to know as Bill), and talk about a site. I explained to Claflin that I had three suggestions — the site now occupied by part of Holyoke Center, the one now occupied by Quincy House, and the southeast corner of the Yard. I preferred the latter.

We saw President Conant. He was living in the Dana-Palmer House on the site that I preferred. He did not want to move and did not like the suggestion. I said I believed that this was very much the best site. It was on the way between the Harvard Yard, where the Freshman dormitories were, and the Freshman Union, where they took their meals; consequently it was an ideal place to catch them during their first years in college. The site was also between student classrooms and the houses where the other undergraduates lived. I very much wanted to have the library there. He was still unhappy, but said he would refer the matter to the Corporation, and I was given opportunities to talk informally with several of its members. The decision was to use the Yard site that I wanted.

A little later President Conant asked me if I had an architect to suggest. I said, "I have worked with Harry Shepley on Littauer, the New England Deposit Library, and, unofficially, in planning for an undergraduate library during the last six years, and I would like to have him." Conant replied, "I don't think he would give us as distinguished a building as some other architects to whom we could assign the task, but I will refer the matter to the Corporation." The Corporation again accepted my suggestion, and when the President told me about it, I said, "I suppose you will notify Mr. Shepley and then I can get in touch with him." The answer was, "Since you have selected him, you can tell him and can take charge of working with him."

This, of course, put me in an unusually good situation; Shepley felt that he was to plan a building under my direction. We almost immediately reached an agreement along the following lines. I was to have the final say on the internal arrangements. Since I was ignorant of such things, it never occurred to me that there ought to be a program outlining the requirements, but I did talk with him about the number of readers to be accommodated, the number of volumes, and the various special facilities that I thought desirable. Shepley would have the final say about the façade and the architectural style of the building. Each of us would feel free to ask questions and make suggestions about decisions assigned to the other; but they would be suggestions only.

Shepley then said, "I am going to assign one of the young men in my firm, James F. Clapp, to the project. He will make proposals under my direction and will come to talk with you about them at any time. He will be at your disposal from now on."

By this time I had partially recovered from the pleasurable shock of being able to go ahead on my long-hoped-for undergraduate library. I realized that there were other problems to be faced in addition to going ahead with the plans. The first was that the site agreed upon was on a small hill, running perhaps thirteen feet above the ground level at the Widener building, so it would be possible to have a deep basement; this should be used for book storage, and might provide an ideal place for additional stack space needed by Widener and Houghton. I also realized that funds for operation and maintenance of the building would be required and that it was Harvard's custom to keep these costs in mind at the time of construction. A talk with Shepley indicated that this might take $75,000 a year, or the income of an endowment fund of $1,500,000.

I talked both problems over with President Conant. As a result, the Harvard Annual Alumni Fund agreed to use its receipts for one or more years for this purpose. When an estimate for the cost of a two-level basement bookstack was obtained, the Corporation approved a building budget of approximately $2,300,000. Unfortunately, by the time we were ready to break ground, just after Commencement in 1947, costs had gone up enough to make it evident that this sum would be insufficient. Inflation had risen rapidly during the years immediately after the war. The Corporation agreed to a larger figure.

I am glad to be able to report that, when the building was completed at the end of 1948, the total bill — including the cost of selecting, acquiring, cataloging, and moving a collection of some 80,000 volumes, of connecting the building with plumbing, and of providing lighting, sewage facilities, and landscaping — came to $250,000 less than the sum that had been approved. An endowment of $1,500,000 for operation and maintenance had also been raised. I understand that this was the first time in recent Harvard history that an entire building project had been completed within the budget finally approved.

As soon as the Shepley firm began work on the plans, I arranged with Paul Buck, who was the Provost of the University and Dean of the Faculty of Arts and Sciences, and President Conant for the appointment of two building committees to help with the planning. The faculty was represented by one of these committees, and students by the other. Fortunately for me, there were no serious problems with the faculty committee. Before the building had been completed two and a half years later, three student committees had been appointed, one for each year, the first two selected by the Dean of the College, and the third by the student senate. I met with each of the three and always began by saying, "This building is to be planned with you in mind, and we want it to meet as far as possible your specifications. On the other hand, you will have to understand that no plan can be satisfactory to everyone, and, while we welcome any suggestions you care to make, the final decision may not suit all of you. But I can assure you that we want to make the building as satisfactory as possible for those who use it."

I concentrated the discussions with each student committee on a number of items — the question of checking books out at the exits, what they wanted to do about coatrooms and smoking, and the types of seating accommodations preferred. They readily agreed on smoking regulations. All books should be checked out before leaving the building. They did not want a coatroom, but coat-hooks would be provided in inconspicuous corners of the reading areas, where they would be in sight of readers. In those days, men did not carry umbrellas; when the fashion changed, I regretted that no provision had been made for them. The students did not want smoking in the main reading rooms; but they wanted a smoking area on each of the levels, and this was agreed upon, for the first time, I think, in an academic library. I believe that the result has been satisfactory, and I am glad to report that there have been practically no complaints. On the whole, smoking rooms have been used less than the non-smoking areas; as a result, two of the seven areas where smoking was permitted originally have been taken over for other uses. It should be added that Radcliffe women were not admitted to the Lamont Library during its early years except while summer school was in session, and we had trouble with smoking by them until the restrictions were called to their attention.

Other problems arose during the course of planning. The students asked for a snack bar; but I persuaded them that this would be unwise because it would inevitably attract vermin, and food and drink would be taken from the room where it was dispensed to other parts of the building, which would be undesirable. Since there were a number of eating places just across the street, anyone who felt that he must eat or drink would not have far to go.

Another question was whether or not Radcliffe women were to be admitted. Soon after I came to Harvard I had arranged to let them use the main reading room in Widener. Before that, Radcliffe graduate students had been permitted to use the main bookstack up to five o'clock in the afternoon, after which time it was thought they would not be safe there. Undergraduate women could use the small Radcliffe Study, as it was called, with only about a dozen seats, the current periodical room, and the public catalog; but women could not enter the main reading room. During my first year at Harvard, one of the senior professors in the Classics Department rushed into my office, looking as if he were about to have an apoplectic stroke, and gasped, "I've just been in the reading room, and there is a Radcliffe girl there!" I am glad to report, however, that admitting women to the reading room caused no complications.

I talked over the admission of women to Lamont with President Conant and Dean Buck, saying that detailed plans for the building's layout would be affected by the decision. I was still old fashioned enough to believe that, if women were to use the Library, the toilet installations would have to be changed, and we should probably not have the small, unsupervised reading rooms that we were planning. We wanted to have these rooms. It was agreed that Lamont Library was to be used by men only. This decision was vigorously opposed by Benjamin Wright, Chairman of the General Education Committee, who later became President of Smith College. He refused to have his office in the building. There was a good deal of controversy. Relations with Radcliffe became closer after my retirement; residence halls eventually were made coeducational, and women were admitted to Lamont before this. No changes were regarded as necessary then, except that two of the five toilet rooms were assigned to women.

To return to the account of planning, I had sessions with James Clapp (whom I quickly knew as Jimmy) several times a week, and one with Shepley nearly every week. In the course of making continual changes as plans developed during the months that followed, Shepley and Jimmy taught me many things that have been useful to me ever since. We had only one serious disagreement. This was about two of the stairwells, one near each end of the building. I had told Shepley that I wanted the students to have to go through the stack areas, which were to be in the center of the building, in order to reach the large reading rooms on three of the five levels, and he planned the stairs accordingly. I did not like the result and asked him to change them, but he still thought he was right. He then suggested that he make two mock-ups of them and put one pair on his desk and the other on mine, where we could study them for a week. He came back a week later and started the conversation by saying, "I have decided that you are right, and will go ahead on that basis." I then spoke up and said, "I've decided that you were right, and since it's agreed that I make the final decision, we'll do it your way."

As has been said, the façade of the building was left up to him, and he wisely prepared three plans, each of which would fit the internal arrangements that I had approved. One was for a traditional Georgian building that would have fitted in with a large share of Harvard's buildings at that time. The second was what he called contemporary architecture, more like what was being built at the time. The third he described as a modern building; it would be the sort of building toward which he thought architects were tending. Sketches for each of the three were presented to the Corporation, which approved the second or "contemporary" building and suggested that I take a model of it to show Thomas Lamont in New York. He was 76 at the time, not well, and he felt it unwise to travel to Cambridge.

I made an appointment to see him at his home on the Upper East Side. The model was some three feet long, and was accompanied by detailed plans showing the proposed layouts. I had a very difficult time getting the model into the taxi to take me to the station. I took a drawing room on the train, and then, after a difficult trip by taxi to the Lamont residence, I had trouble getting it into the house.

I suggested that Lamont look at the internal plans and suggested layouts first, and then I explained what we were trying to do. Finally I asked if he liked what he had seen. He studied the model for a few minutes and then turned to me and said, "Yes, I do like them." But he added, "If I didn't, I wouldn't tell you, because I want Harvard to do what it thinks best." Could anyone ask for a finer and more understanding donor?

I then spoke of the fact that there was a space over the entrance where we would like to have *Thomas W. Lamont Library* carved in stone. He replied, "I didn't ask for this, and I don't like it and don't think it desirable." I then said, "Please remember we have the Widener Library and the Houghton Library, and this must have a name. We don't want it to be called the undergraduate library, because it should be available to any student who cares to use it." I ventured to add that a grandson of his who had been at Harvard was lost in the submarine service during the war, and that this building could memorialize three generations of Lamonts who had attended Harvard. Finally I suggested that, since the building's main entrance jutted out a little, we might have just the word

Lamont in the space at each end of it. When the building was approached from the front, the name would not be visible. This was agreed to and approved by everyone concerned.

Having had our plans approved by the donor, we invited bids. They came within the architect's estimate, and construction began immediately after Commencement in June 1947. A deep excavation was required; the lowest basement level was to be 36 feet below the entrance, which was up just one step from the sidewalk and could be approached from the side by a ramp, so that students in wheel chairs could easily enter the building. Work proceeded rapidly. Shale was found a short distance above the bottom of the excavation, which was only 19.5 feet above sea level; but it was soft enough to be excavated with a steam shovel, and no blasting was needed. After heavy storms, it was found that the water table came a little above the lowest point, and pumping was necessary. Satisfactory waterproofing has prevented any leaks during the thirty-five years since the building was completed.

I should admit that, with the lowest level so far underground, we thought it would be wise to brighten it up to some extent, and I suggested the use of cork on the floor of the lowest level, as in the Houghton and Widener buildings. I had been told that cork should never be used below ground level because it would not stick to the concrete and that vinyl or plain concrete should be used. I retorted by saying that cork had been used only five feet higher in the sub-basement of Houghton and three feet higher in Widener, with satisfactory results in both cases. It was installed. Within two years, however, though there were no leaks of any kind, the cork refused to stick to the floor and had to be changed at a cost of $20,000. Obviously I deserved a good share of the blame. Apparently it was not a question of water but of ground temperature, which is about 50° that far down in the Boston area. The temperature affected the glue attaching the cork to the concrete base. Basements of the two other buildings were not so far beneath the surface, since the ground level of their sites was lower than Lamont's. It should be added that the whole basement level of Lamont was surrounded by a narrow service tunnel through which pipes of all kinds ran, and to which access could be provided without breaking through walls.

Interior layouts, with a few exceptions, will not be described here. An account of them is given in articles that Henry Shepley and I contributed to the Winter 1949 issue of the *Harvard Library Bulletin* (Vol. III, No. 1). Shepley and his assistant, Jimmy Clapp, did a wonderful job of carrying out my uneducated ideas and still providing an attractive building. The following points seem to be worth recording here. The air conditioning has been satisfactory; there are different installations for the three different parts of the building. The first and simplest provides slower changes of air in the two-level storage stack well below ground, where there are few readers and little change in temperature. For the smoking areas, the air is changed more rapidly and is not recycled as it is in the non-smoking areas that occupy most of the building.

The lighting, even by 1947 standards, was sub-standard; while more effective tubes with the same wattage have come into use and the intensity has moved up, it is still below the level maintained in most other buildings. The fluorescent tubes in the entrance lobby are in pairs, with one of each pair on one switch and the other on another. One set is used one week, and the other the next, so the intensity is only half as great as in the reading rooms. Anyone entering the building passes through the lobby to the reading rooms, where he feels that he is going into a bright room, and users appear to have been satisfied. Only 1.5 watts of current per square foot are used instead of the 4 or 5 that are common, but the results have been satisfactory. This saved some $15,000 a year twenty-five years ago, and I know that the sum must have been multiplied several times since then.

Two of the main reading rooms were two levels high, making it possible to have two levels of stack for each of them. This was customary at the time. For the third reading room, which had nothing above it and could easily have been given any height desired, I asked Shepley to pull the ceiling down as far as he thought it safe to do in a room more than 140 feet long and nearly 35 feet wide. He brought it down to 9.5 feet in the clear, but divided it with screens going part way across, breaking the room into three sections, each some 47 feet long. I have had the pleasure of taking several hundred architects into the room, and not one of them has complained that the ceiling is too low.

The building cost about ten percent more per square foot than most other buildings of its time, but Boston building costs exceeded the national average by more than that. Its capacity was some twenty percent greater than its size would have been expected to provide; good use was made of space without giving an effect of overcrowding.

Each of the reading rooms can be entered at five different points on one of its long sides, so no one need go any great distance to find a seat after entering the room unless nearly all the seats are occupied. Carrels are along the walls, 4.5 feet on centers, and there is ample space in them; the working surface in each measures 42 by 21 or 22 inches.

I should add that, in my opinion, there were several serious mistakes in planning that were my fault. The first was in reading room seating. We had a larger percentage of individual seats than had been provided in libraries up to that time, but slightly more than twenty percent of the individual seats were small lounge chairs. These have always been used less than the carrels or other individual seats, and ten percent would have been a better figure than twenty for Harvard, where students tend to take their work very seriously. We had too many long tables, which provided some forty percent of the seating; they have been less popular than carrels in spite of the fact that the tables were four feet across and that each reader had a space fully three feet wide at his disposal. In the center of the building on each of the three reading room levels there are twelve alcoves, each with one table and two chairs. Each alcove was thirteen feet wide, or eleven and one half feet in the clear since there was shelving on both sides. If these alcoves had been one and one half feet wider, the number of seats could have been doubled without crowding, since tables for four could have been provided.

In spite of mistakes, I believe that the Lamont Library has been remarkably successful for a building that was the first of its kind. Some librarians are not convinced that a separate undergraduate library should always be planned in a large university; but Lamont was followed by a good many undergraduate libraries. As a result of my connection with it, I have been called upon as a building consultant for more than 550 libraries; it might be said that the Lamont Library determined the way I have used my time since I retired from Harvard in August 1955.

Chapter 9

Building Problems and Changes in Buildings

T HREE NEW BUILDINGS provided space that was urgently needed by Harvard's growing library during my years as Director, and problems involved in their planning and construction have been described in the three preceding chapters. But my proposal for dealing with the space problem called also for retaining the Widener building as the largest physical unit of the College Library. It had been occupied for more than twenty years, and problems were to be expected, some of them resulting from wear and tear, and others from changing requirements and from the availability of new types of lighting and other facilities. Changes were made; some of those that would have been desirable were not financially practicable until after my retirement.

This chapter will deal with changes in the Widener building. Many of these were made in order to protect the collections from fire, water, adverse atmospheric conditions, and theft, vandalism, or unauthorized borrowing. Others, including renovation of lighting and elevators, contributed to the well-being of the Library's users. The problems considered here are typical of those arising in libraries constructed between 1905 and 1955 while I was working as a librarian. Some of them are still with us, and some of them have become even more serious since my retirement.

FIRE PROTECTION

At the time the Widener stack was built, it was believed that one of the best ways to preserve books was to make sure that they were properly ventilated. I suppose that this was because of fear of mold; to prevent it, open-bar shelving was used and, in the multi-tiered stacks that were standard before World War I, it was customary to have ventilation slits on both sides of each stack range. Widener's ten-level, multi-tiered stack presented two serious fire hazards, which were inadequately mitigated by the fire extinguishers available at conspicuous places throughout the stack.

The ventilation slits were similar to those in the New York Public Library and the original Library of Congress building, now called the Thomas Jefferson Library. The stacks in all three buildings had been designed by the Snead Company, with which I had dealt in my New York days. Because of the slits, the whole installation might have been regarded as a large collection of chimneys that would help a fire to spread rapidly from floor to floor. The hazard would be increased if housekeeping were poor and there were loose papers lying about. The problem was aggravated in Widener by the fact that there were no doors in the wide entrance to the stack area at the rear of the building on the first floor. (Unauthorized entrance to the stack was prevented by an iron grill.)

On the second floor there were two entrances to the eighth of ten levels of stack. Here there were doors, but they had always been kept open. I had double doors installed at the wide entrance on the first floor, and arranged to make sure that the doors on the second floor were closed at night. This did not solve the problem of temperature control during severe summer or winter weather. On days when the outside temperature was above 80° or below 20°, the stack temperature increased about one degree for each level from the bottom to the top of the ten-level stack, so it would be nine or ten degrees warmer at the top than at the bottom.

Except for the doors that have been mentioned, nothing was done during my years in the Library to reduce the fire hazard created by the ventilation slits. Subsequently, however, I am glad to report that the ventilation slits have been closed on every other level. An incidental result of this is that a pencil, small book, or pamphlet that has been carelessly dropped can no longer fall more than one floor. The stack stairways have also been enclosed on every other floor, and smoke detectors connected with an alarm system have been installed throughout the stack. After some fifty years, the danger of a disastrous fire had been reduced to reasonable proportions.

Another serious fire hazard in 1937 was a messy carpenter shop in the front of the sub-basement. This was removed before my first year was over.

As has been noted above, the Houghton Library has been protected from the time of its construction by carbon dioxide fire extinguishers, which can be used effectively with little risk to the lives of its occupants. Some newer buildings are automatically flooded with this chemical in the event of fire, and the occupants have only a very short time to get out safely. The new halon system, which is more effective and much safer, was installed in the new Pusey building, which is connected with Widener, Houghton, and Lamont by tunnels.

After the Cocoanut Grove fire of 1942, which caused the death of nearly five hundred persons, the Boston area became conscious of the danger of inadequate exits from buildings occupied by large numbers of people. Widener's main entrance, with its monumental thirty steps, had been supplemented by a service entrance on the east side. This was open only until 5:00 PM, when it was closed in order to save the salary of an evening control office. We realized in 1942 that we must have two entrances open at all times, and that this side entrance was unsatisfactory in any case, because one had to go down either unprotected steps or a steep ramp to reach the ground floor. The side entrance was closed to the public, and the back door on the Massachusetts Avenue side of the building, which had not previously been used, was opened, with a check-out counter controlling the exit. This also made it possible for persons with stack permits to enter the stack through doors on either side of the corridor leading from that entrance, and it provided an entrance near a public elevator.

WATER HAZARDS

I gave no thought to the dangers of water damage when I took over responsibilities for the Harvard Library buildings. No dangers of this kind had been faced during my eight years in the Oberlin College Library, which had no excavation or basement below ground level. We had no water problems during my twenty-five years in the New York Public Library. The 1938 hurricane, a year after I had come to Harvard, took place while I was in England; it resulted in no water damage to Harvard libraries, and I assumed that we need not worry about floods or dampness,

In the summer of 1944, however, there was another hurricane; it followed several days of heavy rain and brought with it an unprecedented twelve inches of precipitation within twenty-four hours. Water backed up from the floor drain in the front of the Widener sub-basement. Practically all of the building's lowest level, including the book-stack portion of it, was flooded, up to an inch deep in some places. Fortunately there were no books on the floor. Much of the water was disposed of within a short time by the two automatic sump pumps that were in the area, one at the foot of the ramp between Houghton and

Widener and the other at the back of the floor at the Massachusetts Avenue side of the building, and, after the rain ceased, by drainage back through the floor drain from which the water had come. The water vacuum apparatus supplied by the Department of Buildings and Grounds helped to mop up the remainder. Practically no damage resulted, except that we discovered a few days later that mold was developing on the lower shelves throughout the bottom level of the stack. The volumes there were wiped off promptly; there was no permanent damage, and the mold did not return.

I might add that Elinor was on her way to Cambridge after doing errands following her work at the Boston Athenaeum that afternoon. She reached the subway at Charles Street by going through deep water in the underground tunnel there, which fortunately is no longer in existence. When I came up from the Widener basement, we both emptied our shoes into the basin in the closet off my office.

I was worried about what had happened. I learned to my horror that Widener had been built directly over the main storm sewer that drained a good share of the Harvard Yard and adjacent areas. The Cambridge building code provided that there must always be an open drain on the lowest level of a building. I had learned many years earlier at my home in White Plains, New York, that I had to have an open drain in my basement laundry room, and I found this very useful when, too often, I spilled water on the floor. But the house in White Plains was not built over a main storm sewer. We appealed to the Cambridge authorities and obtained permission to close the drain whenever we had what might be called a cloudburst.

We had no further trouble until eleven years later, in August 1955, just before I retired as Director. Then there was another torrential rain. The Widener floor drain was securely closed; but that afternoon I was called to the sub-basement, and rushed down to find little geysers, some of them nearly a foot high, coming through the concrete floor in many places around the closed drain. The storm did not last long, but several of us on the staff got our feet wet moving boxes that the Harvard University Press had stored on the concrete floor under the main entrance to the building. The geysers soon subsided, and there was no damage to the Library's collections, but the Press lost books worth about $1,000. I understand that this experience has not recurred during the twenty-eight years since my retirement and that the storm drain was re-routed, when the Pusey Library was built, to the area between Widener and Houghton.

Widener was not the only Harvard library that suffered from the 1944 storm. Langdell Hall, which houses the Law School's library, had toilet installations on the next-to-lowest level of its stack, and water backed up through them from its storm sewer line and then ran down to the floor below, damaging a few books. Arrangements were made to prevent this from happening again under similar circumstances. At the library of the Institute for Geographical Exploration, where books were stored in the basement level, there were windows with area-ways. Rain falling into these area-ways had no other way to escape and leaked onto the floor, but no serious damage ensued. Experience with this storm made me glad that special precautions had been taken to prevent water damage in the Houghton Library, where most of the collections were stored in two completely underground levels. These precautions have been described in Chapter 7.

Plans for the Lamont Library called for its lowest level to be some three feet below the lowest level in Widener, to which it was connected by a 150-foot tunnel with an inclination of one foot in fifty. There was a sump pump in Widener near the entrance to the tunnel, and another in the tunnel, just outside Lamont, at the lowest point of the three connected buildings, Widener, Houghton, and Lamont. If a downpour should ever flood the lowest level of Houghton the water would run down a ramp to Widener, where there is a sump pump, and any water that this pump failed to dispose of would flow on to the sump pump near the tunnel entrance in Widener; if any water still remained, it would flow down the tunnel to the sump pump just outside Lamont. There are doors to each of these inclined tunnels, but there is a gap beneath each of the doors through which water could run. Walls of the Widener-Lamont tunnel have been stained by small leaks, but there has been no other trouble, and no water has reached Lamont.

The lowest basement level of Lamont, which has been used as an overflow stack for Widener and a reading area for newspapers, microforms, and government documents, is 19.5 feet above sea level, 36 feet and four stack levels below the entrance levels of Lamont and Houghton, which, 55.5 feet above sea level, exactly match the level of Widener's first floor. Since there were accommodations for readers and staff on this lowest basement level of Lamont, toilet facilities were installed there and, because the nearby city sewer line was considerably above the 19.5 level, a sump pump was provided to drain them. During the thirty-five years of Lamont's operation up to now, only one accident has occurred, and it was not serious.

Parenthetically, the storm of August 1955 caused trouble at home as well as geysers in the Widener basement. I was greeted by Elinor with the news that the storm sewer in our house had backed up, and we had a couple of inches of water throughout our cellar. It was the first time this had happened in the eighteen years I had lived there. She had tried to find a way to shovel it out the back door but had been unsuccessful. I was just bright enough to realize that, since the level of the ground dropped off at the rear of the house next to the back door, I could use our long garden hose to siphon it out easily.

Another flooding crisis arose in Widener after my retirement, and this should be recorded here because I was at least partially responsible for it. To provide water for the air conditioning of Houghton and Lamont, a water tower was installed on the roof of Widener in a place where it could be hidden from view, which would not have been possible on either of the other buildings. During one of the tremendous wind storms that occur occasionally in our part of Massachusetts, the wind blew a considerable amount of water from the tower through the gaps between the louvre boards, and it came down through the roof into the public catalog room on the second floor. More than a thousand cards were damaged and had to be retyped.

ATMOSPHERIC CONDITIONS

During my eighteen years as Director, the collections of the Harvard University Library undoubtedly suffered much more damage from unsatisfactory atmospheric conditions than from fire or water. Harry Lydenberg had made me understand in 1913 that deterioration of paper and bindings was a very serious problem. As I have related in Part II of these Recollections, he struggled to improve the situation, and he realized that much of the deterioration was caused by the Library's uncontrolled atmospheric conditions. No solution had been found for the New York Public Library by the time I left, and I soon found that I had not left the problem behind me when I moved to Harvard.

When Widener Library was built, something called "forced ventilation" was installed; but, as had been the case at the New York Public Library, operation of the system proved to be very expensive, and it was turned off; many of the air ducts had been removed by 1937. Windows were available for air changes, and those near the ground level were protected by heavy iron grating. The walls were so thick that the building did not heat up badly in summer except after a prolonged spell of extremely hot weather; then, of course, it took a long while to cool off.

While we were fortunate to be able to do something about atmospheric conditions during the years that followed, I would be the first to say that the problem was not solved while I was Director, and is still far from solved. The major forward step in my time was to provide controlled temperature and relative humidity for rare books and manuscripts in the Houghton building, which was opened in 1942. We did not know then that paper would deteriorate less rapidly if kept at a temperature a little above 32°; but we did arrange to keep the stacks in Houghton at 68° instead of in the low 70's, as was desirable in the staff and reading quarters. The relative humidity was kept as close as possible to 50 percent, which apparently is ideal. As has been noted in Chapter 7, temperature and humidity were recorded constantly and never varied more than a degree or two from these levels. Air filtering was also provided; we were well aware of the damage done by dust and polluted air.

The unsatisfactory atmospheric conditions in Widener were similar to those in other libraries throughout the University. The Law School Library had the finest collection of early English law outside the United Kingdom, much of it bound in pigskin. A few years after coming to Harvard, I found that, in order to safeguard it, this collection was kept in a locked basement room, directly over some hot-water pipes. The air had been dehydrated to such an extent that some of the bindings had warped and pulled the covers off the boards. In my advisory capacity as Director of the University Library, I insisted that the Law School either transfer its rare books to Houghton or provide suitably air-conditioned quarters within its own Library. The latter course was taken at the Law School; but a good many of the smaller departmental libraries sent their rare books and manuscripts to Houghton.

In 1936 the Graduate School of Business Administration's Baker Library acquired a great collection of pre-1850 business and economic literature assembled by Herbert S. Foxwell, and prepared a special room for it. I attended the grand opening soon after I came to Harvard. There was a fireplace in the room and, since this was a festive occasion, a fire was started in it for the first time since the building had been opened. The damper was closed in the chimney, and smoke poured into the room until the situation was quickly corrected.

I believe that Houghton was the first university library building with satisfactory air conditioning. Three years later, when World War II was over, libraries in academic institutions throughout the Deep South began to use air conditioning. When the New York Public Library's new Circulation Center was constructed with private funds, it was planned with air conditioning and windows that could not be opened. The City, which was to pay staff salaries because this was part of the Circulation Department, said it could not pay salaries for anyone who worked in an air-conditioned building; if it did so, it would be forced sooner or later to air condition all its buildings occupied by City employees, and this would cost an enormous sum. Later on, fortunately, the decision was changed, and the building was opened with air conditioning.

I remember my first visit to the library of the North Carolina Women's College, as it was then known, in Greensboro. It was quite satisfactory except that it was not air conditioned, because the State had decided that it could not afford to air condition any of its buildings. As time went on, however, air conditioning was installed without question all over the United States and, for that matter, in Canada, even as far north as Edmonton. This, unfortunately, has not solved our problem of paper deterioration, but it certainly has helped.

Shelving, of course, can also hasten the deterioration of books. When I came to Widener in 1937, part of the rare-book collection was kept in the basement, in the room under the administrative suite, and, in one section of this room, there was an early version of compact storage, completely filling an area between two large columns and the wall. The ranges could be pulled out by hand to make the books available. I found a somewhat similar situation twenty years later in the basement of the Warren Hastings Manor in Calcutta, presided over by Dr. Kesavan and used for one of the national libraries of India. The Widener installation was quite unsatisfactory because one had to jerk the ranges to pull them out; this often made books fall off the shelves, and now and then a book was crushed. I had the compact shelving removed, and we added to the space available for rare books on level one of the stack, which was adjacent to the rare-book reading room.

At the beginning of Chapter 7 there is an account of our attempt to humidify the rare-book area in Widener by means of a fine spray which, unfortunately, deposited a layer of very fine dust on the books. Likewise, I have told there that we air conditioned the Widener Memorial Rooms and then found that double windows had to be installed in order to prevent moisture from condensing and running down into the exhibition cases.

THEFT, UNAUTHORIZED BORROWING, AND VANDALISM

Ever since libraries began, they have had problems with theft and vandalism. In mediaeval libraries, we should remember, books were often chained to prevent their removal. As has been reported in Part I, Chapter 4 of these Recollections, I read the shelves and took the only inventory at Oberlin that I knew of during my years there; losses had been few, and almost everything that should have been there was found.

When I went to the New York Public Library in 1911, I found to my surprise that there were uniformed officers at both public entrances who told (asked) you to leave in an adjacent checkroom your brief case and any books you might have with you. In those days, the New York Public Library had very little trouble in its main building with book thefts, except for those by professional thieves, of whom I have written in Part II, Chapter 9.

At Harvard I found an attendant at the main entrance, with turnstyles that had previously been used in the entrance gates of the athletic fields. These had been installed some years earlier, when it was found that books were being stolen on a large scale by students as well as by professional thieves. In particular, reserved books, which could legally be taken from the building only for overnight use, had often disappeared for indefinite periods.

The turnstyles were far from handsome. Between the turnstyles and the front door there was a checkroom for coats and other belongings. We decided that this could be given up; a checkroom is bound to be unsatisfactory in an academic library where many students enter or leave during the brief intervals between classes. Provision was made for coats and hats at various places in the reading room, we no longer had to pay a coatroom attendant, and the room was useful for other purposes. A small, plain checkout desk was placed to the right of the exit when the turnstyles were removed, and silk cords were used to divide the entrance from the exit passageway.

I should confess that no provision was made for umbrellas because, in the 1930s and 1940s, neither students nor professors were in the habit of using them. In my own undergraduate days, umbrellas had been carried whenever the weather was threatening, and we had to provide racks for them in the Oberlin College Library. Fashions have changed again in recent years, and umbrellas are now a problem in many libraries.

Regarding the loss of reserved books, the Superintendent of the Reading Room told me that checking at the building exit had reduced temporary losses by ninety percent. It had also been made clear that any student caught removing books from the Library illicitly would have his connection with the College severed.

We had some difficulty not long after my arrival in Cambridge with students who underlined passages that they considered important. Individuals who had been doing this (fortunately with pencil rather than pen and ink) were identified on a couple of occasions and put to work erasing the underlining while supervised. Word of this got around, and we had little trouble for some time afterward.

We had a great deal of difficulty with mis-shelved books in the stack during the war years. Members of the staff were invited to volunteer for shelf-reading. When an inventory was taken after the war, we found that there had been a loss of only forty books a year during the preceding fifteen years.

As I have said before, the world has changed since then. I still believe, however, that college students will hesitate to steal books from the library if they know that they will be expelled from the institution for doing so. It is unnecessary to publish this fact; when a student is suddenly required to leave college, the reason for it gets around, and the result is perhaps even more salutary than it would be if the penalty for stealing were officially publicized. This, at least, has been the case at Harvard and other colleges during my time.

LIGHTING

Of the building problems that I had to face during my first years at Harvard, none was more serious than library lighting, a subject in which I have been very much interested ever since.

The lighting in Widener's main reading room had unusual features. Installed in 1915, it was typical of installations during the first thirty years of this century, though less satisfactory than the one in Oberlin's 1908 building or in the New York Public Library, which was completed in 1911. In the Oberlin College Library, the reading room ceiling was not more than eighteen feet high, and there were chandeliers for general lighting in addition to table lights. The main reading room of the New York Public Library had a much higher ceiling than Widener's, but there were large, tall windows on both east and west sides, as well as ceiling chandeliers. I was also familiar with the lighting in the main reading room of Columbia University's Butler Library. At the dedication of that library, which was held in its reading room about 1930, I had heard the dean of the Engineering School at Columbia say, "For the first time we have a great reading room with satisfactory lighting."

I was sure that it was not satisfactory, though it was better than the lighting in Widener.

I learned soon after coming to Harvard that for years there had been a great many complaints by students about inadequate lighting in the Widener reading room. There was cove lighting over the tops of the tall windows, some twenty feet above the floor; there were two table-lamp fixtures on each of the room's long tables; and there were gooseneck lamps over the shelving around the walls that was used for the reference collection and for open-shelf reserved books. Improved table lights had been installed the year before I came; this had ameliorated the situation enough so that in 1937-38, to my surprise, no complaint reached me about the lighting, although I realized that it was far from adequate.

In the fall of 1938, however, complaints came again from individual students, and there were comments in the Harvard Crimson, the student daily newspaper. The room was sometimes called "the black hole of Calcutta." I talked with Charles Mahady, who been in charge of the reading room since 1915; after looking over the lighting, I said, "It looks to me as though we are not getting as much help from the cove lighting as we should. Are you sure that all the bulbs are on?" "No, I'm sure they're not," he replied. "Why not?" I asked. "You know the students are complaining." I was amazed when he explained, "In 1917, after we went into the war, Mr. Lane [then Librarian of Harvard College], who was very much worried about the cost of lighting the building, said to me, 'Turn off half the bulbs and never turn them on again unless I tell you to.' Mr. Lane never told me to turn them on, so they are still off." Lane had retired in 1928, nine years before I came to Harvard. For twenty-one years, then, only half of the original general room lighting had been used.

The coves were cleaned, bulbs were replaced, and all the lights were turned on; still, when I looked over the situation again, I realized that it made very little difference. There was barely enough light in the room after sunset to register on a light-meter. The gooseneck lighting around the walls made it possible to locate books without too much difficulty. The table lights provided what seemed to be adequate light if a book were placed directly under a light. The tables were twelve feet long by four feet wide; there were four chairs on each side, and two lights per table. With four persons using each fixture, a student's book was three or four feet away from a fixture unless he interfered with one of his neighbors. The general room lighting provided only three or four foot candles, and a student was lucky if he had more than five or six foot candles on his book or papers, even if there were no one in the adjoining chair and he could place his work close to the fixture.

I must confess that it took quite a number of years to solve this problem. It seemed unwise to do anything until we could determine whether it would be desirable to install a new floor above the reading room, reducing its height to the level of the building's fourth floor. This would have left a flat ceiling with some twenty feet in the clear below it. Henry Shepley drew up plans for this. There was no question that it would facilitate lighting the reading room, and the space on the new floor could be used for stalls and studies for graduate students and faculty, which we needed desperately. After careful consideration, however, we decided against making the change. The cost would have been great. We were not sure how the ventilation, which was not too satisfactory to start with, would be affected, and it would have meant giving up the handsome barrel vault of the monumental room.

We still realized that something must be done. Shepley and I conferred with Willard Thompson, who had successfully done the lighting for Houghton and Lamont and for the Widener public catalog room. He made a number of suggestions, none of which was acceptable to Shepley or, for that matter, to me. Finally, on the fifth or sixth try, he proposed an installation that we thought satisfactory. The ceiling of the central part of the reading room had three rows of skylights, each about nine feet square, nearly fifty feet above the floor, with the central row at the top of the barrel vault. The skylight glass was opaque, the reading room was on the north side of the building, and little sunlight came through it except on bright summer days. The high windows on the north side of the room gave some satisfactory light, of course; but they were some eight feet inside the monumental columns and outside porch, which reduced their value. Artificial light was needed for most of the hours of opening.

Thompson finally proposed that the skylights, which had always been a problem, be replaced. Several of them had leaked more than once, and we had to place pails on the reading room floor to catch the water that came down during a heavy rain. On one occasion, a large block of ceiling plaster had fallen to the floor while the Library was open; fortunately it did not hit anyone. Thompson proposed that the skylights be covered over, that eight forty-watt fluorescent tubes eight feet long be placed where each of the skylights had been, and that the table lights and gooseneck lamps over bookcases be removed. This was done; it increased the light on the table tops from between three and five foot candles to between fifteen and twenty or even more. This system has been in use now for more than twenty-five years; with modern, more efficient tubes, the intensity has been increased, yet the total quantity of electric current used is less than was required by the original installation of 1915.

The main reading room was by no means the only lighting problem in the Widener building. In Chapter 7 I have mentioned the cold cathode lighting used in Houghton exhibition cases; I had first seen this in a shoe store on Fifth Avenue near the New York Public Library. Before installing it in Houghton, we tried it out in a room then occupied by the Catalog Department typists. It proved to be satisfactory, though I must admit that it provided little more than ten foot candles. Andrew Osborn, who was in charge, told me that this lighting was so much more satisfactory than the original installation that card production by the typists increased more than fifty percent.

Fluorescent tubes replaced incandescent bulbs in the official catalog room and in the Order Department after Lamont was opened. After the Farnsworth Room was moved to Lamont, the room it had occupied in Widener was made available, with changed lighting, for portions of the Catalog Department. I experimented with lighting in my own office and other sections of the administrative space. Different colors of fluorescent light were tried. The new lighting was entirely satisfactory for me, though my successors have increased it considerably, for which I do not blame them.

The catalogers who had been in the same room with the official catalog were shifted to the area that had been the rare-book reading room before Houghton was built. The lighting was changed here as well as in the entrance lobby, which served also as an exhibition area. The four large exhibition cases there had been selected by my predecessor, who was six feet, four inches tall, and were made for persons of that height; they had never been entirely satisfactory with the former lights. The new lighting helped to improve the situation.

Widener bookstack ranges were only four feet, two inches on centers, several inches less than is generally considered standard. There were stalls (as we called them) along most of the outside walls, two for each three ranges, making them six feet, three inches on centers. They were generous in size, and deeper than necessary in both dimensions, but made so that each had a window. There was room back of each chair for a small bookcase. The lighting was simply a dropped incandescent bulb with a lampshade; when the reader leaned forward his head shadowed the book or paper on which he was working. These lights were replaced by fixtures with two two-foot fluorescent tubes in them, which provided much more satisfactory lighting.

The stack aisles had been lighted with fifteen-watt incandescent bulbs; these were replaced by forty-watt bulbs, but the lighting, though improved, was still not satisfactory. The stack aisles had ranges eighteen inches deep from front to back, which left a thirty-two-inch aisle; but there was a ventilation slit on each side of each range, so the space available for walking or operating a book truck was less than twenty-eight inches, which meant that four-foot book trucks like those I had found in the New York Public Library would have been unsuitable. Those in use were only thirty inches long.

Almost all the lighting in the building was changed from incandescent to fluorescent during my eighteen years at Harvard. Exceptions were the current periodical room and the second-floor lobby, from which one reached the public catalog, main reading room, periodical room, and stairs to the third floor. Incandescent light was retained there, because I wanted to show what the lighting for the building as a whole had been. These rooms have been re-lighted since my retirement; this was desirable because the lobby is now used for an extension of the public catalog and an information desk, both of which require good lighting, and it had become increasingly evident that the current periodical room was inadequately lighted.

OTHER BUILDING CHANGES

The two ends of the main reading room, at the northeast and northwest corners of the building, had ceilings only about twenty feet high instead of the forty to fifty feet under the barrel vault in the main part of the room. Between them, they added about 2,800 square feet to the area of the reading room, and they formed part of it, but were used for special purposes. One of them, containing several large alcoves with shelving on their sides, was assigned to current periodicals, which had previously been kept in a portion of the stack adjacent to the periodical room. The other was used for portions of the reference collection, which was rearranged.

Additional reference and bibliographical works were placed on the shelving in the main part of the reading room; much of this had been used for open-shelf reserves before undergraduate services were moved to the Lamont Library. The large reserve-book desk at the center of the north side of the room was removed. In the corner nearest to the public catalog and quite close to the main charging desk, a reference desk was installed, giving us for the first time a satisfactory place where two reference librarians could work at one time.

This reference desk was several inches higher than the reference desks then used in most other libraries, and the librarians there were given high swivel chairs and kneeholes under the desk; the furniture was planned so that they could easily leave their chairs. In this way the attendants at the desk were seated with their eyes at approximately the same level as those of persons consulting them. This was much more satisfactory than a seating arrangement that requires librarians to look up and readers to look down when they are talking with one another.

We did not attempt to give "readers' advisory service" as it is called, which would have made it desirable for librarians and readers to sit down together while conferring at length. With the reader standing, he was not likely to talk longer than necessary. This did not mean that we were not willing to do all we reasonably could for users of the Library. Our philosophy was that we should get the inquirer started, but that it was better for him in the long run to do his own work rather than have us do it for him.

The low-ceilinged ends of the reading room had 21-foot tables, each of which was cut up, making one 12-foot and one 9-foot table, and the building staff of the College was able to make the additional decorated end-supports that were required. The 12-foot tables in the central portion of the reading room had, unfortunately in my opinion, been placed where they did not match the windows and so did not get as much sunlight as they should have. These were now shifted, and the room looked as if it had been planned, and not as though the tables had simply been dumped in wherever they would fit.

President Conant called me one day and said that one of the friends of the University had spent a large sum to pay for construction of three dioramas showing the Harvard Yard and environs as they were in 1675, 1775, and 1936. Tom Barbour, Director of the Museum of Comparative Zoology, had made the arrangements for these and had planned to install them in the Museum; but he had retired and his successor did not think it was a suitable place for them. Would we be interested in having them in the Library? I was delighted. Those for 1775 and 1936 were placed in the corners of the corridors at either side of the main stairway to the second floor, where they could readily be seen by visitors but where persons looking at them would not interfere with traffic. The 1675 diorama was placed thirty feet farther down the right-hand corridor to the back of the building.

There were stairs that had troubled me ever since I first came to Harvard. The architect of the Widener building seemed to have regarded stairs as an architectural feature rather than a functional necessity. As one left the entrance lobby there were two steps, then a landing about ten feet long, and then the main stairway to the second floor. There were corridors on either side of the main stairway; in each of these, two steps went down again to the main-floor level. A book truck could not be wheeled from the front of the building down these corridors to the back. A more serious drawback became evident during my first year at Harvard, when I found that, on the average, at least one person per week stumbled or fell on one of these three sets of two steps, often with unfortunate results. I was able to have them replaced by ramps. A contract provided for installation of non-slip ramps that would match reasonably well the marble of the stairs and the entrance lobby. Unfortunately, however, they did not match. I had kept a sample of the material that the company had agreed to install, and I suggested that we refuse to pay for them but was overruled.

The marble treads of the main stairway had worn down considerably, in some places as much as an inch, reminding me of sandstone steps in Ohio buildings to which I had been accustomed; at Harvard, as in Ohio, the irregularities were dangerous. The stair treads in Widener were reinforced with carborundum, which is still there, and has not worn down in forty years. From the first floor to the mezzanine level at the entrance to the Widener Rooms, each stair tread is nearly fifteen feet wide, which was dangerous even with the non-slip carborundum because there was no center railing. A double railing was installed there, with railings also on both sides, as well as on both sides of the narrower stairs that go on from the mezzanine to the second floor. Safety was increased appreciably.

Elevators throughout the building were also a problem. Those installed in 1915 were very different from those available by the middle of the century. During my first year at Harvard I went through the building from top to bottom every day, but I walked up and down stairs for exercise, and failed to realize how unsatisfactory all six of the elevators were. There was one conveniently located in each side of the bookstack. Another was in the back hallway, which opened onto the stack levels where there were faculty studies; professors and librarians with keys could also reach the stack through this hallway. There were two elevators just off the main entrance lobby. Eventually it penetrated to my slow brain that all the elevators were very poor. They were rewired and improved, and the two small ones off the entrance lobby were replaced by a single larger one. This cost nearly as much as all the other work on the Widener building, including relighting, that was done during my time. Yet, I must confess, the replacements have never been completely satisfactory.

The stack ranges on the long east and west sides of the building are nine sections long, and I took it for granted that the sections were thirty-six inches on centers, which was considered standard. To my surprise, I soon discovered that they were something over forty inches long. I got in touch with Angus Macdonald, then the President of the Snead Stack Company, who had been involved in the installation, and found that his company had not been consulted on basic planning of the building. When it was assigned the task of installing the stacks, it made the ranges as long as possible in the space available. The longer sections had been a means of providing the maximum capacity practicable, and had been used throughout. It was a multi-tiered stack, so there were no supporting columns.

Realizing, in view of our plans for the future, that we ought to install all the shelving we could in Widener, I had a large amount of inexpensive shelving placed in the front of the sub-basement under the main entrance to the building. This provided shelving for infrequently used portions of the University Archives until the Pusey Library became available. Shelving was also installed along walls on the first floor's wide east-to-west corridors; catalogs of the Library of Congress and the British Museum were placed here, conveniently accessible to staff of the Catalog Department and Order Department as well as to the public.

We made a study of the cost of installing compact storage shelving in filing drawers; this would have replaced the regular shelves on the lowest stack level, where the additional weight would not have been a problem. The capacity of that level would have been doubled, making it 500,000 volumes instead of 250,000; but, taking into account the cost and the inconvenience that would have been caused, it was decided to reject the idea.

Another proposal that was not carried out will be reported in Chapter 12, which tells of my suggestion to the Faculty of Arts and Sciences that central public services be transferred to the first floor of the Widener building.

This section should not be closed without noting that there were further changes in the main reading room following the relighting and other alterations that have been reported above. Douglas Bryant, who joined the staff in 1952, was bright enough, as I had not been, to propose that the walls of the room be painted and made more attractive. The result was excellent.

Altogether, more than $250,000 was spent on alterations in the Widener building during my eighteen years there. Most of this was accounted for by the elevators, the new lighting, the new reference desk, the change in the entrances, and shifts in assignment of space. Annual appropriations providing for the upkeep of each building are part of the University's annual budget, and these covered a good share of the funds required. These appropriations accumulate year by year when they are not used. Manpower was scarce during the war, so there were substantial accumulations at that time; after the war the University employed several hundred painters for more than a year.

Special appropriations were required for elevator renovation and relighting, and these were granted when I requested them, despite the fact that at the time of my retirement money was not as plentiful as it became in the later 1950s and 1960s. Another twenty-five years have now passed. Special appropriations are needed today as they were forty years ago, and money is tight again as it was in my early Harvard days. I understand, however, that large sums are now available; they will be put to good use in preserving the Widener building.

Naturally enough, my interest in building planning was increased by the experience I gained in work on building changes between 1937 and 1955. The experience proved also to be very useful during my retirement, a large part of which has been spent in work on planning library buildings.

Chapter 10

James Bryant Conant

A S REPORTED in the last chapter of Part II of these Recollections, President Conant had convinced me, before I decided to come to Harvard, that he realized the importance of the Library to the University, and that he would support me in my attempts to deal with the problems I would have to face as Director of the University Library. In the first chapter of this volume I have told of my talks with him during my first year at Harvard. They clearly demonstrated that he was interested in the Library's needs, including improvement of the staff, better service, building up the collections, space, and increasing use of microphotography. He was himself a reader with broad interests in the humanities, philosophy, and the history of science as well as in his own special field of chemistry.

As I have reported, I spoke to him of the outside activities in which I had engaged during my last eight years in New York and of my hope to continue to work with the Association of Research Libraries, American Library Association, and other library groups. I said that I thought it would be desirable for me to visit and study two or more other academic or research libraries each year as a means of helping me to keep in touch with new developments. He heartily approved. A few years later, when invitations to consult on library problems in other institutions began to come to me, honoraria were offered. President Conant agreed that it would be both proper and useful for me to do such work. I said I would turn in any honoraria I received beyond my expenses, and I continued to do this until some time after World War II. Then I was told that many members of the faculty doing outside consultation work were keeping the honoraria, and that I should do likewise.

I made up my mind in 1937 that at least once a year I would try to write an article dealing with library problems, in addition to my annual report. I knew all too well how difficult it was for me to write but realized that it would be good experience for me even if not useful to others. President Conant said at this time, "If you have an opportunity to go abroad for some purpose connected with libraries, don't hesitate to do so, in spite of the fact that, as an administrative officer, you do not have sabbaticals or leaves beyond the regular one-month vacation."

In the spring of 1938, he spoke to me of the Nieman bequest, which was to be used in ways decided upon by the Harvard administration "to promote and elevate the standards of journalism in the United States." He asked me if I could suggest uses for some of the income from the fund, since the Harvard Corporation had not yet decided what to do and was looking for ideas. I proposed that we microfilm a large number of foreign newspapers, and it was agreed that we should have $5,000 per annum for this over a limited number of years. Beginning in the fall of that year, the remainder of the income was assigned to support the Nieman Fellowships, and Archibald MacLeish came to Harvard in September 1938 to head the program. As reported in Chapter 4 above, I was able to obtain from the Rockefeller Foundation a revolving fund with which to start a cooperative foreign newspaper microfilm project.

Soon after we came to Cambridge, Mart and I were invited to a dinner at the Conants where we were the honored guests, and where my lack of social experience caused me to make another mistake. (The earlier mistake is recorded in Chapter 1, telling of my failure to dress appropriately for my first meeting of the Thursday Evening Club in the President's house.) Other guests at dinner were local members of the Corporation and Board of Overseers, senior administrative officers, and at least one outside librarian, Elinor Gregory of the Boston Athenaeum. Mart and I had an opportunity to talk with the others, and I think things went well until ten o'clock, when glasses of water were brought around. We failed to realize that this was the signal that it was time to leave, and that we, as guests of honor, should begin to say our goodbyes. We made no move, and eventually the wife of one of the Corporation members stood up rather impatiently and announced that she and her husband were about to leave.

Several times during the year I was invited to the Conants or to meetings at which the President was chairman. At one of the meetings with members of the Governing Boards and Harvard administrators we talked over the financial situation of the University and discussed the question of whether the University ought to undertake a general campaign for a large sum of money. An effort of this kind had not taken place since 1919, except for a rather unsuccessful attempt at the time of the Tercentary in 1936. John Price Jones, who had been Chairman of the 1919 Harvard Endowment Campaign, was one of those who commented, I recall, and the decision was not to attempt a campaign. As it turned out, none was to take place until the mid-1950s, after both Conant and I had retired. At another meeting, President Conant spoke of his fear that, with Harvard's high tuition, then $400 a year, it might be difficult to balance the budget by attracting enough students who could both meet the entrance requirements and afford to come. The budget for the entire University was then less than half as much as the University Library budget was to be forty years later.

President Conant was asked to speak in November 1939 at a meeting of the Harvard Library Club, a Library staff organization, following dinner at the Faculty Club. Before introducing him, I spoke briefly of the Library's problems; in addition to improvement of services, space, and book funds, I mentioned some of the difficulties arising from the great decentralization of the University Library. I said that I understood the need for decentralization and, indeed, its inevitability in an institution with Harvard's history. I did not object to it if it could be kept under control, and I suggested that one of my chief tasks was to provide, to as great a degree as possible, what I called "coordinated decentralization."

After having spoken as might have been expected of his interest in the Library and its needs, President Conant said that he had been delighted to hear the term "coordinated decentralization," which he would thereafter use to describe the administration of the University as a whole. Both he and I continued to use these words, and the president of a foreign university where I had worked as a consultant has recently spoken enthusiastically of his belief in coordinated decentralization.

I think it was sometime in 1940 that President Conant was asked to head the Committee on Scientific Aids to Learning. He asked me to be Chairman ot its Subcommittee on Scientific Aids to Libraries, which was to concern itself particularly with microphotography. I had no idea what this assignment would lead to during the rest of my library career; it was one of the most important I have had.

My committee decided to undertake two special tasks. The first was to design an inexpensive reading machine for microfilm. Those available on the market at that time were quite expensive; as use of microfilm rapidly increased, the need for new machines in our research libraries was growing rapidly.

We were fortunate in finding at MIT a man capable of designing what we needed; the Spencer Lens Reading Machine was the result. If I remember correctly, it cost no more than $15. The designer was drafted and killed in World War II. By the time the war was over, other types of microreproduction had come into use, and the Spencer machine was completely obsolete.

Our second task was to study eye-fatigue, particularly as related to reading microfilm. We were able to persuade Leonard Carmichael, then President of Tufts University, to take charge of the study; he was a scientist with an interest in reading. He chose Walter Dearborn of the Harvard Graduate School of Education, among others, to help him. The results were finally published in 1947 by Houghton Mifflin in a 483-page volume entitled *Reading and Visual Fatigue*. Carmichael, by this time, had moved to the Smithsonian Institution in Washington, and it had been forgotten that the study was financed by the Subcommittee on Scientific Aids to Libraries. I did not know of the results until they were reported one evening by a member of the Harvard Shop Club. The findings could be summarized as follows:

Harvard students preferred seventeen foot candles on reading material in book form or microfilm as the intensity for comfortable reading. At this light intensity it was found that the students could read for as much as six hours at a stretch with no measurable physical signs of fatigue or reduction in speed of reading, understanding of the text, or retention of it after a period of one week.

I had already been concerned with the intensity and quality of light in Widener and Houghton areas where we used cold cathode tubes for the first time in a library, and in the New England Deposit Library, where we wanted to use as little electricity as possible. I was working on the lighting for the Lamont Library at this time and kept the intensity there at from eighteen to twenty-five foot candles, rather than the seventy-five or more that the Illuminating Engineering Society was recommending by this time. In 1955, at the time of my retirement, the cost of lighting, if we included the cost of new tubes and replacement of old ones as well as the electricity, came to two cents a kilowatt hour. We were then paying $10,000 a year less for lighting Lamont than we would have paid if we had followed the Illuminating Engineering Society's recommendations as many other libraries did. Costs have increased rapidly since then, and most Harvard libraries are lighted with less than the standard intensity; I estimate that our libraries are now costing about $1,000,000 less per year to light than they would if the Society's recommendations were followed. I might add that new and more effective tubes have now become available; with these, the intensity in Lamont when tubes are new has increased to between thirty-five and fifty foot candles.

One further note on Lamont lighting should be added. Apparently there have been no objections by students that the building is inadequately lighted; but one day the *Crimson*, looking for misdeeds of which the Harvard administration could be accused, ran an article asserting that fluorescent light is very much more dangerous to the health of students than the old incandescent light had been.

It is easy to see why I became even more interested in lighting than I had been before, and why I paid special attention to it in my *Planning Academic and Research Library Buildings* (1965) and wrote a separate monograph, *Library Lighting*, on the subject. The latter was sponsored by the Association of Research Libraries, which published it in 1970.

To return to the 1930s, I was called into President Conant's office in University Hall from time to time to talk over library problems and other matters, and I remember one occasion when he complained that I did not ask for appointments with him as often as he would have liked. He could not have been more friendly and cordial. Any doubts that I may have had about coming to Harvard soon disappeared.

In the late spring of 1940, when the Nazis invaded France, Belgium, and Holland and threatened to overrun all Europe, Conant became involved in national affairs and in furthering the American effort to aid Britain and the other allies. The time soon came when he was spending a good share of each week in Washington, though he almost always managed to be in Cambridge every other week for the regular meetings of the Harvard Corporation, as well as for the monthly faculty meetings. He left almost everything except policy-making in the hands of others, with Henry Shattuck, for a time as Acting President, and then Paul Buck, as Dean of the Faculty of Arts and Sciences and later as Provost of the University, in charge of routine matters. Except at faculty meetings, I saw little of him until the summer of 1945.

There were personal reasons of mine, in addition to President Conant's absences from Cambridge, that helped to account for this. Following the death of my first wife, Martha Gerrish Metcalf, in the summer of 1938, my daughter Margaret lived with me in Belmont while attending school in Boston during 1938–39 and while working as Secretary of the *Harvard Law Review* the following year. She was to be married in September 1940, and I would then be left completely alone. I realized that I could not be comfortable in the house in Belmont and that plans should be made for the years ahead.

As has been mentioned in Chapter 6, at meetings of the group of librarians who organized the New England Deposit Library, I had been particularly attracted to Elinor Gregory, and at one of these meetings when the group had luncheon in the Bellevue Hotel on Beacon Street, I realized that I wanted to marry her. I then ventured one day to invite her to have dinner with me at some place that would be satisfactory to her to talk about the proposed storage library. She suggested that I join her in Cambridge at the home of her uncle, Professor Lawrence J. Henderson, who was at that time head of the Fatigue Laboratory at the Harvard Business School as well as Senior Fellow of the Society of Fellows and Chairman of the Society. He had been a Harvard professor for some twenty years; I had met him during my first year in Cambridge when I was checking on the shortage of faculty studies in Widener and found that he had one that was comparatively little used, since he made his headquarters at the Business School. When I talked with him, he readily agreed that he ought to give up the Widener study, and he promptly did so.

When I arrived at the Henderson home on Willard Street, I found that there was another guest, Mrs. Theodore Richards, the widow of the professor in Harvard's Chemistry Department who many years earlier had been the first American to receive the Nobel Prize for chemistry.

After a pleasant dinner, I was left alone with Elinor in the living room. We talked over the New England Deposit Library, and she encouraged me to go ahead with it. As the months went by, I saw more and more of her and naturally was interested in her family connections. To my surprise, I learned something that was upsetting in some ways. Elinor's mother, with whom she was living on Lexington Avenue in Cambridge, was a sister of Professor Henderson's wife, who was terminally ill, and also a sister of Mrs. Richards, whom I had met before, when she was giving up her house on Follen Street in Cambridge some ten years after her husband's death. At that time she had asked me to take the books that we could use in the College Library.

I found also that Elinor's father, who was a graduate of the University of Pennsylvania and of the Princeton Theological Seminary, had been perhaps the first American to become a professor in a German university. He had taught at Leipzig, where Elinor was born and brought up. He was *the* authority on the New Testament codices and had become acquainted with Lucy Thayer, whom he married and who was Elinor's mother, as a result of his contacts with Joseph Henry Thayer. The latter, Elinor's maternal grandfather, had started out as a Congregational minister and had been a professor at the Andover Theological Seminary, which he left because he was unwilling to sign the fundamentalist Congregational Creed that donors to the Seminary had insisted upon.

At that time he had been a member of the Harvard Corporation. After his resignation from the Corporation, he had been appointed to a professorship in the Harvard Divinity School, where he continued his work as Chairman of the New Testament Revision Committee and as editor of the English edition of Grimm's New Testament Greek Dictionary, which he had translated from the German.

I had also discovered that Mrs. Richards was Mrs. Conant's mother, so Elinor and Mrs. Conant were cousins. I realized that, if I were to marry Elinor as I desired to do, I must be very careful not to seem to take advantage of her relationship to President Conant. But I decided, after due thought, to go ahead and continue my effort to persuade Elinor to marry me. It was nearly a year and a half before I was successful; but in June 1941 I won out, and we were married the next month.

During the summer of 1945, when it was apparent that the war was drawing to a close, I came into direct contact with President Conant on three special occasions.

The first was when I was included in a group of heads of College departments whom he invited to dinner in the rooms of the Society of Fellows. When he spoke following the dinner he said that he hoped additional funds would become available after the war. He knew that each department would want increased funds for its own use; each of us was then asked to express an opinion regarding the greatest needs of the College as a whole, leaving out the needs of his own department. Each believed that the Library should have the first priority. It can readily be imagined that this was very helpful to me in obtaining additional funds as they were apportioned during ten years that followed before I retired.

The second occasion was early in September 1945. Atomic bombs had fallen on Hiroshima and Nagasaki, and President Conant had returned to full-time work in Cambridge. He asked me to come to his office and spoke approximately as follows:

"We are living in a very different world since the explosion of the A-Bomb. We have no way of knowing what the results will be, but there is the danger that much of our present civilization will come to an end. We do not want to lose permanently a large part of that civilization, as happened when Rome fell fifteen hundred years ago. I think I am correct in saying that the greatest disaster in connection with that loss was the destruction of a large part of the information that was then recorded only in manuscripts that were destroyed or lost. It has seemed to me that, in the world's present situation, it might be advisable to select the printed material that would preserve the record of our civilization for the one that we can hope will follow, microfilming it and making perhaps ten copies, and burying these in ten different places throughout the country. In that way we could insure against the destruction that resulted from the fall of the Roman Empire. How many volumes would have to be copied, and what would it cost to make ten microfilm copies of them? The funds required, even if very large, can be found. How should the material be selected? How should it be organized? Please report to me in two weeks on any proposal you are ready to make."

You can imagine that I did a good deal of thinking during those two weeks. I then reported to President Conant somewhat as follows:

In order to preserve material on which our present civilization is based, we would need to film 500,000 volumes, averaging 500 pages each, or a total of 250,000,000 pages; ten copies would make 2,500,-000,000 pages in all. This would include the great literature of all countries that should not be lost, such as everything written by Shakespeare, Tolstoy, Dante, and Goethe; but there would be no need to preserve more than a few of the thousands of volumes written about these writers and their works. This would be true also for other great authors, music, books about the fine arts, the important records of world history, philosophy, economics, sociology, etc., and, perhaps especially important, our scientific developments in the broadest sense of that term. It would be difficult to select the material, but I think it could be done reasonably well.

I then went on to say that I thought it would be a mistake to try to go ahead with the proposal; it could not be done without the world learning about it, and everyone would be so upset at the idea of such a catastrophe as the destruction of what we call our civilization that it would be unwise to undertake the task. I then added that copies of practically all of this material would be found in university and college libraries that were not in large cities. In the libraries of Dartmouth, Stanford, Iowa State College, Oberlin, and other institutions at a distance from large cities, nearly all of the volumes in question would be available. It must be remembered that this was before the hydrogen bomb and other more recently developed instruments of destruction.

Conant accepted my report. We did not discuss costs, and I heard nothing more about the proposal.

The third occasion in 1945 that involved relations with him came in the fall of the year, after we had been assured that funds would be provided for building the undergraduate library. As has been explained in Chapter 8, I had decided that the site for it ought to be the one occupied by the historic Dana-Palmer House in the southeast corner of the Harvard Yard. Conant had moved into this house after he had begun to spend most of his time in Washington, and the President's House had then become the headquarters for Naval units stationed at Harvard. He wanted to continue to live in the Dana-Palmer House instead of returning to the mansion that President Lowell had built and given to the University as a residence for its presidents. I asked him to put the problem before the Corporation, which he did, and my recommendation was accepted. He appeared to be disappointed, and I was afraid that he would never forgive me, but he did. When the plans that I proposed for the building included additional space in the basement to house material from Widener and Houghton, he obtained funds for this purpose from the Corporation. And later, in *My Several Lives*, his autobiography, he wrote enthusiastically of the project.

The Dana-Palmer House reminds me of an incident that was connected with it. This was during the war, while President Conant was living there. Winston Churchill, after attending one of his meetings with President Roosevelt on this side of the Atlantic, had come to Harvard to receive an honorary degree. As I parked my car back of Widener that morning, David Little, then the Secretary of the Corporation and Master of Adams House, was rushing by; but he stopped to ask, "Do you have a good fountain pen?" When I told him I had, he asked if he could borrow it, explaining that the Secret Service men apparently had cleared the Conant residence of all pens, fearing that they might contain small bombs. "I'm looking for one with which Mr. Churchill can sign his name in the Library's guest book, which you turned over to me yesterday," he concluded. He took my pen and returned it a day or two later, saying that he did not know whether or not Mr. Churchill had used it in signing the guest book, but he had signed the book. I kept the pen for years as a souvenir; but, among the many old pens that I have accumulated, I must confess that I am not sure which one it was. I am afraid that, although I am an accumulator, I am not a collector.

When President Conant finally persuaded me to come to Harvard in 1937, one of the reasons for my decision, though a minor one, was that I knew I was four years older than he, so I took it for granted that I would not have to deal with another president before I reached retirement age. It came as a surprise and a shock to me when he retired in 1953 at the age of sixty to become our High Commissioner, and later Ambassador, to Germany. Elinor and I were fortunate enough to continue to see him and his wife, Patty, until his death in February 1978. We agree enthusiastically with the eulogies given at the memorial service for him.

Chapter 11

The Library Staff After 1938

MAJOR APPOINTMENTS during my first year at Harvard have been reported in Chapter 2, and some account has been given there of each of the eight men in question — Grieder, Halvorson, Hofer, Jackson, Osborn, Palmer, Peiss, and Shipton. Men and women who held key positions on the staff at the time I came have also been mentioned; but I have not told of the young Harvard men, some of them still undergraduates, who were working for the Library in 1937. Before dealing with other appointments of 1938-1955, it seems appropriate to devote the first section of this chapter to seventeen Harvard graduates whose library careers included work in the Harvard Library during my years there.

HARVARD MEN WHO BECAME LIBRARIANS

During the years when I was trying to build up the staff of the New York Public Library, I had observed that few Harvard men seemed to be going into library work, and the few whom I had been fortunate enough to employ in New York had apparently not been interested in working at Harvard. To my surprise and pleasure, however, I found a number of recent graduates of Harvard working in the Library in 1937, as well as a few student assistants, and several of these men earned their library degrees, in most cases by attending summer school at Columbia.

Frederick G. Kilgour, a Harvard graduate of 1935, was one of those who was already on the staff. In 1938, at the suggestion of Walter Briggs, I brought him into the office as my personal assistant to help in any way he could, run errands, and pick up information for me. He proved to be extremely useful, to put it mildly, and enabled me to cover much more ground than I could otherwise have done.

In 1940, because of increased use of the Library and competition for clerical workers in the Boston area, we found that circulation service in Widener was breaking down. I asked Fred to take charge of the circulation desk and propose changes in the system that would help it to run more smoothly. A very large percentage of books called for were not on the shelves in the stack where they belonged. Inadequate and incorrect records at the circulation desk were part of the problem. Fred went to the Business School and checked with faculty members there who were interested in record-keeping. He was told about the McBee-Keysort, a punch card system, which would enable us to identify much more quickly the books that were overdue, and to recall them.

This solved only a portion of the circulation problem. Several hundred carrels in the stack were assigned to graduate students. Each carrel had shelving for eight running feet of books on the desk and on a shelf above it, with a bookcase behind the chair holding as many more. There were also about sixty faculty studies, each with shelving for a thousand or more volumes. Professors and graduate students had found that the best way to make sure books would be available when wanted was to sign out at the beginning of the term everything that might be needed for months ahead. This, of course, made it difficult for others to obtain the books. We removed the additional shelving from stalls, asked the faculty to return books or check them out annually, and did not hesitate to "re-borrow" any book in a stall or a faculty study when another reader called for it. As a result, the number of books we could supply was considerably increased, and circulation went up more than forty percent during my first four years at Harvard.

The McBee-Keysort system was not, I regret to say, a permanent solution. As time went on, more and more clerical positions became available in the Boston area at higher salaries than we were paying; it grew harder than ever to find satisfactory clerical help, and the system broke down like its predecessor. It was not until after my retirement that Foster Palmer worked out and installed an IBM punched card circulation control.

Fred Kilgour managed to spend three summers at Columbia in order to obtain his library degree. In 1942, Professor Langer asked him to join the Office of Strategic Services, where he did valuable work during the war, after which he served as Deputy Director of the Office of Intelligence Collection and Dissemination in the Department of State until 1948. He was then Librarian of the Yale Medical Library, as well as lecturer on the history of science and medicine; he had always wanted to be a doctor but had been unable to finance a medical education. From 1965 to 1967, he was Associate Librarian for Research and Development at Yale. Scientific aids to learning had always interested Fred, and in 1967 he left Yale to organize and direct the Ohio College Library Center (now the On-line Computer Library Center), which has done a great deal to prevent cataloging costs from increasing as they tended to do during the earlier years of this century. OCLC has been used by more and more libraries, both American and foreign, and I understand that it now provides more catalog cards for libraries than the Library of Congress.

I wish that Fred's Harvard classmate, Theodore Nordbeck, had not left librarianship, in which he could have had a distinguished career. He was working in the Catalog Department in Widener when he decided to go to Columbia. His application apparently was misinterpreted, and he was asked to take the entrance examinations despite the fact that he had been graduated *cum laude*. As it turned out, he passed them with the highest grade that had ever been given up to that time. In 1941, however, he went into the Army and then, like Fred, into the Office of Strategic Services; he never returned to library work.

A third member of the Harvard Class of 1935 was Robert W. Lovett, the only one of the Harvard men who, with intermissions for Army service in North Africa and Italy and summers in library school at Columbia, remained at Harvard throughout his career, chiefly in archival work, which has been outlined in Chapter 2. From 1948 until his retirement in 1979, Lovett's title was Curator of Manuscripts and Archives in the Baker Library of the Graduate School of Business Administration.

Arthur Hamlin, Harvard 1934, has been mentioned in Chapter 5 as the Curator of the Woodberry Poetry Room to whom I turned over the William Dean Howells correspondence for arranging and listing. He had headed the Poetry Room since 1936 and enjoyed his work; when I first talked with him about library school he was not interested, saying that he would be content to stay at Harvard for the rest of his career. I pointed out that prospects of advancement would be greatly increased if he had a professional degree. When he was graduated from the library school at Columbia in 1939, we did not have a suitable position to offer him; after working in the New York Public Library and the University of Pennsylvania, he served as Executive Secretary of the Association of College and Research Libraries from 1949 to 1956, when he was appointed Director of Libraries at the University of Cincinnati. Then, from 1968 until his retirement in 1979, he was Director of Libraries at Temple University. Before he left Cincinnati, its library, in an old building that had been adapted for library use, suffered greatly from water and fire damage. Because of the experience he gained at that time in rehabilitating books that had been soaked, he was called upon to go to Florence, Italy, to assist in rehabilitating materials damaged by the flood of 1966, and was cited by the Italian government for the work he did there. *The University Library in the United States: Its Origins and Development* was published in 1981, and I recently enjoyed reading this interesting and important contribution of his to library history.

Hugh Montgomery, a classmate of Hamlin's, was also working in Widener when I came there. He worked in the New York Public Library while earning his library degree at Columbia. After Army service, he returned to Harvard and was in charge of the Littauer Library of the Graduate School of Public Administration from 1946 to 1952. He was then Librarian of the University of Massachusetts, Amherst, until 1967, when the political situation there became impossible. After a short time at the Wentworth Institute in Boston, he went to the University of Southeastern Massachusetts, where he worked with Frank Jones until he retired in 1976.

Morrison C. Haviland had worked in the Adams House Library before his graduation from Harvard in 1937, and had decided that he wanted to become a librarian. I had taken him on at the New York Public Library during the summers of 1936 and 1937, and he received his degree from the Columbia library school in 1938. During the four years that followed, he filled several positions in the Harvard Library before going into the Navy. In 1946–47 he completed a second year of library school at the University of California, Berkeley, and then returned to the Harvard Library for three years. Subsequently he was Librarian of Wabash College (1950–1955), Director of the University of Vermont Library (1955–1961), Chief of the Reader Services Division of the Air University Library, Maxwell Air Force Base (1961–1964), Assistant Director of the Tulane University Library (1964–1965), Associate Librarian for Administration at the University of Massachusetts, Amherst (1965–1967), and Director of the Readers Services Division at the State University of New York in Albany. Following the death of his wife in 1976, retirement, and world travel, Morrison returned to Boston, where he is now doing useful volunteer work in the Countway Library of Medicine.

Walter W. Wright was a Harvard classmate of Haviland's. He had not worked in the Library as an undergraduate, but he came to my attention almost immediately after my arrival at Harvard, when a letter from Charles C. Williamson, Dean of the Columbia University School of Library Service, stated that his School had an application from a Harvard graduate of 1937; they were not quite sure of his qualifications and asked if I would oversee examinations for him. I was reminded of

April 1911, when Azariah Root gave me examinations before I was admitted to the Pratt Institute. The young man's father was a professor in the Romance Languages Department at Harvard. I gave Walter the examinations, and he was admitted; when he received his library degree the next spring, I asked him to come back and start work on gifts and exchanges, which I thought had been neglected. He organized the Library's operations in this area; but we had no suitable promotion to offer him after 1941, and I did not try to keep him at Harvard. After working in the New York Public Library, the Harvard Club of New York City, and the Johns Hopkins University Library, he went to the University of Pennsylvania Library, where I saw him when I surveyed that library. In 1957, at my suggestion and recommendation, he became Librarian of Ohio University in Athens, Ohio, succeeding Frank Jones, of whom I will write later. He went to Dartmouth in 1968 as Curator of Rare Books and Chief of Special Collections, where he remained until he retired in 1980.

The Humphry twins, James and John, were working as student assistants in the Catalog Department when I came to Harvard; they were graduated *cum laude* in 1939. One day they came to me and said they wanted to go into library work but would expect to work in the same library. I advised them that it would be desirable to go to library school but probably not wise for them to go at the same time. If one of them would apply at Columbia for admission in 1940, I thought I could arrange for him to have a position at the New York Public Library. When he finished library school, he could return to Harvard, and his brother, who would then have been in the Harvard Library for an additional year, could go to Columbia while working in the New York Public Library. I suggested that they should realize that separation was necessary if they were to get ahead in library work. They reluctantly accepted my recommendation.

John Humphry, after having returned to Harvard and then having been in the office of the Chief of Naval Operations until 1946, was successively Director of Book Processing at the Enoch Pratt Free Library in Baltimore, Director of the Springfield (Massachusetts) City Library (1948–1967), Assistant Commissioner of Education for Libraries in the New York State Education Department (1967–1977), and Executive Director of the Forest Press (Lake Placid), which publishes the Dewey Decimal Classification.

James Humphry, after service in the Army, was Chief of the Map Division of the New York Public Library (1946–1947), Librarian and Professor of Bibliography at Colby College (1947–1957), Chief Librarian of the Metropolitan Museum of Art in New York during a period when new quarters were being constructed (1957–1968), and Vice President of the H. W. Wilson Company.

Herbert Cahoon worked in the Library as a student assistant before his graduation from Harvard in 1940. He was greatly interested in rare books. He stayed in Widener for a year following graduation, attended the Columbia library school, and worked in the New York Public Library until 1954, when he became Curator of Autograph Manuscripts in the Pierpont Morgan Library, where he has been responsible for many exhibition catalogs.

Francis P. Keough came to my attention in 1939, when I learned that he was not happy in the Boston Public library, where he had worked for five years; he gladly accepted my invitation to join the staff of the Harvard University Archives. Frank received his Harvard degree in 1940, having earned it by taking University Extension courses. After war-time service and library school at Columbia, he worked at MIT for a year and then returned to Harvard as a reference librarian. He was Director of the Framingham (Massachusetts) Public Library from 1951 to 1964, and then succeeded John Humphry as director of the Springfield City Library, where he remained until retirement in 1978. At Framingham he was responsible for a fine new central library building, and he has been active as a building consultant since 1964.

William Van Lennep was graduated from Harvard in 1929, and was awarded a Harvard Ph.D. in 1934. He had worked at the Folger Shakespeare Library and the Huntington Library before coming to the Harvard Library as Curator of the Theatre Collection in 1940. Unfortunately, ill health caused him to resign in 1960, and his untimely death followed in 1962.

Philip H. Dolan, Harvard Class of 1935, had worked in the Newton (Massachusetts) Free Library and served in the Army before coming to Widener as Chief of Circulation in 1946. After only three years, he left to become director of our good neighbor, the Cambridge Public Library.

William B. Ernst was a Harvard graduate of 1939 who took advanced work in the history of art and, after war-time service, came to the Widener staff in 1946 on the recommendation of E. Louise Lucas, Librarian of the Fogg Museum. In 1948, when he had earned his library degree at Simmons College, he was assigned to reference work in Lamont Library; and he served as Librarian of the Lamont Library from 1956 to 1960, when he went to the State University of New York at Buffalo, where he was successively Assistant and Associate Director of Libraries. In 1969, he became Director of the Chicago Circle Campus

Library of the University of Illinois, where I tried to help him solve a difficult library building problem.

George William Cottrell, Jr., who was graduated from Harvard in 1926, was not a professional librarian, but he was the eminently successful Editor of the *Harvard Library Bulletin* from its beginning in 1947 until publication was temporarily suspended in 1960. During more recent years he has continued his research in ornithology at the Museum of Comparative Zoology and has served on the Overseer's Committee to Visit the University Library.

Charles C. Colby of the Harvard Class of 1945 is now Associate Librarian for Boston Medical Library Services in the Countway library of Medicine, and something will be said of his career in Chapter 13.

At a meeting of one of the Boston library organizations not long after I came to Harvard, I became acquainted with Frank N. Jones, who was then at the Boston Public Library. He had been graduated from Harvard in 1930 and had returned for work in the Graduate School of Arts and Sciences. After working in the Boston Public Library and briefly in the Newburyport Public Library, he had returned to Boston as head of the Science and Technology Division; but he feared that there was no future for him in the Boston Public Library. We discussed the situation, and I found that his father, who had been a trustee of the library of Reading, Pennsylvania, had come to see me in New York in 1928 to ask for help in finding a librarian. I had been unable to help then, but I told Frank that, if he would go to library school, I would take him on for three years at Harvard, giving him a different assignment each year in order to provide the broadest possible experience.

He worked in the New York Public Library while in library school and then had a year as Williamson's assistant at Columbia. After four years in the Army, he came back for the three years I had promised at Harvard. He helped in various places, and I remember with particular pleasure his time as assistant in my office, his work with a small group of the staff going through second-hand bookstores in Philadelphia and New York to find copies of books that Ed Williams had listed as desiderata for Lamont Library, and his leadership in moving the Engineering Library up several levels in Pierce Hall, where there was no elevator. He was in charge of a group of young men who had a good time in spite of the task of carrying heavy books up the stairs.

Frank became Librarian of Ohio University in Athens in 1949. I remember the day in 1951 when I was visiting my brother Harry, a country doctor in Hendrysburg, Ohio, and Frank appeared after a long drive, accompanied by a handsome woman named Leona Felsted, who was Dean of Women at Ohio University. He said he had come to ask me for permission to marry her. I gave it, and all concerned have lived happily in the thirty years since then.

After having been Director of the Peabody Institute Library in Baltimore from 1957 to 1966, Frank became the first Librarian of Southeastern Massachusetts University in North Dartmouth, where he remained until he retired in 1973. I had the pleasure of attending the dinner given in his honor at that time nad realized what a fine job he had done there. Frank and Leona are now in a retirement home in Dallas, Texas, and we keep in touch with monthly letters.

APPOINTMENTS OF 1939–1942

Notable contributions to the profession have been made by the Harvard men who worked in the Library during my time; but none of them, except Bob Lovett, remained at Harvard throughout most of a long career. Of the eight men I brought to Harvard during my first year, Hofer, Jackson, Palmer, and Shipton remained here, as did Margaret Currier, whose appointment in 1939 has been mentioned in Chapter 2. Among those who came after 1939, several were to devote many years to the Harvard Library.

Notable appointments of 1940 brought Donald T. Clark and Edwin E. Williams to Harvard. Something will be said of the former, who stayed at Harvard for twenty-two years, in the section of Chapter 13 dealing with the Business School Library; the latter retired after forty years in the Harvard Library.

Ed Williams, with whom I have worked more closely than with any of those who joined the staff later, was born in California, graduated from Stanford, and earned an M.A. for two years of study in the School of Librarianship at the University of California, Berkeley. He went to Chicago in 1937 as assistant to Carl Milam, Executive Secretary of the American Library Association, and in 1940, realizing that Ed was too good to keep in that position, Carl talked with me about him. This was when I wanted to have Fred Kilgour straighten out our circulation problems. I welcomed Ed as General Assistant in my office, where he stayed most of the decade, though he had a number of special assignments, which included acting as secretary of the Library Committee and editing everything that I wrote for publication, as he has done ever since.

When construction of the Lamont Library was authorized, Ed took charge of making ready the 75,000 volumes that we wanted to have in the new library when it opened in January 1949. Selecting the books and obtaining copies of them was a tremendous task. Ed talked with a representative of each department of instruction in Harvard College, giving him a list of the titles in his field that were already available on undergraduate reserved book shelves and could be transferred to Lamont. He obtained all the help he could from the faculty in selecting additional titles that they thought should be available in an undergraduate library, and then added a good many more that he thought desirable. It should be remembered that this was the first time that a great university had set up an undergraduate library with a building of its own, and Ed was covering new ground. The whole collection turned out to be so satisfactory that, at the request of the Carnegie Corporation and with the help of a grant from them, a copy of the catalog was printed a few years later and made available to other libraries.

After the list had been made up, there was the difficult task of finding copies of those of the titles that were out of print. A special appropriation for purchases had been approved, so there were adequate funds. Under Ed's direction and with great help from Frank Jones, second-hand bookstores in the Boston area were searched, and members of the staff pursued the hunt in New York and Philadelphia. The collection was fully classified, catalogued, and on the shelves when Lamont opened. Books were moved from Widener, where they had been assembled, into Lamont through the tunnel between the buildings; there was snow on the ground during the Christmas holidays of 1948.

After 1950, when Ed became Chief of the Acquisitions Department, he continued to work closely with the Librarian and Director, particularly in preparation of the Annual Report and its statistical tables. He edited Paul Buck's *Libraries & Universities* (1964). In 1966, he was appointed Associate University Librarian, and one of his responsibilities from 1968 to 1980 was to edit the *Harvard Library Bulletin*. In 1983, three years after his theoretical retirement, he is still in charge of the Library's preservation microfilming program.

His work away from Harvard has been equally noteworthy. His survey of resources of Canadian university libraries for research in the humanities and social sciences (1962) was, in my opinion, the best survey of its kind that has ever been made; in an amazingly short time thereafter the picture in Canadian academic libraries was transformed. His survey of theological libraries in the Boston area was an important contribution to library cooperation, as was his earlier study of the United States Book Exchange.

I have written of Fred Kilgour's efforts to improve our circulation services. A major post-war effort in this direction was the inventory that Roland Moody supervised. Roland had come to us in 1941, following his graduation from Dartmouth and the library school at Columbia, but was in the Army from 1943 through 1946, serving with distinction in the Italian campaign. While we had done our best to "read" the shelves as often as we could, there had been no complete inventory in some fifteen years. We discovered that, of Widener's more than 2,000,000 books, 6,000 were missing, with no record showing where they were. However, after diligent searching during the following year, this number was reduced to 600, which meant that, on the average, only forty books a year had disappeared during the past decade and a half. This, I should emphasize, was in the 1940s, and I fear that no library in the country could do equally well today.

Roland was Circulation Librarian in Lamont from 1948 until 1953, when he left to become Director of the Northeastern University Library, where he has now been for thirty years.

Robert L. Work was another young man who joined the staff in 1941. A graduate of Albright College and the Columbia library school, he had worked in the Albright College Library before coming to Harvard to take charge of exchanges. As I have already mentioned, he became the first Librarian of the New England Deposit Library in 1942. Following service in the Navy, he returned to Harvard in 1946 to do reference work, and became Librarian of the Museum of Comparative Zoology the following year. In 1951, however, he was called back to duty in the Navy and chose to remain there rather than return to librarianship. He was one of the most popular members of the staff during his years at Harvard.

Chapter 13 is the appropriate place for writing of Arthur Pulling, who became Librarian of the Law Library in 1943. Two other noteworthy additions to the staff came during that year.

John L. Sweeney would not claim to be a librarian, but he served ably for twenty-seven years as Curator of the Woodberry Poetry Room, first in Widener and then in its more satisfactory new quarters in Lamont. As Subject Specialist in English Literature, he also had an important role in book selection, and he taught General Education courses in the College. Jack retired in 1969, and is living in Ireland.

Philip J. McNiff, a Boston College graduate, had been a student assistant in the Brookline Public Library during his high school and college days, had filled various positions in the Newton Public Library, and had gone to library school at Columbia for summer sessions. He came to Harvard as a reference assistant in 1942, and was appointed Superintendent of the Reading Room the next year. In 1948, when I was looking throughout the country for someone to take charge of Lamont when it opened, I realized that Phil, already on the Harvard staff, was the ideal person. He gave Lamont a fine start and stayed there until after my retirement. From 1956 to 1965, he was Associate Librarian for Resources and Acquisitions in the College Library, with the further title, after 1962, Archibald Cary Coolidge Bibliographer. In 1965, he became Director and Librarian of the Boston Public Library, the position from which he is retiring in 1983. I will not attempt to outline his career further, except to say that he has also done important work for libraries and librarianship generally in addition to all he has accomplished for Harvard and the Boston Public Library.

APPOINTMENTS OF THE LATER 1940s

William H. Bond, a Haverford graduate, was awarded a Harvard Ph.D. in 1941 and spent the following year abroad as Research Fellow of the Folger Shakespeare Library. He then served in the Navy. In 1946, Bill Jackson selected him for the Houghton Library staff; after two years as Bill's assistant, he became Curator of Manuscripts, and did remarkably good work in that department for sixteen years. After Jackson's death, he was appointed Librarian of the Houghton Library in 1965; he was also Lecturer in Bibliography from 1964 to 1967, and has been Professor of Bibliography since 1967. In 1982, he retired as Librarian, but continues to teach. Houghton prospered under his administration as it had under his predecessor's.

Jerome T. Lewis came to the Library as an assistant in the Widener reading room during 1946, the year after his graduation from Colby. He earned his library degree at Simmons while on the Harvard staff, and worked in several departments, in both Widener and Lamont, until 1959, when he went to the Newton Free Library to head the Processing Department. After having been Librarian of Bryant and Stratton Junior College, he went to the Cambridge Public Library, where he was Associate Director in 1976, when he died at the age of fifty-four. His name is perpetuated by a scholarship fund for graduates of Cambridge public schools and by a memorial room in the Cambridge Library. Jerry was a popular member of the staff; I regretted that we did not have a position that would have kept him at Harvard, and I regret that he and Mrs. Smith are the only blacks who appear in this account of appointments.

Richard O. Pautzsch came to the Catalog Department in Widener during 1946; he was a graduate of Boston University and was awarded his library degree by Columbia in 1950. Soon afterward he went to the Brooklyn Public Library, where he held several cataloging positions and was Coordinator of Cataloging from 1956 to 1971, when he moved to the Chicago Public Library as Assistant Chief Librarian for Technical Services. He retired in 1975. Dick was active in library association affairs.

Bartol Brinkler, a graduate of Princeton and the Columbia library school, came to the Library in 1947, and his thirty-five years there were largely devoted to classification; he was Chief Subject Cataloger from 1950 to 1965, and Classification Specialist from 1965 until his retirement in 1982. He served the Library superbly in these positions. It should be added that, prior to adoption of the Library of Congress system in 1976, classification in Widener involved development of the Library's own system.

James E. Walsh came to the Houghton Library as a cataloger at about the same time that Brinkler came to Widener. He became Head of the Division of Rare Book Cataloging in 1951, and has been Keeper of Printed Books since 1965. At the time this is being dictated in 1983, the Houghton library and the Goethe Society of Boston have just published a festschrift, *Essays in Honor of James Edward Walsh on his Sixty-Fifth Birthday*; there was also a symposium in Houghton on Goethe to celebrate the occasion. I like to recall the task that Jim carried out early in his career at Harvard when he selected thousands of volumes from Widener's classical literature and history collection as candidates for transfer to the New England Deposit Library. As reported in Chapter 6, members of the Classics Department found only a dozen instances in which they wished to overrule Jim's recommendation.

Mrs. Hiawatha H. Smith, a graduate of Lane and of the library school at Atlanta University, came to the Catalog Department in 1947 after having been a reference librarian at Tuskegee. She was a first-class cataloger, but she left us in 1952 to go the University of California at Los Angeles, where I was glad to see her in the early 1960s when I was working on the plans for a new building there.

David C. Weber came to us in 1948 as a cataloger under Andrew Osborn after having been graduated from Colby and from the library school at Columbia. In 1950, I took him away from Andrew, who was displeased at losing him, to serve as my assistant in the office, where he remained until my retirement. In 1957, Paul Buck promoted him, and his title became Assistant Librarian of Harvard College and Assistant

Director of the University Library. He went to Stanford in 1961 as
Assistant Director under Rutherford Rogers; since 1969, when Rogers
went to Yale, David has been Director of Libraries at Stanford.

(Parenthetically, I wish that universities would follow Yale's example
and use the title *University Librarian* instead of *Director*).

Laurence J. Kipp also came to Harvard in 1948. A graduate of Valley
City State College in North Dakota, with an M.A. from the University
of Colorado and a library degree from Illinois, Larry began his library
career as Librarian of Eureka College, where Ronald Reagan had been
graduated ten years earlier. After Army service, he was Assistant
Director and later Director of the American Book Center for War-
Devastated Libraries, with headquarters in Washington. Soon after
coming to Harvard as my assistant, he took charge of loan services in
Widener. He moved across the river to the Business School in 1954;
after serving as Assistant and then Associate Librarian there, he succeeded Don Clark in 1963 as Librarian of Baker Library. Larry retired
at the Business School in 1978; but, in the spring of 1979 he was
persuaded to serve as Acting Librarian of Harvard College pending the
appointment of a successor to Louis E. Martin. This intermission in
retirement lasted until the middle of 1980. Larry's career also included
a year of surveying libraries in India on behalf of the Department of
State, 1960–61, followed by a long return visit seven years later for the
Ford Foundation.

Walter W. Curley worked in Lamont while attending Northeastern
University and library school at Simmons College. After several years
as a reference librarian in the Providence Public Library, and then as
Business Manager and Assistant Director there, he became Director of
the Suffolk Cooperative Library System on Long Island. My daughter,
Margaret Metcalf Small, then the Director of the Bellport Public
Library, was enthusiastic about his work. Later he was with the Arthur
D. Little Company in Cambridge, was Librarian of the Cleveland
Public Library, where he encountered problems that I missed by not
going there fifty years earlier, and subsequently headed Gaylord
Brothers, the library supply company.

APPOINTMENTS OF THE 1950s

Carol Ishimoto came to the Catalog Department in 1950, two years
after her graduation from Simmons College. She was a reference
Librarian in Lamont for two years, and then was a cataloger at the
University of Pennsylvania Library from 1958 to 1960. Fortunately she

then returned to Harvard and to the Catalog Department; in 1973, she became Head of the Cataloging and Processing Department in the Harvard College Library, an exciting position in these days of automation and the Distributable Union Catalog on microfiche.

Thomas F. O'Connell was graduated from Boston College in 1950, earned his library degree at Columbia, and came to the Circulation Department in Widener in 1951. He headed that Department in 1952, and was also in charge of the stacks from 1955 until 1963, when he went to York University in Canada as Director of Libraries. Since 1976, Tom has been back in the United States as Director of Libraries at Boston College.

During the 1947 American Library Association conference in San Francisco, I met for the first time Douglas Bryant, who was then Assistant Librarian of the University of California, Berkeley. I decided that, if I had my way, he would sometime come to the Harvard Library. I had no suitable position for him then. In 1950, as will be recorded in Chapter 18, I met Doug in London, and talked with him about Harvard. He was then Director of Libraries for the United States Information Service. Two years later he came to Harvard as Administrative Assistant Librarian. I fear that he was disappointed when he did not succeed me in 1955. The story of my successor's appointment is told in Chapter 23. President Pusey apparently had an unhappy experience with his librarian at Lawrence University in Wisconsin and wanted a man with a professorial background.

I was naturally very much pleased in 1972 when Doug became Director of the University Library and Professor of Bibliography. Since his retirement in 1979, he has been serving as Executive Secretary of the American Trust for the British Library.

Walter Grossmann, a native of Vienna and graduate of Yankton College with a Ph.D. from Harvard and a library degree from Simmons, joined the Widener staff in 1952. He was appointed Assistant Librarian for Book Selection in 1961 and Archibald Cary Coolidge Bibliographer in 1965. He left us in 1967 for the University of Massachusetts, Boston, where he has been Director of the Library and Professor of History since 1968; he has also taught at McGill and has had a Guggenheim Fellowship.

Fortunately his wife, Maria, a native of Vienna and graduate of Smith College with a Ph.D. from Harvard and a library degree from Simmons, has not left the Harvard Library. She came to the Andover-Harvard Library of the Divinity School in 1956 as Order Librarian, and was then Assistant Librarian (1960–1965) and Librarian (1965–1974). After five years as Librarian for Collection Development in the Harvard University Library, she returned to Andover-Harvard, again as Librarian, in 1979.

Wolfgang Freitag was one of my last appointments; he came to the staff in 1955. He was born in Berlin, had been graduated from Freiburg and earned a doctorate at Albert Ludwigs Universität, and had worked in the United States Information Center in Frankfurt before coming to the United States. He attended Simmons while working as a cataloger in Widener, and received his library degree in 1956. His Harvard career was interrupted by two years at Stanford, but he has been Librarian of the Fine Arts Library and Senior Lecturer on Fine Arts since 1967. I am indebted to him for help in the bibliographical work for my volume on *Planning Academic and Research Libraries*. His wife, Doris, is Book Conservator in the Harvard University Library.

Y. T. Feng, I am glad to say, was also appointed while I was Director, though I can claim no credit because it was Doug Bryant who offered her the position as reference assistant that she accepted in the summer of 1955. She was a graduate of the University of Shanghai, with an M.A. from Colorado State College, a Ph.D. from the University of Denver, and a library degree from Columbia; she had also been a trainee at the New York Public Library. She came to start work at Harvard on a day when Doug was away, and I heard who she was while she was talking with Helen Powers just outside my office. I welcomed her to the Library. She was, I think, the last professional staff member employed during my eighteen years at Harvard.

She was also one of the best. Reference work was followed by book selection from 1957 to 1965, and she was Assistant Librarian for Documents from 1965 to 1967, when Phil McNiff persuaded her to come to the Boston Public Library as Assistant Director for Research Library Services. From 1977 to 1980, she was Librarian of Wellesley College, and in 1978 she and Phil were married. In 1980, she was appointed Librarian of Harvard College, the first woman to hold that title, which was first held by Solomon Stoddard in 1667. I am very happy to see the position filled by a librarian with the ability she has demonstrated.

REFLECTIONS AND REGRETS

In Part II, Chapter 7 of these Recollections, I mentioned a list of seventy-five persons, "all first-class librarians, who joined the reference department of the New York Public Library while I was in charge of personnel work," some of whom "stayed with the library for the rest of their careers, while others went on to serve in important positions elsewhere." The Harvard list is shorter; but it does not include staff members in the specialized libraries at Harvard or those whom Bill Jackson brought to Houghton. There are other omissions, and I hope that I will be forgiven by those not mentioned here who came to Harvard during the 1940s and early 1950s.

I have been pleased at the number of Harvard graduates from the 1930s who chose to become librarians; most of them went to the library school at Columbia, and many of them worked in the New York Public Library while doing so. I regret that this did not continue during the post-war years, in part because I was very busy with other matters, and also because there were few suitable vacancies on the Harvard staff.

It has seemed particularly important to me to attract well-qualified men to librarianship because I have always felt, and still believe, that, if women are to be paid properly in library work or in other professions, there must be men doing similar work, and not in the top positions only. I fear that salaries will always be unduly low in a profession that is considered to be primarily feminine. The great increase during the past sixty years in salaries for librarians, both men and women, has in my opinion been due primarily to the increasing number of men in the field. Equal pay for equal work will finally come. It is encouraging to see that women now direct a greater percentage of large libraries than ever before.

More should have been written of the women like Gertrude Shaw, Gertrude Sullivan, Margaret Currier, and Susan Haskins, on whom the Library depended during my eighteen years. An attempt to mention all of them would have greatly lengthened this chapter.

I hope at least that what has been written in this chapter will demonstrate my conviction that Edwin Hatfield Anderson was right in believing that nothing is more important than to build up a library's staff, and that, if suitable promotions are not available for those who have been employed, better positions elsewhere must be found for them. Harvard's record from 1937 to 1955 might have been better, but I think I need not be ashamed of it.

Chapter 12

The Council, the Faculty, and the Faculty Library Committee

A T THE TIME I came to Harvard the Statutes of the University provided that the Director should be, *ex officio*, Chairman of the Council of the College Library, and that this Council, consisting of the Chairman and six other persons appointed annually by the Corporation, with the consent of the Overseers, should have the "general control and oversight" of the College Library, make rules for its administration, and "apportion the funds applicable to the purchase of books."

My relations with the Council went smoothly and failed to present the problems that I feared they might. On the few occasions when my proposals were questioned, Professor Alfred Tozzer of the Peabody Museum was particularly helpful in coming to my rescue. The book-selection work seemed to be going well; as reported in Chapter 5, I had persuaded the Council to turn over to me responsibility for allocating book-fund income. My proposals for dealing with space problems had been discussed with heads of College departments as well as with administrative officers of the University.

The first years after World War II brought us a much larger student body and one that took its academic work more seriously than its predecessors ever had done. Faculty members were increasing their demands on the Library for more books and serials and tended to be dissatisfied because their departments were not provided for as adequately as they would have liked. At the same time, they feared that pressure from the Library for additional funds might take money that they wanted for other services in their departments. As had been the case throughout the Library's history up to that time, appropriations for acquisitions were restricted to current gifts for the purpose and to the income of endowed book funds. This income was inadequate, and too often the individual funds were restricted to limited fields.

Without consulting me, Paul Buck, the Provost of the University, had arranged in 1945 to have Professor of Bibliography added to my previous titles, which were Director of the University Library, Librarian of Harvard College, and Member of the Faculty of Arts and Sciences; this was meant to enhance my status. In 1948, the President and the Provost decided, with my approval, that the Library and its problems should be a topic for discussion at one of the monthly meetings of the Faculty of Arts and Sciences. At this meeting, one of the senior members of the Economics Department, a very prolific writer who published at least one volume a year, suggested that the physical expansion and the budget of the Library could be brought under better control if it discarded the half of its collections that, as far as he could tell, was never used. As an example of what ought to be weeded, he then added that the Library had a large collection of children's books, which he thought it perfectly absurd for a college to house.

Wondering what to say in reply, I thought of the story I had heard of Alfred North Whitehead before I came to Harvard. He was said to have engaged in a similar discussion with a group of senior faculty members, one of whom proposed that the collection be reduced in size by perhaps one half. He then said, "Yes, I can see how you feel about it, and here is a suggestion. We will ask each department chairman to examine the books in his field and divide them into two groups, one half to be kept, and one half to be discarded." (I am sure he knew that none of them would find more than a handful of titles in his own field that he was willing to give up.) I might have said, "This is an interesting proposal; but I will look over the volumes suggested for discard and will find that they are probably the only copies of these books in an American library. It would be a great mistake to dispose of them. Those that you propose to keep are duplicated in many of our university libraries and so are of comparatively little importance, and we might well discard them."

But before I had an opportunity to say anything, Professor Samuel Eliot Morison stood up and spoke briefly and wryly, saying, "I confess I have never examined the collection of children's books to which the previous speaker referred, but I am ready to suggest that, if we look ahead another generation, this collection will be more valuable and will be used more than the large number of volumes that he is producing." This ended the discussion.

The University administration, however, was quite properly worried about the increasing financial needs of the College Library for staff salaries and acquisitions. I had frequently said that these costs would tend to increase more rapidly than those of other parts of the University, because the Library continually added to its collections while discarding very little. The College took in new students annually as the Library took in new books, but students left the scene eventually and did not accumulate. Moreover, as the Library's collection grew larger and larger, it became more and more expensive to catalog each new item. There would inevitably be continued pressure for appropriations from unrestricted funds for both services and acquisitions, and these would be difficult to grant. The Statutes provided that "The central collection, known as the Harvard College Library, is for the use of the whole University," and it had never been fully realized that the College Library was primarily a facility for the Faculty of Arts and Sciences. Theoretically at least, as a part of the institution receiving tuition, this Faculty might more easily find funds for its support than the Corporation, which, under the present system, had to finance the Library from general funds of the University.

A change was approved, making the College Library a department of the Faculty of Arts and Sciences rather than a department of the University. At the same time, the Corporation, "acknowledging the responsibility of the University as a whole for maintaining a great research library center of a size beyond that necessary to provide suitable library facilities for the Faculty of Arts and Sciences," set aside a fund "the income of which should be used to provide one half of the general overhead of the Library."

Under the new arrangement, I continued, as Director of the University Library, to serve as advisor and coordinating officer for the University Library, which, according to the Statutes, "consists of all the collections of books in the possession of the University"; but, as Librarian of Harvard College, I reported to the Provost, Paul Buck. He and I then talked over the Library problem and decided that the University Library Council should be replaced by a Library Committee of the Faculty of Arts and Sciences, with the Director its Chairman, *ex officio*.

We realized that it would be desirable to appoint to the new committee a number of professors who were inclined to criticize the Library. It was appointed shortly before the Lamont Library opened. Ed Williams produced the minutes of the second meeting and of nearly all those that followed until, after the 201st, he retired in 1980. Members included two professors from physical sciences departments who were naturally more interested in their own laboratory science collections than in the Library as a whole, two social scientists who had been and continued to be vocal in their criticisms of the Library, and two representatives of the humanities who did not always agree with what was being done. One of the latter complained bitterly and vigorously about the selection of books in his field for the Lamont Library. I asked him for a list of those to which he objected. Of the six that he specified, I found that three had been written by members of his department, while the remaining three had been recommended for the collection by other members of his department. One of the social scientists had spent a good deal of time in Washington, working on the Federal budget. He could not understand why the College Library needed, in addition to me, more than one person who might be considered to rank with members of the faculty.

I must admit that I spent a rather difficult year or two as a result of the new committee; but no serious problems with the faculty arose except in connection with proposed changes in use of space in the Widener building, as will be explained below. Following this controversy, things began to go smoothly again, and there were no difficulties with the committee through the remainder of my administration.

When the Lamont Library was completed in 1949, its basement levels provided space for nearly 500,000 volumes of overflow from the Widener and Houghton collections. Separate tunnels connected Lamont with the older buildings. With this, as well as the space that had been freed in Widener by sending material to Littauer and to the New England Deposit Library, we had, for the first time in many years, ample space for the next decade's growth of the Widener collection. It was hoped that further space could be provided by comparatively small and inexpensive additions to libraries for the fine arts, the Graduate School of Design, the Divinity School, and the Graduate School of Education, since portions of the collections for each of these fields were in Widener. There were also proposals for a central science library to house extensive files of periodicals from Widener as well as from the specialized science libraries. All of these hopes have been realized since my retirement. Underground construction was also proposed in 1938, and this has been provided by the Pusey Library.

I had been dissatisfied with the assignments of space in the Widener building. The public catalog, reference collection, main reading room, and stack entrance for students were all on what was called the second floor of the building; it was actually the third level, more than seventy steps up from the ground level outside. No suitable elevator was available. The only access to the stacks for students was from the circulation desk, four steps up from the so-called second level; this took one to the eighth of ten levels of the stack. If one then wanted to get to the lowest level of the stack, one had to go down seven flights of stairs or take one of the two slow, inadequate elevators, which were approximately one hundred yards apart, one on the east side of the building and one on the west. The one on the east side did not go down to the lowest level. If a student on the lowest level wanted to use the public toilet, he had to go up to the eighth level and then down to the basement, seventy steps down the main stairs. This was the situation when I came in 1937; the toilet problem was partially solved by installation of toilets in the stack in place of two faculty studies on the fifth of the ten stack levels. I have sometimes said that, as far as graduate students are concerned, I will go down in history as the man who provided toilet facilities in the Widener stack.

After the Houghton Library was opened in 1942, the order and cataloging staffs were conveniently and adequately provided for on the main entrance level; at that time the catalogers had been moved from the congested union catalog room into what had been the rare-book reading room. The problem that called for debate in my opinion was the location of the central public services, then seventy steps above the Yard outside. In an article published in the winter 1950 issue of the *Harvard Library Bulletin* (Vol. IV, No. 1), I proposed that most of these central public services be transferred to the east half of the first floor, which would bring the circulation desk, stack entrance, public catalog, and bibliographical and reference collections to a level thirty steps above the ground. Copies of this statement were distributed to the faculty, and comments were requested. Only a handful of replies were received, and I was in a quandary. I was not at all enthusiastic about my suggestion but had made it largely in order to get faculty reactions; I had been naive enough to think they would welcome the opportunity. The proposal called for turning over the east side of the first floor to public services, leaving only the west side for the processing staff; this was one objection to it, I realized, because, unless automation and cooperation between libraries came rapidly, the staff would soon need more space than this, and convenient quarters could not easily be provided.

Arrangements were made for a meeting of the Faculty of Arts and Sciences to discuss the proposal. Two senior members of the Faculty distributed a petition, for which they obtained as many signatures as they could, opposing the plan. There was violent opposition at the meeting. After hearing the discussion, President Conant turned to Archibald MacLeish, who had returned to Harvard after serving as Librarian of Congress and then as Assistant Secretary of State, and asked his advice. MacLeish said he did not feel that he was in a position to comment, except to say that he would be inclined to follow any recommendations made by the Director of the University Library.

I had failed to realize that scholars, liberal as they might appear to be, were basically conservative as far as their own work patterns were concerned, and did not like to change them. Although I had initiated the proposal, I confess that I was very much relieved. If accepted, it would have called for large expenditures and, except for saving a thousand or more persons from going up and down stairs daily, would in many ways have provided arrangements less functional than those then in use. I was irritated by some of the criticism and sorry that I had not made it clearer that I was simply trying to make the Library easier to use and more satisfactory for the professors and graduate students who, since the opening of Lamont, were the major users of the Widener Library.

I had refused to discard a large number of books that some professors regarded as useless, and many members of the Faculty of Arts and Sciences had opposed my suggestion that central public services be transferred to the first floor of Widener. With these two exceptions, I was surprised, amused, and pleased at how good my relations were with the Faculty and its Library Committee during my eighteen years at Harvard. Several factors helped, I am sure. President Conant had feared that a new central library building would be demanded and was relieved when it was not. Provost Buck was interested in the Library. There was general agreement, I hope, that the building program was reasonable and that reasonably satisfactory service to students and faculty had been maintained during difficult times without taking a larger share of the University's resources than those who used the Library thought it ought to take.

Chapter 13

Libraries of Departments, Research Institutions, and Faculties Other than Arts and Sciences

I HAVE TOLD something in the first chapter of this volume about getting acquainted with libraries throughout the University that serve departments of the Faculty of Arts and Sciences, research institutions, or graduate professional schools under the faculties of Business Administration, Design, Divinity, Education, Law, Medicine and Public Health, and Public Administration (now Government). These libraries, though not administratively responsible to the Director of the University Library, reported to him at least annually and, theoretically, called upon him for advice. The financial support of each library came from its own department, institution, or faculty.

There have been changes since 1937, when the College Library, essentially, was Widener. Houghton and Lamont were units of the College Library by 1955. There have been seven additions to the College Library since that date. These are the Fine Arts Library (1963), Hilles, an undergraduate library formerly administered by Radcliffe College (1971), the Cabot Science Library (1973), Littauer (1974), Harvard-Yenching (1976), the Eda Kuhn Loeb Music Library (1978), and the Tozzer Library of the Peabody Museum (1979).

These were all in existence prior to their transfer to the College Library, except for the Cabot Science Library. A science library had been proposed during my time, however, by Edwin Cohn, in honor of Theodore Richards, President Conant's father-in-law and the first American Nobel Prize winner in chemistry, and of Lawrence J. Henderson, Chairman of the Society of Fellows, head of the Fatigue Laboratory, and brother-in-law of Mrs. Conant's mother. Dr. Cohn, who greatly respected these men because their research made possible his own important study, which resulted in the fractionation of blood, died prematurely, and nothing came of his proposal. Because of Elinor's relationship to both Richards and Henderson, I felt that I should not urge President Conant to act on the plan. This may have been a mistake on my part; but a long struggle would have been required at that time to persuade the large science laboratories to give up their early material, though this seemed to me to be a good idea. In any case, I was pleased when the Cabot Science Library was established, and have been glad to watch my successors in the College Library support its development under Alan Erickson, its librarian.

This chapter, then, will deal with libraries that were not part of the College Library in my time, though some of them have subsequently been annexed to it administratively.

THE LAW SCHOOL LIBRARY

Eldon James, who had been Librarian of the Law School Library since 1923, left for temporary war work in Washington during 1942, and became Law Librarian of Congress the following year. Dean Landis of the Law School wanted to appoint as his successor a man whom I have known for many years, but who, I felt would make a better contribution to his profession elsewhere. Landis left Harvard at this time, and I was able to arrange with Acting Dean Edmund Morgan to appoint Arthur Pulling. In my opinion, this turned out very well. Pulling was helpful in avoiding unnecessary duplication between the Law School Library and other libraries in the University.

When Pulling reached Harvard's retirement age in 1954, he accepted a position as head of the law library at Villanova, where he could continue to work after the age of sixty-six. Earl Borgeson, who succeeded him at Harvard, had earned degrees in both law and librarianship and had worked for Pulling while attending the University of Minnesota. He remained here until 1970, when he went to Stanford as Associate Director of Libraries.

Erwin Griswold became Dean of the Law School in 1946. His father and mother had been graduated from Oberlin in the 1890s, and he had been graduated there in 1925, fourteen years after I was. I had met his parents in 1928 at Oberlin meetings and had known his father's brother in Youngstown, Ohio, in the summer of 1911, when he was Principal of the Rayen High School and I was in charge of a playground there in the slum district; but I did not meet Erwin until after I came to Harvard. We became good friends, but he always insisted that the Law School

Library was completely independent of the rest of the University Library and that I had no responsibility for it. In this he was following the practice of Law School deans throughout the régimes of Lowell and Conant. Indeed, the independence of law school libraries was customary throughout the country at that time. In *My Several Lives*, President Conant wrote that, "In dealing with the Law School Faculty, I found it to be the most quarrelsome group of men I ever encountered."

THE BUSINESS SCHOOL: BAKER LIBRARY

The Dean of the Graduate School of Business Administration, Wallace Donham, and his successor, Donald David, were always very friendly, as was the Librarian, Arthur Cole. I regularly attended the meetings of their library committee; in 1938 or 1939 the committee talked of calling on me to study their library problems, and a little later Dean Donham invited me to do so. Andrew Osborn and I looked into the situation. The book selection and cataloging were going well, but we thought that it would be useful to have a good administrative assistant to help Cole. Donham agreed and asked me to suggest someone.

Breaking my rule against taking advantage of my knowledge of the New York Public Library staff, I suggested Donald Clark, who had made such a good impression on me that I was ready to recommend him. He was a native of Seattle, had been graduated from the University of California, Berkeley, had earned a degree from the library school at Columbia, and had joined the staff of the New York Public Library in 1935. At Harvard, he was able to earn his M.B.A. while working in the library. When Cole retired in 1956, Clark succeeded him and headed the Business School library until 1963, when he left Harvard to become the first librarian of the newly organized University of California at Santa Cruz. In 1967, I had the pleasure of working with him in planning an interesting new library building for that university.

Clark's appointment enabled Cole to give more time to book selection; as has been noted in Chapter 1, he was chiefly responsible for selection of materials in economics and sociology for Widener and helped to select for Littauer. It was highly desirable to have his help in coordinating the acquisitions of Widener, Littauer, and the Business School.

I continued to work closely with the Business School until my retirement. One of the professors there who had been graduated from Bowdoin was responsible for the invitation I received to consult with that college about its library problems, something that I was particularly glad to do because my father had been a Bowdoin graduate of 1847.

My son-in-law, Maxwell Small, his father, and one of his sons are also Bowdoin men.

My experience with problems of library lighting encouraged the Business School to call on me to work with them on lighting their very large reading room, which has a high ceiling. If I am not mistaken, the lighting there was considerably improved.

THE MEDICAL SCHOOL LIBRARY

At the Medical School, as reported in Chapter 1, I found the Dean, Sidney Burwell, the Librarian, Anna Holt, and the library committee easy to deal with; but there were difficulties in relations with the Boston Medical Library resulting, at least in part, from the unsuccessful campaign of 1929 to raise money for a building in which the two libraries would have been housed.

Soon after coming to Harvard I became acquainted with James Ballard, Librarian of the Boston Medical Library, and Dr. Henry Viets, the dominant figure representing the medical profession on its board. It was evident that both were anxious to remain independent of the Harvard Medical School Library. However, at the invitation of the Board of Directors, Andrew Osborn and I surveyed the situation and made some critical comments on the way Ballard was dealing with crowded conditions in the Library. Uncataloged books were piled up in the basement like cord-wood. Ballard and Viets took offense, and their verbal attack on Osborn was violent. Apparently they were not quite ready to treat me in the same way; but certainly nothing came of the study.

I felt strongly enough about the matter to appeal to Dr. Roger Lee, a member of the Harvard Corporation who, I knew, was influential in Boston medical affairs. He, apparently, was as dissatisfied as I was with the situation in the Boston Medical Library but felt that it was hopeless because of Ballard's reputation as a collector; and he did not want to become involved.

While I continued to work closely with the Harvard Medical School and its library committee, nothing was accomplished in improving relations with the Boston Medical Library until after I retired. Then, after Miss Sanda Countway had given $3,500,000 for construction of the Francis A. Countway Library to house Harvard's medical collection, an agreement was reached in January 1960 to unite the two libraries under one roof and one librarian.

Apropos of the Boston Medical Library, I might add that I was involved, in 1949, in the appointment of a capable young man, Charles

Colby, to serve as assistant librarian under Ballard and to try to keep things running as smoothly as possible. Colby, a Harvard graduate of 1945 with a library degree from Simmons College, stayed for five years; then, after having been Librarian of the University of Missouri Medical Library for two years, he returned to head the Boston Medical Library. In 1965, he became Associate Librarian of the new Countway Library of Medicine.

THE ANDOVER-HARVARD LIBRARY OF THE DIVINITY SCHOOL

Difficulties at the Divinity School Library have been mentioned, but these were resolved when Professor Henry Cadbury became responsible for general oversight of the Library, with Jannette Newhall as his associate. Dr. Newhall left in 1949 to teach at Boston University and head the library of its School of Theology; but Cadbury continued to direct the Andover-Harvard Library until 1954.

Cadbury was a distinguished scholar; but I cannot resist telling of a mistake of his that I never ventured to report to him. After Elinor retired from the Boston Athenaeum in 1946, we purchased (in celebration of the event, you might say) the *Dictionary of American Biography*. One day I asked her about her grandfather, Joseph Henry Thayer, and she said, "Why don't you look him up in the *D.A.B.*?" When I did so, I found that Henry Cadbury had written his biography there. It stated that Thayer had married in November 1859. Elinor's mother had been born in September 1859, two years after Grandfather Thayer was married, not two months before, and Elinor changed the *9* to a *7* in our copy and, perhaps wickedly, in the Boston Athenaeum copy.

At the Andover-Harvard Library, Cadbury was severely handicapped by the fact that the Divinity School's endowment was far too small to support the Library adequately, and the University administration was not interested in supporting it from unrestricted funds. The book budget was completely indequate, and I finally appealed to President Conant. He was not sympathetic because he believed that President Eliot's adage that each department should "stand on its own bottom" financially ought to apply to the Divinity School as much as to any other part of the University.

I found that Willard Sperry, Dean of the Divinity School, was easy to deal with, but he was not a money-raiser. Widener still had a good collection on church history, including periodicals, which it was keeping up; but I felt that something must be done, and I told the President as strongly as I could that, whatever the present generation might feel about theological collections, a later generation might feel very differently about them (this turned out to be the case), and much of the material that I thought should be acquired at the time it was published would be difficult if not impossible, and certainly more expensive, to acquire later. He relented and agreed to provide a somewhat more satisfactory book fund, enabling the School to purchase important theological periodicals currently, as well as other essential publications.

Increased funds became available to the Divinity School about the time I retired, and in 1960 an addition to Andover Hall provided space for more than 100,000 additional volumes as well as for readers and staff. Some of the space was used for materials transferred from Widener, in accordance with plans I had suggested for shifting collections that were of primary interest to more specialized Harvard libraries.

The Andover-Harvard Library was involved in our acquisition of the archives of the American Board of Commissioners for Foreign Missions, one of the interesting developments of my Harvard years. At one time these archives had been stored in the headquarters of the American Board in the Congregational building next to the Boston Athenaeum on Beacon Street. In 1929, when the Divinity School was more prosperous than in my time, and was eager to build up its collections, they had been deposited as a loan in the Andover-Harvard stacks. But the affiliation of the Andover Theological Seminary with Harvard was challenged in the courts, the affiliation was dissolved, and conservative members of the faculty left to join the Newton Theological Institution, forming the Andover Newton Theological School in Newton Center, Massachusetts. The book collection, however, was left in the Andover-Harvard building with the understanding that it would be as readily available to Andover Newton faculty and students as to Harvard people.

The American Board's archives included not only the correspondence between the Board and missionaries all over the world, but publications for which they had been responsible, often the first items printed in native languages and, therefore, of great value to bibliographers and collectors. During my New York years I had been able to acquire for the New York Public Library a large collection of these publications that had been assembled by a Harvard professor and Franz Boas, the noted Columbia University professor of anthropology who had once taught briefly at Harvard. New York would, of course, have been very glad to acquire the Board's own collection of printed material and its archives.

I believed that the American Board archives ought to be kept in the Boston area and given the special care that we could provide in the

Houghton Library. I had several meetings with representatives of the Harvard Divinity School, the Andover Newton Theological School, and the Congregational Library Society in Boston. Andover Newton was eager to obtain title to the material, but the Harvard representatives were finally successful in persuading the Congregational Society to have the archives remain at Harvard with the understanding that they would be kept in Houghton. I was naturally delighted, all the more because perhaps a quarter of my high-school class at Oberlin had been made up of American missionaries' children who had been sent from posts throughout the world where the climate was believed to be particularly undesirable for children in their teens.

I might add that, when the discussion was concluded, the Andover Newton representative very generously offered a prayer to give thanks that the Spirit of the Lord Jesus had descended upon us and settled a very difficult problem. I was sitting beside the representative of the Congregational Society, who whispered to me, "Not the Spirit of the Lord, but Keyes Metcalf brought about the decision."

THE GRADUATE SCHOOL OF EDUCATION

In 1937, and for a number of years before and after, the headquarters of the Graduate School of Education and its library were in Lawrence Hall, an old building just east of Littauer. A part of the site is now occupied by the west end of the Science Center. There was room for little more than half of the School's library collection in Lawrence Hall in 1937; the other half, consisting chiefly of primary, elementary, and high-school textbooks, college catalogs, and other college publications, was in Widener. The textbooks were moved to the New England Deposit Library when that building was opened in 1942, though serious consideration was given to transferring them to Teachers College at Columbia. It was decided to keep them at Harvard because interest in them might increase.

I remember arriving at my office one morning and receiving a call from the Department of Buildings and Grounds, saying that at least half the books in the Education Library must be moved immediately because there was danger of the building collapsing. Fortunately, though it was not easy, we found space for them. It was considerably later that Larsen Hall was built for the School on Appian Way; still later, in 1972, the Monroe C. Gutman Library, at the corner of Brattle Street and Appian Way, was opened, and the School of Education for the first time had satisfactory quarters for its library.

THE GRADUATE SCHOOL OF DESIGN

Two libraries, occupying different floors of Robinson Hall, were maintained by the Graduate School of Design, the Architecture Library and the Landscape Architecture and Regional Planning Library (later called the City Planning and Landscape Architecture Library). Many of the books, particularly works on architecture, were shelved in Widener. In 1972, long after my retirement, Gund Hall was opened, housing the School and both of its libraries, which were combined. Architectural books from Widener were also moved there, completing the transfer from Widener of books in subjects covered by the graduate professional schools, and leaving in Widener primarily the collections in the humanities, history, and those of the social sciences outside the scope of the law, business, and government schools.

FINE ARTS

Relations between the College Library and the Fogg Museum Library were always good. There was a first-class librarian at the Fogg, E. Louise Lucas, who gave a great deal of attention to book selection and to avoiding duplication between her collection and Widener's. In 1963, construction of an underground bookstack addition to the Fogg made it possible to move the research collection in fine arts from Widener and combine it with the working library in Fogg. As this is written, an addition to the Fogg Museum is under construction, and there are plans for increasing space assigned to the Fine Arts Library in the Fogg building.

THE HARVARD-YENCHING INSTITUTE

As has been explained in Chapter 1, I was particularly interested in the Chinese-Japanese Library of the Harvard-Yenching Institute because its basic endowment had come from Charles Martin Hall, the Oberlin graduate who did so much for Oberlin. I have also mentioned the interest of John K. Fairbank and Edwin O. Reischauer in building up holdings on contemporary history and civilization of the Far East. Reischauer, of course, was later our ambassador to Japan.

The Institute's librarian, from 1927 to 1965, was Alfred Kaiming Chiu, with whom I became acquainted in 1924, when he was attending the New York Public Library Library School. With more than 600,000 volumes, the Harvard-Yenching Library is surpassed in size at Harvard only by Widener and the Law School Library, and it is the largest Far Eastern collection in an American university. In 1957, it was moved from rather unsatisfactory quarters in Boylston Hall to the building formerly occupied by the Institute of Geographical Exploration on Divinity Avenue.

OTHER HARVARD LIBRARIES

Not long before I retired, the Gray Herbarium Library and the non-horticultural portions of the Arnold Arboretum Library were placed adjacent to each other in a new Harvard University Herbarium building. Here they are next door to the Museum of Comparative Zoology Library and the Farlow Reference Library (cryptogamic botany), as well as to the Biological Laboratories Library and the Economic Botany Library of Oakes Ames in the Botanical Museum. It was later found desirable to return some of the materials from Arnold to the horticultural headquarters of the Arboretum in Jamaica Plain; but a single librarian is now responsible for administration of this collection as well as the two libraries in the herbarium, and some duplication of botanical collections has been eliminated.

During my early years at Harvard, funds given by Dr. Ernest Stillman provided a new building at Petersham, Massachusetts, in which the Harvard Forest Library occupied more satisfactory quarters than had previously been available. There is also a working collection at Cornwall, New York, for the Harvard Black Rock Forest, which was bequeathed to the University in 1949 by Dr. Stillman.

A major addition to the University Library came in 1940, when the Dumbarton Oaks Research Library and Collection in Washington, D.C., was given to Harvard by Mr. and Mrs. Robert Woods Bliss. Three libraries are included. The research collection covers all aspects of Byzantine culture, the Garden Library includes many early and rare publications in its field, and the Bliss Pre-Columbian Collection maintains a small working library.

Chapter 14

Service on *Ad Hoc* University Committees

D URING MY EIGHTEEN YEARS at Harvard, I was appointed by President Conant to three University *ad hoc* committees. These dealt directly or indirectly with problems affecting the University as a whole. My assignments involved wartime defense questions and the selection of new directors for the Fogg Museum and the Harvard University Press. All three provided interesting additions to my education and to my acquaintance with Harvard and with my colleagues.

THE WAR DEFENSE COMMITTEE

President Conant had been among the first of the influential Americans who believed that we ought to do our best to help Britain in its struggle against Nazi Germany. By the time we entered the war in December 1941, he realized that there would be at least a possibility of damage to University property by sabotage or bombing. Harvard's buildings stood in a strategically dangerous location; bombers might well have an almost straight run from the ocean over the Massachusetts Institute of Technology, Harvard, and then on to the Watertown Arsenal, which at that time was an important and busy military installation.

As a result, the University's Defense Committee was appointed. Its chairman was Donald Scott, Director of the Peabody Museum, who had long and successful administrative experience as a publisher. Other members included Irving Parkhurst, the Superintendent of Buildings and Grounds, and Aldrich Durant, the Business Manager of the University. The Committee continued until the end of the war, nearly four years later.

I welcomed the opportunity to become well acquainted with Scott, who, before coming back to Harvard, had been connected with the Century Publishing Company in New York, like his father, who was known as "Great Scott." (The Century Company archives had come to the New York Public Library during my time there. From the age of twelve, I had used the *Century Dictionary, Book of Names,* and *Atlas,* which we had at home in Ohio and which had come to me in White Plains after the death of my sister Marion in 1930.) Donald Scott was a delightful person in every way as well as a first-class administrator, and my association with him, first on the Defense Committee and later in connection with the Harvard University Press, is one of the Harvard experiences that I look back on with special pleasure.

It was evident that the University, even in an emergency, could not move all of its activities out of Cambridge; but we had to consider the question of valuable works of art, other museum materials, and collections of books and manuscripts. The situation was similar in other institutions in the Boston area and along the East Coast. Some of them moved valuable collections to locations that were believed to be safer. I understood that the Boston Public Library had deposited some of its manuscripts and rare printed books in Boston bank vaults. Some of the most valuable collections of the Boston Museum of Fine Arts were moved to the western part of the state. We considered what should be done with the Museum of Comparative Zoology's glass flowers, which were irreplaceable, extremely fragile, and a popular attraction. The story went around that a group of elderly Cambridge women sent one of their number to see the glass flowers every day, believing that, as long as they were still in their regular location, it would be safe to remain in Cambridge; but, if the collection were moved, it would be time to seek safer living quarters elsewhere.

The Library had large and irreplaceable collections of books and manuscripts in Widener, in Houghton (when that building was occupied, soon after Pearl Harbor), and in the libraries of the Medical School, the Law School, and other parts of the University. I talked with the Treasurer, Bill Claflin, about insuring the collections. He laughed at me, naturally enough, saying that the cost of insurance made this out of the question, but that, if any part of the Library were destroyed, its replacement, as far as possible, would have first call on Harvard's unrestricted endowment after the war.

The Defense Committee readily agreed, however, that we should be prepared for removal of the Library's most valuable possessions if the situation were to seem critical. I was assigned two tasks. The first was to suggest a place to which collections could be moved, as well as methods of getting them there if an emergency should arise. The second and more difficult task was selection of the material to be moved. I went to work on both problems.

Where would we put what was selected for removal? The Harvard Forest, thanks to the generosity of Dr. Ernest Stillman, the man who had made possible the Harvard dioramas in Widener, had recently received funds for construction of a new building at the Forest, in Petersham, Massachusetts. The University owned a large tract of land in that area. Parkhurst and I thought seriously of excavating a cave in the Forest. It was known by this time that Germany had buried in caves many of its most valuable art, manuscript, and book collections. We selected a spot near the Harvard Forest building that seemed to be suitable but finally decided that it would be undesirable because of the difficulty of controlling atmospheric conditions and making the cave safe from water damage. Plans were prepared, instead, to provide the space that would be needed in the new Forest building.

I worked out a plan for moving. We knew that, if we decided to act, there would undoubtedly be a tremendous number of people attempting to move westward at the same time, and that the main highways then available (Routes 2 and 3) would probably be almost impassable. I had been interested in the countryside ever since coming to Massachusetts; eight generations of my family had lived in one small town or another east of the Connecticut River. I had become acquainted with practically all the good roads in the Petersham area and picked the route that I thought would be most suitable for getting to the Forest. I learned also that Aldrich Durant, a member of the Committee, had spent his summers for many years in his ancestral home in Princeton, not far from Petersham. When I took my proposal for our escape route to him, I found to my pleasure that it was the one he had used year after year when driving out to his grandmother's home. Our route, at least, was selected.

Moving, obviously, would call for packing material. I was already closely involved with Parkhurst because of library building and the move into the New England Deposit Library, which took place during the weeks following Pearl Harbor. With his help, we purchased suitable lumber for making a large number of boxes quite similar to those I had used in moving the Oberlin College Library during 1908 and at the New York Public Library in 1933. He planned a production line to put the boxes together. Suitable packing material was also acquired; this, plus the lumber, cost a total of $4,000, a sum that went much further then than it would forty years later. Parkhurst had a crew of men available for assignment on short notice to construction. It was agreed that quite a number of the University's trucks and drivers would be assigned to the move.

It was much more difficult, of course, to select what was to go. Each Harvard library was asked to designate the material it would want to send. The largest amount was to come from Houghton; but the libraries of the Law School, Medical School, Museum of Comparative Zoology, and Gray Herbarium were among those calling for special attention. Then, with Bill Jackson's help, I drew up lists of books and manuscripts to be moved, with priorities, and we felt that we were ready to act at any time. The emergency, fortunately, never arose, and I am glad to be able to report that, at the end of the war, the lumber and packing material were sold for more than enough to cover the original cost plus interest.

The University was concerned for the safety of its faculty and students as well as for the preservation of irreplaceable collections, and it became my responsibility to have plans for action ready in case a sudden bombing attack were threatened. Alarms to alert the whole area were provided. It was decided that, if an alarm should come during library hours, the occupants of Widener and Houghton would be directed to Widener's sub-basement, two levels below ground. There were tests on two occasions to see how the plan would work. Once during daylight hours and once during the evening, we were able to herd readers and staff down into an area that was believed to offer protection from bombs. Everything worked out reasonably well; those who had to move were amused, though to some extent annoyed at being taken from their work.

Scott, the Chairman of the Defense Committee, continued during the war to spend summer vacations in the Southwest, doing anthropological field work, and I was left in charge as Deputy Chairman. For 1942, 1943, and 1944, Elinor and I gave up our regular two-week summer vacations in the Catskills, and stayed at the Ark in East Jaffrey, at the foot of Mount Monadnock, from which we could have returned to Cambridge in our own car within two hours or less if an emergency had threatened.

Since there was no attack on Harvard, one might say that the whole program was a waste of time; but it was a very interesting experience for me, and I retain pleasant memories of my friendship with the other members of the Committee.

DIRECTORSHIP OF THE FOGG MUSEUM

My second *ad hoc* University committee was appointed to recommend a new director for the Fogg Museum following the retirement of both its director and associate director. The retiring director was Edward Waldo Forbes, a grandson of Ralph Waldo Emerson, whom he resembled in appearance. His associate, retiring at the same time in 1944, was Paul Sachs. The two men had worked together with amazing success for nearly thirty years and had trained a large proportion of the directors of fine-art museums throughout the country.

As was customary when a position of this type was being considered, the Committee included members who were not at Harvard. Fortunately for all concerned, my responsibilities were lighter than they had been on the Defense Committee. We considered a number of museum directors from all over the country, some of them from museums in large cities and some from academic institutions. Those whom we thought suitable were not interested; those who were interested did not seem to be what we wanted.

I finally suggested a non-Harvard member of the Committee and was authorized to try to persuade him to accept. This was Huntington Cairns, a lawyer who was Secretary and Treasurer of the National Gallery of Art in Washington. I did my best, but he was unwilling to come, and the Committee reported that it had no one to recommend at the time. An acting director was appointed.

Finally, three years after the retirement of Forbes and Sachs, John Phillips Coolidge was selected. He was a son of Julian Coolidge, who had recently retired as Professor of Mathematics and Master of Lowell House. John was also a nephew of Archibald Cary Coolidge, the first Director of the Harvard University Library; he had received his Ph.D. at Harvard and had taught at Vassar and the University of Pennsylvania. He proved to be a good selection. He seemed to us to be quite young, but he has now been retired for several years.

THE HARVARD UNIVERSITY PRESS

My connection with publishing before I came to Harvard was slight and indirect. Harry Lydenberg had been greatly interested in printing and publishing, and had kept in his own hands the management of New York Public Library activities in these fields. His competence, combined with the designing genius of John Archer, who was in charge of the Printing Office, resulted in the publication of a number of important volumes, several of which were so well designed and printed that they were selected for recognition when the American Institute of Graphic Arts made its annual awards.

I had not been at Harvard long before I met Dumas Malone; he had become Director of the Harvard University Press in 1936 after a successful career of teaching history at Yale and the University of Virginia, followed by his work as editor of all but the early volumes of the *Dictionary of American Biography*. I saw something of him during the next half-dozen years. He found it difficult to adapt himself to the financial problems of a university press in a university with an administration that was struggling to balance its budget and did not want to subsidize its press, which had practically no endowment.

Harvard's new Treasurer, William H. Claflin, who took office in 1938, looked into the finances of the University Printing Office and the University Press, which had been dealt with as one unit, and found that charges for printing billed to the various departments of the University seemed to be unnecessarily high; exorbitant rates for printing had been a means of balancing the budget for the combined units of publishing and printing. Malone left Harvard in 1943, and was a professor of history at Columbia; he retired in 1959, but continued work on his great biography of Jefferson, of which the sixth and final volume appeared in 1981.

Malone's place as Director of the Harvard University Press was filled by Roger Scaife, who had been with Houghton Mifflin and then with Little Brown in important positions. His experience enabled him to improve the financial situation of the Press, and for the time being it was in less danger of being discontinued. Scaife, however, was past the regular retirement age for administrative officers at Harvard, and a University *ad hoc* committee was appointed to make recommendations on selection of a new director. I was appointed Chairman, and Donald Scott, with whom I had worked closely on the Defense Committee during the war, was a very helpful member. We were asked to report as promptly as possible.

The directors of several other university presses applied or were suggested, but we were not prepared to recommend any one of them. We finally decided that Thomas J. Wilson was the man we preferred. His father had been a professor at the University of North Carolina. Wilson had gone there for his undergraduate work; this had been followed by a Rhodes Scholarship, and he had earned a doctorate at Oxford. He had taught Romance Languages at Chapel Hill and then had been with a good publisher in New York City for twelve years, working in several positions, including administrative ones. During the war, he had spent four years in the Navy, serving with distinction and rising to the rank of Commander. He was now in his first year as Director of the University of North Carolina Press.

I went to Chapel Hill to talk with Wilson as a representative of the Committee. I stayed with the Librarian of the University, Charles Rush, whom I had known for nearly twenty years during his varied experience in public and academic libraries. I remember that, outside the breakfast-room window, he had a bell rigged up; when he rang it, the bird-feeding station was immediately filled with birds, rejoicing to find their breakfast waiting for them. I was able to talk with Louis Round Wilson, who had been Director of the University of North Carolina Library for more than thirty years before going to the Graduate Library School of the University of Chicago to serve as Dean for ten years during its most brilliant period. He had been one of the early chairmen of the American Library Association's Board of Education for Librarianship and also President of the ALA. After retiring, he had returned to his old home in Chapel Hill. He was not related to Tom Wilson but of course had known him and his family. It was evident that the University did not want to lose the new Director of its Press.

Tom Wilson was interested, but hesitated to leave Chapel Hill, where he had just begun his work for the Press. I asked him to come to Cambridge and look the situation over, which he did. He arrived on one of the rare days in the Boston area when the temperature stays below zero. I had invited him to come to dinner with me in Belmont that evening with Penelope Noyes, Justin Winsor's grand-daughter, whose mother had been a close friend of Elinor's mother in Cambridge during the 1880s. She was the only other guest. Tom, Penelope, and Elinor joined me in my car, which had been parked behind the Library all day.

I had been worried about starting the car because of the cold; but there was no difficulty, and we headed up Concord Avenue toward Belmont. Just beyond the Commander and Continental Hotels, where the road is normally three lanes wide, but where the heavy snow had narrowed it to two, my engine suddenly died, and I could not start it again. This was during the rush hour, and heavy traffic in both directions came to a complete standstill almost immediately. The next morning, I remember, Elinor had a call from her friend Marion Eaton, Librarian of the Boston Reserve Bank, who lived nearby; Marion wondered if Elinor had heard of the terrible traffic jam of the previous evening.

Fortunately, the police arrived soon, extracted our Dodge, and hauled us to a garage less than a mile away, where we thawed out and then went on our way. Apparently we had started with a full carburator, but the line to it from the gas tank had frozen.

The evening ended with no further problems, but I feared that Wilson had seen enough of New England weather and would say he was not interested in coming to Harvard. He did express interest, however, provided that we could wait until he had completed a full year at Chapel Hill. The Committee recommended his appointment; but, when I drew up the terms that I thought we should offer, there were objections from Edward Reynolds, the Administrative Vice President, who was the watchdog over the budget. With the help of my good friend, Donald Scott, we were able to satisfy both Reynolds and Wilson and to reach an agreement.

Tom Wilson came to Harvard later in 1947. The Harvard Press, like Oxford's, had a Board of Syndics, an editorial advisory committee whose chief function was to pass on the Director's recommendations for publication. A business Board of Directors was now appointed for the first time. I was already on the Board of Syndics and was asked to join the Board of Directors too; for a time I was the link between these boards. I continued to serve on the Board of Directors after my retirement until I left the country for a year, on my round-the-world trip of 1958–59.

Tom Wilson and I became good friends. My years as a Syndic taught me something of the problems of selecting books for publication, and, as one of the Directors, I learned of publishing's financial problems. One day my Wellesley sister asked me to ask Wilson if he would publish a volume on Eleanor of Aquitaine that a friend of hers had been trying unsuccessfully to have published. After reading the book, I passed it on to Tom, reporting that I hesitated to recommend it because it seemed to me to be too colorful for the Press. Tom and other readers to whom he referred it did not agree with me. It was published and for some years was the best seller that the Press had ever had. This seemed to show how little I knew about book publishing.

When the Press needed more space for storage of its back stock, we were able to provide it in the sub-basement under the front steps of Widener. As reported in Chapter 9, there was a problem of flooding here.

I kept in close touch with Tom until he left Harvard to join the Athenaeum Press in New York, where he could continue past Harvard's regular retirement age. Unfortunately he died prematurely, partially, perhaps, as an indirect result of a severe attack of pneumonia that he suffered during his days in the Navy.

In Part IV of these Recollections, I will report how Tom came to my rescue in connection with the publication of my *Planning Academic and Research Libraries*.

Chapter 15

Three Librarians of Congress

ARCHIBALD MACLEISH

I N PART II of these Recollections there are a number of references to Herbert Putnam, who became Librarian of Congress in 1899, when he was thirty-eight. He continued in the position for forty years. Throughout this time he was generally considered to be our leading librarian. But in my opinion, despite some noteworthy accomplishments during his last ten years, it might have been better for him, for his library, and for his profession if he had retired at a more normal time. (Perhaps I am prejudiced because I am in my nineties.)

Putnam had always been a shy man who did not make friends easily. Most of his contemporaries had died or had dropped out of the picture by the 1930s. Members of the next two generations of librarians stood in awe of him, and few of them became well acquainted with him. Because he lost contact with most of the profession and because the salary budget was inadequate, the quality of his staff declined. There were difficulties in finding replacements when senior staff members retired or junior members went to other libraries. There was a decline in the quality of service. It was apparent that Putnam was not popular with the Congress or with President Roosevelt. Since the Librarian of Congress did not come under the regular civil service rules, Putnam could stay on, unless dismissed by the President, until he decided to resign.

When it became known that he would leave office sometime in 1939, an American Library Association committee was appointed to wait on President Roosevelt and suggest a suitable person or persons as Putnam's successor. Five former presidents of the Association made up the committee; they were Harrison Craver, Harry Lydenberg, William Warner Bishop, Linda Eastman, and Louis Round Wilson. Despite requests for a hearing, President Roosevelt did not communicate with Craver, who was the Chairman. There were efforts to reach the President through persons who were believed to have access to him and influence with him. Then, since Craver was scheduled to go abroad, he asked Harry Lydenberg to serve as Acting Chairman. The story of the committee's efforts to influence the choice of Putnam's successor has been told in detail by Peggy Sullivan and others.

Before continuing the story and telling my part in it, I ought to summarize my dealings with Archibald MacLeish before Roosevelt decided to appoint him. I had read some of MacLeish's poetry in the 1920s and 1930s, and was old fashioned enough to be unenthusiastic about it, though I had been impressed by his use of the English language. I knew nothing about him personally before I came to Harvard in 1937.

During the same year, Harvard received Mrs. Nieman's bequest, establishing a fund "to promote and elevate the standards of journalism in the United States and educate persons deemed especially qualified for journalism, in such a manner as the governing authorities of Harvard College from time to time shall deem wise." I have told in Chapter 10 how President Conant asked me, among others, to suggest uses for some of the income from the fund, and how I proposed that $5,000 per annum be allocated to the Library for the purchase of microfilm copies of foreign newspapers; this, with a revolving fund provided by the Rockefeller Foundation, enabled us to launch the cooperative project described in Chapter 4. In his autobiography, Conant wrote that he received only two suggestions and that only mine attracted him at the time.

The Nieman fund amounted to nearly $1,500,000, and only a small part of the income was required for the newspapers. President Conant later worked out a plan of his own for establishment of the Nieman Fellowships. Over the course of forty years, the Fellows have included many of the most influential journalists in the United States, and foreign journalists also have been brought to Harvard during recent years.

Archibald MacLeish was selected to direct the program; his title was Curator of the Nieman Foundation. Conant asked me to do what I could to help MacLeish by providing him a study in the Library and assuring him that we would make a special effort to provide service to the Fellows. As a result, I saw something of Archie in the fall of 1938, was greatly impressed by him, and began to feel somewhat acquainted.

Early in the winter of 1939, Bill Jackson, who had come the year before to take charge of rare books, told me that Wilmarth S. Lewis, the collector of Horace Walpole and member of the Yale Corporation, had asked him to arrange for a dinner at the Harvard Faculty Club to be attended by Samuel Eliot Morison, Archibald MacLeish, Lewis, Jackson, and me. This was my first meeting with Lefty Lewis; in Chapter 17, I will tell of interesting later experiences with him.

Jackson had been fortunate enough to find a Walpole item to give Lefty, which put him in good spirits. As one who has known the others can realize, it was an unusually pleasant occasion, and it proved to be exciting as well. It soon became evident that the dinner had been planned so that Morison and MacLeish could talk with the others about President Roosevelt's plan for a library at Hyde Park, New York, for his archives and other collections. I learned later that there had already been a meeting with Roosevelt in the White House, at which the proposal had been discussed by MacLeish, Morison, Felix Frankfurter, Randolph Adams of the University of Michigan's Clements Library, Julian Boyd, Librarian of Princeton, and others.

MacLeish and Morison approved of the idea and tried to sell it to the rest of us. I am not sure what Lewis' attitude was. Jackson questioned it, and I felt strongly that it would be a mistake; I did my best to discourage it, but was not successful. I thought it would mean that future presidents would follow Roosevelt's example. Higher Federal appropriations would be required to make presidential archives accessible if presidential libraries were scattered throughout the country (as has happened during the forty years that followed), and historians dealing with more than a single president would find it expensive and inconvenient to pursue their research. Rather than have a new archives building every four or eight years, even if it were constructed with funds raised by friends of the retiring president, I thought it would be cheaper for the government and better for scholars if the collections could all be housed in the National Archives, the Library of Congress, or a new, separate, expandable institution readily accessible from Washington. In addition to the one at Hyde Park, we now have presidential libraries in Georgia, Iowa, Kansas, Massachusetts, Michigan, Missouri, and Texas, with more bound to follow.

Sometime in March or April of 1939, MacLeish asked if he could talk with me confidentially. He then told me that President Roosevelt was considering appointing him Librarian of Congress to replace Herbert Putnam, who was retiring later in the year at the age of seventy-eight. He asked what, in my opinion, was involved in the position. He knew that, for a considerable number of years, I had spent at least one day a month, on the average, in Washington, chiefly at the Library of Congress. As best I could, I told him that it was primarily an administrative position in charge of our largest library and its staff. The acquisition and cataloging problems were on a larger scale and more difficult than in any other library. Library of Congress catalog cards were distributed to a large share of American libraries and to many abroad. The Library was responsible for service to members of Congress first of all, and then to all government employees, but it also served scholars throughout the country through interlibrary loan and by other means. I said that the staff was inadequate in quality, chiefly because insufficient funds had been appropriated by Congress. More money was needed for acquisitions; there were sad deficiencies in the program for collecting foreign books. A tremendous backlog of books was waiting to be cataloged. All in all, it was a very large and difficult administrative assignment.

MacLeish then told me that this was definitely not what he wanted to do. His primary interest was in writing, particularly in poetry. I thought, innocently, that the matter was settled; but, as is explained in *The Librarians of Congress, 1802–1974* (published by the Library of Congress in 1977), p. 207, President Roosevelt was not willing to take *no* for an answer. He had consulted Felix Frankfurter, who had recommended MacLeish very strongly.

Archie came to me again about the middle of May, if I remember correctly, to say that he was being urged by the President to accept the position. I went into more detail than before about what I thought the assignment involved, and Archie again said that it was not what he wanted to do. But on 29 May he asked me if we could spend some time together the next morning, on Memorial Day. My office, theoretically, was closed that day, but we had a long discussion there. He told me how anxious the President was for him to accept. Roosevelt had told him that it really would not be a large administrative assignment, saying, "You can do it in the morning while you are shaving." I went over the same ground that I had gone over before but realized that MacLeish was going to succumb. He wrote to the President two days later, saying that he would accept the position.

In the meanwhile I was feeling very uncomfortable. I knew that Harry Lydenberg, under whom I had worked during my quarter-century at the New York Public Library, was Acting Chairman of the American Library Association committee that had tried to reach the President and urge him to appoint an experienced librarian. Harrison Craver, the committee's Chairman, was still in Europe, and Lydenberg was in charge. I realized that many librarians would be upset, but I had promised Archie that our conversations would be kept in confidence, and I could not warn librarians of what I was sure was going to happen.

On 7 June 1939 the *New York Times* reported that the President had named MacLeish to be Librarian of Congress; the nomination was one that must go to the Senate for approval. I was about to leave on an extended trip, first to the Oberlin commencement, where I was to receive my first honorary degree, then to Webster Groves, Missouri, where I was to visit two of my elder brothers and their families, and then finally to San Francisco, where the American Library Association conference was to begin on 13 June. I followed my schedule, and had a pleasant time in Oberlin and with my relatives in Webster Groves, where I received a letter from Felix Frankfurter, forwarded by my secretary, in which he asked me for my opinion of the President's nomination of MacLeish. He asked for an immediate reply because he was about to leave for England, where he was to receive an honorary degree at Oxford. I was in a quandary regarding what to say even if I were able to reach him; but I had no address for him and used that as an excuse for not writing to him at his office in the Harvard Law School. I did not see him or hear from him again until we met at lunch in the Faculty Club during September.

I reached San Francisco as planned. On Monday morning, 15 June, the Council of the Association met and, one might say, exploded. Milton Ferguson, the Association's president, spoke almost violently against the MacLeish appointment. Louis Shores, whom I had employed as a reference assistant at the New York Public Library during his library-school days at Columbia, spoke for the younger generation of librarians, saying that the appointment would make it evident that there was no chance for a library-school graduate to reach the highest position in his chosen profession. Altogether, it was what I would call a disgraceful scene.

Soon after the meeting was over, someone told Ferguson and Carl Milam, the Association's executive secretary, that I must know MacLeish since we were both at Harvard, and they came to me, saying that I must telephone to MacLeish and tell him how strongly librarians felt about his appointment. I could not very well refuse; but it was already too late at night to make the call then.

The next morning, allowing for the three-hour difference in time between California and Massachusetts, with Ferguson and Milam beside me, I called MacLeish from my hotel room. When I started to tell my story, he interrupted almost immediately and said that he had just read the report in the *New York Times* about what had happened in San Francisco the day before. He said that he had learned earlier that librarians were very much upset about his nomination, and he had been prepared to ask the President to withdraw his name. But now he had changed his mind, because he was not willing to withdraw under fire. That was that.

Harry Lydenberg had not gone to San Francisco because, as Chairman of the ALA committee on the librarianship of Congress, he knew that he might be called at any time to appear at the Senate hearing on the nomination. When called to Washington, he presented the Association's objections, but not in the violent terms that had been used in San Francisco. MacLeish was approved with almost no opposition.

At some time in the mid-1970s, more than thirty years after MacLeish's appointment, I received a letter from James Henderson, Director of the Research Libraries in the New York Public Library (a position that I held from 1928 to 1937 under the title "Chief of the Reference Department"), saying that he had been going through the Library's vault for the first time since Harry Lydenberg's retirement in 1941, and had found there a large package labelled, "Not to be opened except by H. M. Lydenberg or Keyes D. Metcalf." Harry Lydenberg had died in 1960. Henderson asked me if I would care to come down to New York and examine it. When I did so, I found that it contained the originals or copies of correspondence of the Committee To Wait on the President in Connection with the Selection of Herbert Putnam's Successor. I was already at work writing my Recollections and did not feel that more should be included in them than I have written in this chapter. I was somewhat embarrassed because I had not been directly involved with the Committee. I arranged to have the material re-packed, sealed, and marked, "Not to be used except by Keyes D. Metcalf or E. E. Williams" (with whom I have been closely associated since 1940). I talked about it with Archie, and he approved its use by anyone I selected.

Fortunately, before the San Francisco conference was over, the incoming president of the ALA, Ralph Munn, spoke in a conciliatory manner, saying that the nomination had been made, and, if it were approved by the Senate, he would do everything he could to have the Association work smoothly with MacLeish. This paved the way for reconciliation. MacLeish, very properly, invited Putnam to visit him at his summer home in North Conway, Massachusetts. The invitation was accepted; and, because Putnam had a severe cold while there, Archie persuaded him to stay much longer than had originally been planned. They had an opportunity to become well acquainted, and Putnam, of course, was able to tell him of the problems he was about to face more fully and more accurately than I had been able to do. I might add that

Putnam continued to keep an office in the Library of Congress during the years that followed but in no way interfered with its administration. On a number of occasions when I was called to the Library and Putnam was not in town, I used his office.

Archie's first year in Washington was a great success. After he became acquainted with the situation, he appointed Luther Evans to the post of Legislative Reference Librarian; a year later, Luther became Assistant Librarian and Archie's right-hand man. They were both able administrators. In the spring of 1940, MacLeish asked Carleton Joeckel, then a professor in the Graduate Library School of the University of Chicago and an author of excellent works on administrative problems of libraries, to serve as chairman of a committee to study reorganization of the Library of Congress. Paul North Rice, who succeeded me at the New York Public Library, and I were invited to be the other members. I was still new at Harvard and felt that I should not take the six-weeks leave that would be required; plans for both Houghton and the New England Deposit Library were at a critical point and seemed to demand my attention. I suggested to Archie that he replace me with Andrew Osborn, who was then in charge of cataloging in the Harvard College Library. Osborn had a remarkable analytical mind and could contribute more than I to solving of the Library's very difficult cataloging problems. Moreover, my background and experience resembled Paul North Rice's so much that it seemed to me better to have a third member with qualifications different from mine.

Archie accepted my proposal, and I agreed to come down and work with the committee over a number of weekends. Its three members worked practically around the clock for six weeks. Joeckel told me that Osborn was an ideal person to deal with the cataloging questions. Before the six weeks were over, it was evident that more help was needed for some specific details of the work; Paul and I suggested that L. Quincy Mumford and Francis St. John would be useful. Mumford was then Chief of the Preparation Division (Cataloging Division), after having filled various other posts in the New York Public Library, including Executive Assistant in the Director's Office, which I had held before becoming Chief of the Reference Department. St. John had wide experience in the New York Public Library, and had been a great help to me when I was Chairman of the Board of Education for Librarianship; he was now Assistant Librarian of the Enoch Pratt Free Library in Baltimore. This was pretty much a New York Public Library group, since five of the six had been on the staff there. They worked well together, and the three members of the Committee prepared a report of more than three hundred pages which I had an opportunity to read before it was submitted.

MacLeish was so impressed by Mumford's work with the Committee that he asked Lydenberg and Rice to lend him to the Library of Congress for a year to reorganize the Catalog Division; my experiences with this Division had been unfortunate when I was Chairman of the ALA Cooperative Cataloging Committee. Mumford undoubtedly learned a good deal that year that was useful to him and to the Library fourteen years later, when he returned as Librarian of Congress.

In 1941, MacLeish appointed the director of an historical society to make a study of interlibrary cooperation, a subject in which he was greatly interested. This ultimately led to the Farmington Plan, of which I will write in Chapter 18. And in 1943, he asked me to go with two other representatives to Peru on a good-will mission following the destruction of the national library there. (See Chapter 17.)

In order to obtain help and advice from outside the Library of Congress, MacLeish appointed an informal group, the Librarian's Council, consisting of librarians and others interested in libraries. I was one of the members. We met a number of times in Washington, and I remember one delightful occasion at Archie's Georgetown house, with its pleasant enclosed back yard, when we had no formal agenda and talked in small groups. I drifted from one group to another during the evening and ran into Belle da Costa Greene, the Director of the Morgan Library, and Bernhard Knollenberg, the Librarian of Yale. They were both highly excited, almost screaming at each other. I broke in, actually fearing that they would become violent. When Belle left the room to join another group, Knolly asked me, "Who was that terrible woman?" I had taken it for granted that they had met earlier; I had known her during my New York years, of course, and assumed that they were acquainted.

Later on, there was a meeting of the Council in Miss Greene's apartment in New York. I have no memory of what happened there but later discovered that I had a fine pencil with *Belle da Costa Greene* imprinted on it. MacLeish had been succeeded by Evans, who was told soon afterward that it was not proper to have a council of this kind that had not been approved by Congress, so the Librarian's Council quietly disappeared.

Beginning in October 1941, President Roosevelt asked MacLeish to take on additional duties, first as Director of the United States Office of Facts and Figures, and then in June 1942 as Assistant Director of the Office of War Information. He spent more and more time on these activities, and operation of the Library was neglected to some extent in spite of his great administrative ability and of the fact that he had greatly strengthened the Library's staff at a time when this was very difficult to do.

Luther Evans, who became Chief Assistant Librarian in 1940, had been Director of the Historical Records Survey of the Works Progress Administration from 1935 to 1939 before serving as Director of the Legislative Reference Service in the Library of Congress. Like Archie, he was not a professional librarian, but he was an excellent choice; as Librarian of Congress after 1945, he was much more interested than Archie had been in strengthening relationships between the Library and the American Library Association and libraries generally.

Very early in his administration, Archie had also chosen Verner Clapp to head the Administrative Department; later he was in charge of the Acquisitions Department. Clapp had joined the staff in 1923 as a junior assistant.

By 1944, MacLeish had made the contributions to the Library that he felt he could make, and he accepted an appointment as Assistant Secretary of State. I think it is fair to say — and this is not in any sense a criticism of him — that he left at just the right time. He had completed the reorganization that had been needed, and it was time for a change, both for him and for the Library.

The whole story can be summarized as follows. Herbert Putnam ranks near the top of American librarians of the late 1800s and early 1900s. But largely because of his natural shyness, which made it difficult for him to keep in touch with younger librarians as he grew older and to make friends among them, he did not have a satisfactory staff, and his relations with Congress and the President had deteriorated; he had stayed on too long. The senior members of the profession still regarded him with such great respect that none of them could have taken over the position and carried out the much-needed reorganization that MacLeish did not hesitate to undertake. MacLeish was the ideal person for the position during the five years he held it. It is true today as it was thirty years ago that any important administrative appointment should go to the person who can do the most important things that need to be done for an institution, and MacLeish, despite the opposition of librarians and his lack of library experience, was undoubtedly the best successor for Herbert Putnam who could have been found in 1939.

It is interesting to note, apropos of this, in the *Quarterly Journal of the Library of Congress* for April 1975, pages 81 and 149, the testimony that Herbert Putnam gave before the Joint Committee on the Library in

1896. He was asked, "What are the qualities that the Chief Administrative Officer of the Library of Congress ought to possess?" He replied, "Administrative ability."

When MacLeish had made his contribution to the Library, he moved to another government position and later returned to the academic field and to writing, which I am sure he enjoyed more than his work in Washington. In 1949, he returned to Harvard as Boylston Professor of Rhetoric and Oratory. His contributions to Harvard during thirteen years in this chair, as well as his work as one of our great poets and dramatists, will long be remembered. His short reign as Librarian of Congress, in our foremost library position, was not the least of his many achievements. He was the right man in the right place, and a great Librarian of Congress.

LUTHER EVANS

I first met Luther Evans soon after MacLeish had persuaded him to come to the Library of Congress as Director of the Legislative Reference Service. Then he became Chief Assistant Librarian and was often in charge while MacLeish was engaged in other government work. I soon had an opportunity to become acquainted with him and was impressed by his competence.

In the winter of 1945, after it had been announced that MacLeish was resigning to become Assistant Secretary of State, Harry Lydenberg and Waldo Leland were concerned regarding the appointment of his successor. Lydenberg was then in charge of the American Library Association's International Relations Office in Washington; Leland, Director of the American Council of Learned Societies, was well known and respected in academic circles. Lydenberg and Leland remembered the complications that had arisen at the time of MacLeish's appointment. They felt that Luther Evans was the obvious man for the position but doubted that the President would appoint him. They knew that the American Library Association, as on the earlier occasion, had appointed a committee to wait on the President, hoping that he would ask for suggestions. Carl Vitz, the president of the Association, was chairman of the committee, and I was a member. As in 1939, the committee had been unable to get in touch with the President.

One day when I was in Washington, I talked with Lydenberg and Leland about the problem. Less than two years earlier, as will be related in Chapter 22, Theodore C. Blegen and I had made a study of the libraries of the State Historical Society of Wisconsin and the University of Wisconsin. Blegen, a professor of history and Graduate Dean at the University of Minnesota, had previously been Superintendent of the Minnesota Historical Society and its Library. I had been greatly impressed by him; I now suggested that he might be a suitable candidate for appointment as Librarian of Congress. He was not known as a librarian, and we were convinced that the President would not appoint a trained librarian.

Leland thought he could obtain an interview for himself and Lydenberg with President Roosevelt, and they said they would present Blegen's name. They approached Blegen, who gave them permission to do so, and agreed to accept the position if it should be offered. Rather to my surprise, as well as Lydenberg's, Leland did succeed in obtaining the interview. Sometime in March 1945, if I remember correctly, they met with President Roosevelt. He was interested, accepted the recommendation, and said he would nominate Blegen. This was only a short time before Roosevelt's sudden death on 12 April.

Carl Vitz learned of what Lydenberg and Leland had done and was understandably upset, because he felt that a trained librarian should have been proposed. Early in his administration, President Truman realized that the time had come to make an appointment, and he quite properly nominated Luther Evans; this was quickly approved by the Joint Committee on the Library and by the Senate. I have always suspected that one reason for the choice of Evans was that he came from west of the Mississippi, and Truman was interested in making appointments from that area.

Evans and I had become good friends while he was MacLeish's deputy, and I continued to go to Washington for consultation work with other departments of the government as well as with the Library of Congress. I saw him from time to time and had the pleasure of sitting in with him and his department heads several times at the daily conferences in which they talked over administrative problems. Luther could and did speak very strongly when he disagreed with members of the staff, but they did not hesitate to express their opinions. When the time came to make a decision, that decision was very definitely Luther's.

As has been noted, the informal Librarian's Council was soon discontinued, because it seemed unwise to have a body of this kind with no official status. In 1946, however, Evans decided to appoint a Library of Congress Planning Committee. Congress had been appropriating money for the Library for more than 140 years and had approved the reorganization under MacLeish, but the Library had never been given a charter. There was no formal document authorizing many of its activities, though these had been recognized in the annual appropriations. Luther thought it would help him and his successors if a proposal for what might be called a charter could be addressed to the Joint Committee on the Library, approved by this body, and then approved by Congress. He asked me to be chairman of the committee, and we talked over its membership. He wanted it to be as broadly based as possible.

Members included Herbert Eugene Bolton, Professor of History, *Emeritus*, at the University of California, Berkeley; Edward Condon, Director of the National Bureau of Standards; Douglas S. Freeman, Editor of the *Richmond* (Virginia) *News Leader* and biographer of George Washington and Robert E. Lee; Wilmarth S. Lewis, collector, editor, and writer; Carl McFarland, a lawyer from Washington, D.C.; Kathryn Mier, Librarian of the Missouri State Library; Lessing J. Rosenwald, book collector, merchant, and philanthropist; Ralph R. Shaw, Librarian of the United States Department of Agriculture; and Walter L. Wright, Jr., Professor of Near East Affairs at Princeton. It was a good committee in my opinion; but I must confess that we had considerable difficulty in reaching agreement on two major points.

The first was the name of the Library of Congress. We finally agreed that the name should include some reference to the fact that the institution was our national library. We knew that Congress was proud that its own Library of Congress was the world's largest library and that this name ought not to be abandoned. We suggested that the name continue to be Library of Congress, but that below this, on letterheads and elsewhere, there should be *The National Library of the United States*. Unfortunately, in my opinion, no action on this has ever been taken.

The second question on which we disagreed involved the relation of the Library of Congress to other government libraries, and whether or not it should be considered the leader of the group, with its librarian *ex officio* the chairman of a committee made up of chief librarians from the group. Ralph Shaw, representing the other government libraries, at first agreed to this proposal; but, after he had presented it to a meeting of librarians in Washington, he changed his mind and said that it would be impossible.

There were also questions regarding the service that the Library of Congress could and should provide to other government libraries, and the titles that should be given to the major institutions in this group. It was agreed that the Army Medical Library and the Library of the Department of Agriculture should be recognized as libraries giving national service in special fields. I am glad to say that this has taken place; the official names of these libraries are now the National Library of Medicine and the National Agricultural Library.

I have never struggled with the wording of a report as much as I did with this one before I finally presented a draft that was approved by the Committee. It had been very carefully edited by Edwin E. Williams of the Harvard staff, who, as I have said again and again, expresses what he knows I want to say better than I am able to do. The final report was submitted to the Joint Committee on the Library by Luther Evans and published as an appendix to his Annual Report for 1946-47. As far as I was able to learn, no member of Congress ever paid any attention to it until 1954, when Senator Jenner of Indiana made use of it in the hearing on L. Quincy Mumford's nomination, as will be reported later in this chapter.

During my work on the report, I went down to Washington from time to time to meet with Luther Evans. One week-end he gave me a written authorization to be presented to the Captain of the Guard, who also had a copy, saying that I was to be admitted to the Library at any time on Saturday or Sunday while the Library was closed. Luther had asked me to have dinner with him and his family at his home in Alexandria, Virginia. It was a very pleasant occasion, as could be expected, and I did not go to the Library that evening. Early the next day, Sunday morning, I presented the authorization and was greeted almost gruffly by the Captain of the Guard with the question, "Where were you last night?"

Luther worked very successfully with the American Library Association during his nine years as Librarian of Congress. Its officers and members appreciated his interest in their needs. I remember one ALA Council meeting late in his régime when he felt he should warn librarians that Congress was probably going to insist that the charge for catalog cards include at least part of the cost of cataloging as well as the printing and distribution costs. He was unhappy about this, as were the librarians; but, while the price of cards inevitably rose as other prices did, he was not forced to include cataloging costs in it.

Evans was apparently handicapped, however, as MacLeish had been, by the fact that he spent a good deal of his time on work outside the Library — particularly, in his case, with UNESCO. This irritated members of Congress and increased the difficulties he faced in obtaining additions to his budget. Appropriations increased, as they had during the MacLeish years, but they were not large enough to provide the service that he and the librarians of the country wanted. I sat in on the budget hearings several times during the years between 1939 and 1953.

MacLeish and Evans, with the valiant aid of Verner Clapp and others of the Library of Congress staff, did a remarkable job of presenting the budget; but they were handicapped by the fact that MacLeish and Evans did not hesitate to express their opinions about political matters. During those fifteen years, when the Library of Congress was expanding its services and becoming a genuine national library even more effectively than it had been up to then, the budget only tripled, despite inflation that devoured a good share of that increase.

Evans resigned in 1953 to become Director-General of UNESCO, a position in which he did excellent work for some five years. Then, following several years of other Government work, he was in charge of the international and legal collections at Columbia University from 1962 until he retired ten years later. There I had the pleasure of working with him on plans for a new Law Library.

L. QUINCY MUMFORD

Charles C. Williamson, Director of the Columbia University Library and Dean of its School of Library Service, sent L. Quincy Mumford to the New York Public Library early in 1929 as a prospective member of our staff. He told me that Mumford was one of their best students and that he had already acquired varied library experience while at Trinity College, which later became part of Duke University. We liked Mumford and offered him a position at the information desk in the Reference Department. He was very satisfactory there, but was so promising that we decided to try to give him broader experience. In 1933, he became Executive Assistant in the Director's office, the position I had held from 1919 to 1927, and one of his major assignments there was to work with personnel. It was evident that he had unusual skill in choosing for the staff the best of the new library-school graduates; during the years that followed before I left for Harvard, he had an important part in the staff selection for which I had final responsibility. He took charge of the Preparation Division in 1936 and remained there until 1943 except for the year when, as noted above, he was lent to the Library of Congress to reorganize its processing work. He had several years in charge of the General Service Division of the New York Public Library, including the information desk, public catalog, main reading room, and main bookstack. No one has had equally broad experience in that library except Harry Lydenberg, Keyes Metcalf, Paul North Rice, and Edward G. Freehafer. In 1946, Mumford left New York to become Assistant Director of the Cleveland Public Library, and he became Director there in 1950. He was unusually successful in each of his positions. In 1953, he was elected Vice President and President-Elect of the American Library Association.

When Luther Evans resigned as Librarian of Congress in 1953, the American Library Association, as in 1939 and 1945, appointed a committee to wait on the President and make suggestions. I was appointed chairman of the committee. We drew up a list of persons whom we thought should be considered; our next task was to try to reach President Eisenhower and make sure that he saw and considered our list. There had been rumors that two college professors were being considered, but, from all we could learn, neither had satisfactory qualifications for the position.

We — members of the committee and other librarians who had been in touch with the Library of Congress during the MacLeish and Evans administrations — agreed that Verner Clapp should be nominated to succeed Evans. The breadth of Verner's experience during three administrations had been unequalled in the history of the Library of Congress. In each of his eleven assignments, which included cataloging, legislative reference, work with the blind, acquisitions, and administration, he had done an outstanding job. He had served as acting librarian in Evans' absence. He had been involved in the organization of the United Nations and had gone to Japan as our representative on a committee for the National Diet Library, among other things. We all thought that he would be ideal for the position.

We soon learned, however, that there was no chance of his appointment. He was considered to have been Evans' right-hand man as his Associate Librarian, and he had also been highly esteemed by MacLeish. Both men had freely expressed their political opinions and had made so many enemies in Congress that approval of Clapp's nomination would have been impossible; evidently it would be a mistake to urge it.

I went down to Washington to see the senior Senator from Massachusetts, Leverett Saltonstall. I remembered having taken him through the New England Deposit Library twelve years earlier, when he had been Governor and had visited the Library because the Massachusetts State Library was involved. I arrived at his office and was greeted cordially by Elliot Richardson, his assistant, who made a great impression on me. I did not have to wait long for the Senator and started our conversation by saying that, as Chairman of the American Library Association committee, I hoped the President would not nominate for Librarian of Congress a man who could be called a political appointment. We thought the Library ought to be kept out of politics. Saltonstall looked at me sadly and said, "Metcalf, you must remember that all appointments in Washington are political."

But, with help from Saltonstall and from Arthur S. Adams, who was then head of the American Council on Education, Waldo Leland and I were able to obtain an appointment with Sherman Adams, who was at that time President Eisenhower's right-hand man. I said to him, as I had to the Senator, that I hoped the nomination would not be a political one. He told us that Verner Clapp could not be confirmed. As representatives of the American Library Association, we gave him a list of suitable candidates for consideration. We did not discuss the individuals on it. We left with Adams' assurance that the persons suggested would be considered very carefully.

I was very favorably impressed by Adams and was shocked and unhappy five years later when we heard, in Australia, that Adams had resigned under pressure because he had (Should we say thoughtlessly, carelessly, or innocently?) accepted a vicuña coat said to be worth $1,000 from a textile manufacturer. Thereby hangs a tale:

Elinor and I had met this textile manufacturer and his wife some time before the Adams affair when we attended a commencement at New England College in Henniker, New Hampshire. (I was there for two reasons. The first was that I had consulted with the College on its library problems. The second was that I was interested in Henniker because I remembered that, in the late 1840s, more than one hundred years earlier, my father had been in charge of planning a railroad right-of-way from Concord to Henniker and on to the Connecticut River. One Sunday morning while at Henniker, he had walked ten miles up the hill to Dunbarton, New Hampshire, to go to church. There he saw for the first time a young woman in the choir who was the daughter of the minister and who, three years later, became his first wife and, in time, the mother of my twelve half-sisters and half-brothers).

We had not been impressed by the textile manufacturer in question. But, before Elinor and I started on our year-long trip in 1958-59, which included New Zealand and Australia in their winter seasons, we had been told by an academic friend who had been there not long before that few of the libraries, hotels, or houses had central heating; we were warned that we ought to take adequate clothing if we did not want to have to return to warmer climates before our assignments were completed, as some other academics had had to do. Elinor had seen a vicuña cardigan at Brooks Brothers in Boston; it was very warm, but would cost $65, which seemed a tremendous sum in those days. She felt that we should not spend that much for it. Just a few days later, however, she received word that the publishers of Grandfather Thayer's English translation of Grimm's German-Greek New Testament lexicon had discovered that royalties had not been paid since the end of the copyright period, though it had been the publisher's intention to continue them at least for a time. Elinor's share, as one of Joseph Henry Thayer's descendants, turned out to be $65. She decided to use this to buy the cardigan for me. It proved to be extremely satisfactory and useful during cold weather down under; but we were a bit embarrassed when Sherman Adams' debacle came and vicuña, which I was wearing, suddenly became notorious.

To return from the antipodes to Washington and to April 1954, some two months before Mumford was to take office as President of the American Library Association, President Eisenhower nominated him for Librarian of Congress. (I have always been inclined to believe that Mumford was chosen, rather than anyone else on our list, because he came from North Carolina and no one seemed to know whether he was a Republican or a Democrat). Senate hearings on the nomination were delayed for some reason. The American Library Association conference was scheduled for the last week in June in Minneapolis, and I went there, going early for the pre-conference meeting on building planning and registering for the full period. A telegram came from Washington, saying that the hearing on Mumford's appointment would probably be called soon and that I had better go to Washington immediately. I arrived there with no hotel reservation, but Julia Bennett, the ALA representative in Washington, arranged to have me sleep in the ALA office in the Continental Hotel. In a day or two I learned that the hearing would not be held until July, so I went back to Cambridge; it was too late to return to Minneapolis.

The hearing on the nomination of Lawrence Quincy Mumford as Librarian of Congress was held on 26 July before the Committee on Rules and Administration of the United States Senate. The chairman of this committee, Senator William E. Jenner of Indiana, had a 100-page staff memorandum that was not available to me at the time. It included a history of the Library of Congress, something about its previous librarians, and a list of the Congressional enactments regarding its use. It did not include the report of the Library of Congress Planning Committee, of which I have written above; but it was evident from the Chairman's questions that he had read that report and was trying to use it to find proposals on which it would be difficult for Quincy to comment. Quincy answered the questions superbly, it seemed to me. Sidney B. Hill, General Manager of the Association of the Bar of the City of

New York, was then given an opportunity to testify. He was followed by Ralph Ulveling, Librarian of the Detroit Public library, who was also a member of the ALA committee. Then I was asked to speak.

As an indication of my regard for Quincy Mumford, I give here my statement as it is recorded in the printed minutes of the Senate committee's hearing.

My name is Keyes D. Metcalf. I am the director of the Harvard University Library. I am here as one of the representatives of the American Library Association, which has 20,000 members. I was chosen because I am the head of the largest library in the country after the Library of Congress; because I am the librarian outside of Washington who has had most to do with the Library of Congress in the past 35 years; and because I am a librarian who has been closely associated with Mr. Mumford for over 25 years.

I have only two points to make. It is a matter of first importance, especially to the Congress, but also to Government departments, to the library world, and to research workers, to have a well-administered Library of Congress. If the Library is not well managed, you and all Government agencies will very soon be handicapped. The Librarian has a tremendous task which involves more technical detail than most other Government administrative positions. This is largely because the Library contains well over 30 million books and other pieces of research material which, if periodical articles are included, consist of many more than 100 million different items that should be readily accessible on short notice. The Library receives about 4 million new pieces each year which must be dealt with, reduced to a million which are to be retained, cataloged, and made available for use. A man without intimate knowledge of research library problems would, however competent, start with two strikes against him in this position.

And this brings me to my second point.

You have under consideration for the position of Librarian of Congress L. Quincy Mumford, who is at present the director of the Cleveland Public Library. I met Mr. Mumford more than 25 years ago when he was taking his professional training at Columbia University. I was then in charge of the central building of the New York Public Library at 42nd Street and Fifth Avenue. I offered him his first position after he completed his training, and he started out by doing general reference work at the library's information desk. The quality of his work was such that, 4 years later when a general administrative assistant was needed in the office, Mumford was selected. Three years later when the largest and most complex division of the library, the catalog division, needed a new chief, he was chosen. I occupied both of those positions in earlier days myself, and I consider them as good training for library administration as can be found anywhere. In both positions, Mr. Mumford's success was outstanding, and I found him the best judge of people I have ever known. In 1937 I left New York to take my present position at Harvard, and my contact with him has not been as close since that time. However, in 1940, I was a member of a group that was called in to advise the Librarian of Congress on the Library's reorganization. We arranged to have Mumford lent for a year by the New York Public Library to the Library of Congress to reorganize the processing department, the largest, and again the most complex, single department in this Library. He did this difficult and intricate job with the most conspicuous success, and then went back to New York where, in 1943, he became coordinator of the general public service in the big building at 42nd Street and Fifth Avenue. He had now had experience in each of the three main parts of the New York Library, general administration and personnel, cataloging, and service to the public. In 1943 he worked with me on a survey of what is now the Armed Forces Medical Library. He continued in New York until 1945 when he went to Cleveland as associate director; in 1950 he was promoted to be director.

You have in Mr. Mumford a man whose training and experience in large libraries is ideal for the position of Librarian of Congress, one who has demonstrated again and again to my firsthand knowledge what he can do under difficult circumstances. In a quiet way he is a man of forcefulness who gets things done. I do not hesitate to recommend him wholeheartedly for the position for which he has been nominated by the President.

The nomination was approved, and L. Quincy Mumford became Librarian of Congress that fall. Thereafter I have seen him less frequently than I had earlier; but, when he was preparing plans for what is now the Madison Library, I was asked to consult on them. I spent a day or two in Washington on several occasions during the 1960s. He had hoped that the blocks behind what is now called the Jefferson Library building could be made available; but this turned out to be impossible, and the block to the south of the existing building was cleared. There the Madison building was completed and occupied during Mumford's administration. I remember, among other things, that the preliminary planning studies dealt largely with the depth below ground that would be available in order to obtain the square footage desired on the site without exceeding height restrictions.

This was long after I retired. While I saw comparatively little of Mumford, I did begin to hear in the early 1960s that there was dissatisfaction with him among academic librarians because, among other things, he had not pushed what later became known as cataloging in publication, and they thought he was not doing enough for them in other ways. Benjamin Powell, Librarian of Duke University until his retirement, knew Quincy in his college days at Trinity in North Carolina. In his biography of Quincy in *The Librarians of Congress*,

1802–1974, which was published by the Library of Congress in 1977, Powell has suggested some of the reasons, though the dissatisfaction seems strange because Mumford was the first professionally trained librarian to hold the position of Librarian of Congress. He had served for more than 15 years in the Reference Department of the New York Public Library, one of the great research institutions in the country, and nine years at the Cleveland Public Library, where the central building had a large reference collection and its service to the public at large was outstanding. But apparently the fact that he was not a university librarian and that the Cleveland Public Library was not a member of the Association of Research Libraries raised doubts in some minds.

As Powell wrote, the Librarian of Congress had assumed a leadership role under MacLeish and Evans in attempting to resolve problems of concern to research libraries and had made commitments that seemed to be natural responsibilities of the national library because they were beyond the capabilities of any university library. Under Mumford there was less Library of Congress leadership in the Association of Research Libraries discussions. He seldom took the floor to commit the Library or to encourage creative projects that could not be developed effectively without his active involvement. He seldom made commitments without discussing their implications with his associates, and this generally was done back in Washington.

On the other hand, Mumford realized that his first task was to make sure that he had Congress behind him in anything he undertook, and in this he was amazingly successful. In his twenty years as Librarian of Congress, he accomplished what his three predecessors, through the period that might be called modern library history, had been unable to do. The budget under Mumford increased from less that $10,000,000 to nearly $100,000,000 a year, and the Library reached a position in which it could and did do more for the library world than it had ever been able to do before.

I am inclined to think that the part Mumford played in library development will eventually be recognized. Each of the four librarians of Congress from 1899 to 1974 was a great librarian. Each made great contributions. The indications are that Daniel Boorstin will follow in their footsteps, and that Herbert Putnam was correct when he told the Joint Committee that the Librarian of Congress must, above all else, have administrative ability. I hope that Boorstin's successors over the next three generations will be as successful as those of the past three.

I might add that I had the pleasure of introducing Daniel Boorstin in 1975, when he spoke at the first American Library Association conference he attended, and I was bold enough to suggest that his new position was a full-time job. Fear that he would not realize this was something that had caused many librarians to oppose his appointment. They had felt that his nomination was a mistake because he had been known primarily as an historian and author, and might be tempted to continue to give much of his time to writing. Apparently, however, he realized the situation and has found it easier to avoid outside work than MacLeish and Evans did.

I suggested also that Boorstin would do well not to continue in his position until he was seventy-eight, as Herbert Putnam did. As has been indicated earlier, the new Librarian of Congress has taken hold very well during the past eight years, and there is every evidence that the Library will prosper in spite of its recent financial problems.

I do not hesitate to say that, other things being equal, it is desirable to have a trained, experienced librarian as Librarian of Congress. But it is even more important to have a man who is a good administrator and realizes and appreciates what librarians of the country expect from the head of our greatest library, who particularly emphasizes improvement of the quality of his staff, and who maintains good relations with Congress.

Chapter 16

Department Libraries in Washington

THE SURGEON GENERAL'S LIBRARY AND ITS SUCCESSORS

As I REMEMBER, it was in 1943, during the spring of my term as president of the American Library Association, that I was called on the telephone by Carl Milam, the Association's executive secretary. He said that Colonel Harold W. Jones, Librarian of the Army Medical Library, after obtaining the approval of the War Department and conferring with his Surgeon General and with Alan Gregg, Director of the Medical Science Department of the Rockefeller Foundation, had asked the ALA to appoint a committee to conduct a study, which the Foundation would support, of his medical library. I had been proposed for the chairmanship of the committee. Would I take the assignment? I agreed to do so.

Harry Lydenberg was a friend and next-door neighbor of Alan Gregg in Scarsdale, and as a result I had already met him. Mrs. Gregg (Eleanor Barrows Gregg) was the daughter of John Henry Barrows, who had been president of Oberlin College from 1898 to 1901. Her brother, Arthur Barrows, had been a college classmate and close friend of my next elder brother, Isaac Stevens Metcalf. Arthur had become president of Sears Roebuck Corporation and later became Deputy Secretary of the Air Force. I am often amazed at how small the world is.

We were fortunate in being able to arrange for an unusually fine committee, consisting of Janet Doe, who was at the New York Academy of Medicine; Thomas P. Fleming, Librarian of Columbia's College of Physicians and Surgeons; Mary Louise Marshall, Librarian of the Tulane University Medical School; L. Quincy Mumford, then in charge of the Preparation Division of the New York Public Library; and Andrew Osborn, with whom I had worked at both the New York Public Library and Harvard. I do not believe that a finer group for this assignment could have been assembled.

Theoretically, the Surgeon General's Library began in 1836, but it was not until John Shaw Billings, a Civil War surgeon, took charge in 1865 that it began to make any real progress. During the first ten years of Billings' régime, it became one of the great medical libraries of the world and began to publish the Surgeon General's Library *Catalogue*, a great series of volumes listing medical books and periodical articles. Billings was also responsible for the monthly *Index Medicus* (later a quarterly), which provided an up-to-date record of medical literature published throughout the world.

Dr. Billings was in charge of the Surgeon General's Library from 1865 to 1895; but during the later years he spent much of his time helping to organize the medical school at Johns Hopkins University and, after that, building up the University of Pennsylvania medical school and its library. He became the first director of the New York Public Library in 1895.

The name of the Surgeon General's Library was later changed to Army Medical Library. After Billings left, the indexing was carried on by his assistant, Robert Fletcher, and later by Fielding Garrison; but the Library began to deteriorate. It became the custom for the War Department to appoint as Librarian a senior Army medical officer, sometimes for his last three or four years before retirement from active duty; the appointment was a means of honoring a distinguished medical officer. (Years later, I might add, many Japanese universities appointed their librarians in much the same way.) Each new librarian would be interested in the Library, but it was generally not until he retired that he came to realize the problems that needed to be faced. As a result, not enough pressure was brought to bear on the War Department and on Congress to keep up the appropriations for books and periodicals, for maintaining a staff of high quality, and for service. I was told that only sixteen volumes were purchased during one of the years in the early 1930s. The building had been well planned for its time by Billings; but upkeep had been neglected, and it was in bad physical condition. There was often water in the basement, and there was an infestation of rats.

Colonel Jones had been appointed Librarian in 1936 and was kept in the position into the 1940s because of the war, despite the fact that he had reached the regular retirement age. Having realized that the Library faced serious problems, he had applied for help in having a survey made. The Rockefeller Foundation had provided adequate funds, $20,000, for the committee's work, and each of the members spent some time during the summer of 1943 at the Army Medical Library in Washington; each of us also visited the Rare Book Section of the Library, which had been moved to the Allen Memorial Library in Cleveland in order to protect it from the bombing that was feared in Washington. The Allen Library was named in honor of Dudley Peter Allen, an Oberlin graduate who had provided the funds for the Allen building for the art collection at Oberlin, of which I wrote in Part II, Chapter 3 of these Recollections. Dr. Allen had removed the appendix of my next elder brother, Ike, in 1901, one of the early appendectomies in that part of the country.

Later in 1943, our committee had a three-day conference in the New York Public Library at which we talked freely about our problems and decided to divide the report into three parts: What the surveyors found, what the surveyors would like to see, and recommendations. Andrew Osborn wrote a large share of the report, combining the suggestions of other members of the committee and summarizing salient features. A draft was forwarded to each member before the end of the year; in January 1944, we met again and agreed upon the final text of the report, which was then submitted to Major General Norman T. Kirk, the Surgeon General of the United States, and to the American Library Association, which published it as *The National Medical Library* later that year. I have a bound, typewritten volume of 169 pages, with 33 appendices that were not included in the printed report. I believe that the result of our work was useful, though years passed before all of our recommendations were carried out.

When we had completed our task, a balance remained in the Rockefeller Foundation grant. On the recommendation of members of our committee, and with the approval of Dr. Gregg and the Librarian of Congress, this was used to develop a new medical classification that could be used by both the Library of Congress and the Army Medical Library.

Before writing of the committee's recommendations, I should note that this survey was only the beginning of my connection with the Army Medical Library, which continued for more than a decade; I was asked again and again to serve as a consultant.

One of our major recommendations was that the Library should have new quarters. It was occupying a building constructed in the 1880s; as has been mentioned, there were water and rats in the basement. The staff was inadequate. As a footnote for library-history enthusiasts, I may report that the bookstacks had iron-grating floors and that the custodian was accustomed to sweep every day, starting on the first floor and then going up. This meant that dirt from the second level sifted down through the grating to the first floor; he then proceeded to the third floor, sending dirt down to the second. He had not previously been persuaded to change, but we managed to institute a reversal of his procedure.

New quarters were a more difficult proposition than sweeping. Very little space was available in Washington during the war. The Library was able to arrange for temporary storage of part of its collections across the street, and funds for planning a new building were provided almost immediately. Eggers and Higgins, the New York architects, were selected, and they planned a building for a site adjacent to the Folger Shakespeare Library and near the Library of Congress. We thought that this was an ideal location, which would help to prevent unnecessary duplication. The plans provided for placing most of the books below ground on a very large level, laid out so that it looked like a map of a cross-section of Manhattan Island, but with an even larger number of main avenues. With stairwells, toilets, and elevators scattered through the area irregularly, the result was a maze. Both main aisles and cross aisles were obstructed by these facilities, and I feared that the staff would get lost. The only illustration in our committee's report was a frontispiece showing the appearance of the proposed building.

In my opinion it is fortunate that funds for constructing this building were not obtained. The three armed forces — Army, Navy, and Air Force — were brought together after the war under the Department of Defense. The Navy was authorized to plan a Defense Department Medical Library, which they proceeded to do some miles to the north, outside the District of Columbia. I was asked to serve as a consultant, and we worked on plans, but no appropriation for construction was obtained.

By this time the Government was building up the National Institutes of Health in Bethesda, Maryland, west of the site selected by the Navy. As will be reported below, the Library was removed from the Department of Defense and, as the National Library of Medicine, was placed next to the National Institutes of Health. The architectural firm of O'Connor and Kilham, which had planned the Firestone Library at Princeton, was selected, and I served as consultant. The rare books were brought back from Cleveland; a reading room for them was provided on the main floor, with the collection readily accessible immediately below. The building has proved to be satisfactory, and the Library has been well supported by Congress. It is now full, and an addition has been constructed, which I saw during an Association of Research Libraries meeting in Washington.

The second of the committee's recommendations in 1944, and perhaps the most important, was that the Library be put under the charge of a professional librarian. This was taken care of partially and temporarily by appointing an experienced librarian under Colonel Jones, whose title was changed to Director, until other arrangements could be made. Francis St. John, who had been at the New York Public Library and the Enoch Pratt Free Library in Baltimore, was appointed. He was in the Army already, and it was easy to arrange for his transfer. After the war, Wyllis Wright, also from the New York Public Library and a good organizer and cataloger, took St. John's place for a short time. He them became the Librarian of Williams College.

Colonel Jones, who retired in 1946, was succeeded by a good Army doctor, but the situation still was not satisfactory. The new Director arranged for a broad-based advisory committee, of which I was a member. A search was made for an Army medical officer who was ready to make librarianship his career. When one was found, the Carnegie Corporation made it possible for him to receive library training, and he was appointed Director of the Armed Forces Medical Library "without limit of time," as we called it at Harvard. Dr. Frank Bradway Rogers, known as Brad by his friends, was the man selected. He became a superb director. Increased appropriations were obtained, and the Library again became one of which we can all be proud. Dr. Rogers resigned to go to Colorado in 1963 and was succeeded the next year by Dr. Martin M. Cummings, under whose direction the Library continued to move forward. Under both Rogers and Cummings it was a leader in the development of library automation. Dr. Cummings has recently been followed by Dr. Dan Tonkery.

With the appointment in 1949 of Rogers as director, an Army officer but without a limit of time, it was possible to improve the situation in many ways; but it was still doubtful that the Department of Defense would support the Library year in and year out on the scale that the survey committee and others desired.

Alan Gregg took the lead and, with such help as I was able to give, succeeded in persuading Senator Lister Hill of Alabama, whose father had invented Listerine, and Senator John F. Kennedy of Massachusetts to come to our aid. They introduced a bill providing that the Library be removed from the Department of Defense and designated the National Library of Medicine. Gregg and I appeared at the hearing. Thanks to the two senators and to Gregg's influence, the bill was approved by the Defense Library Committee and then by Congress; the Armed Forces Medical Library became the National Library of

Medicine in 1956. It has received more and more regular support than ever before and has become the finest medical library in the world. I look upon my connection with it as one of the high points of my library career.

THE ARMY AND NAVY LIBRARIES

I did consultation work for other libraries of the armed forces during and after World War II. My work with the Air Force Library began years later and will be recorded in Part IV of these Recollections.

My work with Army libraries began in 1943, less than a year after the opening of the Pentagon, when a brilliant young Army officer, an assistant to General McNarney, who was one of Eisenhower's right-hand men, was sent to the Harvard Graduate School of Public Administration to obtain an advanced degree. While at Harvard, he came to me and asked if I would be willing to undertake a study of the twenty different libraries that had already come into being in the Pentagon, as well as the Army War College Library and a few other Army libraries scattered through Washington.

It was soon evident why I had been asked to undertake this assignment. The Pentagon libraries had all just grown like Topsy in *Uncle Tom's Cabin*, and there was no plan to connect or coordinate them in any way. Among them was one fairly large library, called the Army library and presided over by an intelligent, hard-working, ambitious young man who had no library experience but knew how to pull strings when necessary. He was eager to coordinate and, as far as possible, centralize under his direction all the Army libraries.

I accepted the assignment with interest but with some reluctance, realizing the complications that might ensue. The Pentagon was, and is, an enormous building; if you set it down in the Harvard Yard, it would extend beyond the fences on all sides. There were hundreds of offices, and when the head of any one of them needed some books, he started a library and had no difficulty in finding funds with which to buy the materials that he thought he needed. Sometimes he found a librarian to take charge and sometimes he did not. I learned a great deal from this assignment. Here are a few of the things that stand out in my memory —

To start with, I had to fill out an application blank, giving my life history in detail, as well as my parents' and my wife's. I was finger-printed and was told that in due course I would receive a button to place on my lapel; this would admit me to the Pentagon at any time. While my work continued, not consecutively but over a period of several months, I did not receive the button until the day I turned in my report. Before that, I had to go to the desk at a specified entrance and call the captain in charge of the central library. He came down or sent someone else to escort me and keep track of me until I left. This was my first experience with strict governmental control. Since then I suppose I have been through the process twenty times, and I often wonder about the stack of FBI and CIA information about me. In Part IV of these Recollections, I shall write about the last occasion on which I went through this process. I cannot resist adding that one day I arrived at the Pentagon a half hour early, before the guards had come on duty, went through the entrance without interference from anyone, and worked in the building all through the day.

The young officer to whom I reported did manage to become the Pentagon Librarian and did what he could to coordinate and centralize the libraries. He obtained as his assistant a trained librarian who succeeded him; but what happened to the Captain I do not know. I remember that he came to visit me in Belmont at least once.

I also remember one evening that I spent with him just across the Potomac River from Georgetown University, at a junk pile full of rats, where he was accustomed to spend the evenings improving his accuracy in shooting. Another thing that particularly interested me about him was that he had a recording device on his desk on which he recorded both ends of many of his telephone conversations. It was my first experience with this type of activity.

The greatest duplication among the Pentagon libraries was in expensive legal publications. This was easy to understand, because many departments of the Army had to deal with legal problems; but to have twenty high-priced sets of the same material in one building, even if it were a very large building, seemed to me to be overdoing it.

One of the largest and best organized of the libraries, which I am sure was useful and was needed as a separate unit, was directed by a capable professional librarian with whom I later became reasonably well acquainted. I found that he was making twenty-five copies of each order for a new acquisition in addition to the one that was sent to the supplier. Each of these twenty-five records had to be filed in a separate place, and something had to be done to it later on when the book was received. I fear that this was a typical example of Army red tape.

I frequently had opportunities to meet the "higher-ups" and was always properly impressed with their individual competence, but was appalled by the difficulties arising from the Army's rapid growth under pressure, and by the inefficiency on all sides compared with what I had known at Oberlin, the New York Public Library, and Harvard. I was particularly bothered by what I saw at the Army War College Library, where I was told by its librarian, with no hesitation, that it was the finest military library on earth. I checked over the collections as well as I could in a couple of days and am ready to admit that it was probably the finest American Civil War library in existence. However, when it came to topographical, ethnic, economic, and climatic conditions throughout the world, particularly in areas outside Western Europe, all I could say was that I was appalled. I ventured to speak up and tell the librarian that I hoped the officers who were sent to the War College — they were, of course, chosen Army officers on their way up the promotion ladder — were directed to go to the Library of Congress to find material on the subjects I have mentioned after they had used what was available in his library. I was told that this was unnecessary. I was also told that one of the reasons that General Eisenhower had been selected to head the invasion of North Africa was that his thesis, written at the end of his term in the Army War College, had dealt with that region. I have often wondered if the reason he had trouble before he reached the end of that campaign was that he did not have a sufficiently thorough knowledge of the terrain, climate, and people with which he had to deal — knowledge that he could easily have obtained at the Library of Congress.

I was told of a library of some 20,000 volumes in a special field that might have been important but could not be found in the Pentagon or elsewhere. It finally turned out, after a long search, that it had been assigned to a young officer who had been told that it was a criminal offense to be in charge of any type of Army material without an inventory of it. He cold not find a list or catalog of it, at least not one that he considered suitable. I never learned whether or not there had been a catalog of the library; but I do know that, in order to protect himself, he had the whole library destroyed.

At the end of my study, I reported to the Army authorities that, in view of the importance of the Pentagon and of the use of materials there, it was not only desirable but necessary to put the library collections under a good administrator, who could either combine all the Pentagon libraries or, preferably, at least coordinate them with a union catalog, providing what we at Harvard called "coordinated decentralization." The latter plan was finally adopted; a reasonably good central library was established, and some of the others were eliminated. My report paid special attention to the legal materials, which were of great importance and could not be entirely centralized. The solution was a reasonably good War College Library that could be reached easily by most of those who would need to use it, and a smaller number of duplicate law books at other points where they would be heavily used. I was called back later to review the progress of the library, and a trained librarian took charge still later.

Toward the end of the war I was asked to survey the Navy libraries in the Washington area. Like the Army, the Navy had about twenty-five libraries, but it did not have a Pentagon, so they were scattered all over the city and its suburbs. It seemed impossible to try to combine them or to place them under a single administrator. Since each of the libraries dealt with a different subject, there was comparatively little needless duplication. In this work I saw a good deal of Walter Muir Whitehill for the first time; he was working with Admiral King and later helped with King's autobiography. In the summer of 1946, Walter succeeded my wife as Librarian of the Boston Athenaeum.

Other Libraries in Washington

During my last ten years at Harvard I was occasionally called upon for advice by other departments of the government. I came to know Ralph Shaw, who was in charge of what became the National Library of Agriculture, and I knew Foster Mohrhardt, who succeeded him when he went to Rutgers.

I studied the library situation in the new building of the Department of Health, Education, and Welfare on Constitution Avenue, where they were trying to combine the Library of the Office of Education with other libraries in the building. The librarian who had built up the health collection was very unhappy with my recommendations, which was embarrassing because she was a friend of Mrs. Metcalf.

I have also been called to Washington from time to time since I retired. When planning began for the addition to the Library of Congress that became the Madison building, L. Quincy Mumford asked me to serve as a consultant with the idea that it would not be an overwhelming job. Two problems arose. One was that government rules prevented the Library of Congress from paying the consultation fees that I, and other library consultants at that time, were receiving; funds obtained in other ways would have to be used. Then it became evident that this was a full-time assignment, which I did not wish to undertake. Robert Rohlf, a native of Minnesota who had held various positions in Minnesota and the Dakotas and who had extensive and successful planning experience, went to Washington on a full-time basis as Planning Officer. After having made a good start on the plans, he returned to Minnesota as Director of the Hennepin County Library and was succeeded by Frazer Poole, who had wide experience in building planning and had served as Director of the American Library Association's Library Technology Project; he had also been Librarian of the Chicago Circle Library of the University of Illinois.

I had a similar experience in another Washington library and told them that, while I would be glad to work for a below-standard fee, it would be undesirable because it would have an unfortunate effect on library salaries throughout the country, particularly on consultation salaries. Government salaries, except for elected officials, had continued to be sub-standard. It should be remembered that Herbert Putnam and Archibald MacLeish were paid only $10,000 a year. In recent years, however, this situation has changed; in the last Association of Research Libraries report it can be noted that, of the librarians in research libraries who are paid $60,000 or more a year, a large percentage are in Federal Government libraries.

Chapter 17

Peru

I LEFT THE Library of Congress on Thursday, 5 August 1943, took the night train back to Boston, and met Elinor at Harvard Square on her way from Belmont to her work at the Boston Athenaeum. We had breakfast together, and I arrived in my office in Widener just before nine o'clock. A few minutes later the telephone rang; the call was from Archie MacLeish, saying that arrangements were being made for a State Department mission to Lima, Peru, to consult with the Peruvian government. Their national library in Lima had been destroyed by fire, and practically all of its collection had been lost. It was the national depository for books and manuscripts, perhaps the finest collection in Latin America, and Peru had been very proud of it. MacLeish had arranged for the mission and wanted me to be one of its three members. One of the others was Wilmarth S. Lewis, whom I have mentioned in Chapter 15, and the second was Lewis Hanke, who had been an instructor at Harvard during my first two years there before he went to the Library of Congress as Director of its Hispanic Foundation. Hanke had travelled extensively throughout Latin America and was well known there. I realized that it would be a very congenial group and an exciting assignment. However, I had a problem. It was just time for Elinor and me to go on vacation. I was to be in Washington on the following Tuesday, and two of the intervening days were Saturday and Sunday; I needed typhoid and smallpox shots. MacLeish had told me that he would have the State Department prepare diplomatic passports for us.

I called Elinor on the telephone and had a hard time convincing her that what I told her was accurate. She said, "I left you only a half hour ago, and you were just back from Washington and said nothing about it." Then she added, "Can't I go along?" I had to tell her that unnecessary travel was not permitted because of the war, and that she would be considered excess baggage. She understood, and agreed that I ought to take part in the mission.

I went directly to the Harvard Medical Center and obtained my typhoid and smallpox innoculations, went back again on Monday for a second typhoid shot, and took the night train to Washington that evening. The three of us received instructions there, took a night plane to Miami, and arrived on a hot August day in time to take a swim in the ocean; I kept my recently vaccinated arm overhead, out of the water. For the first time I saw the sun go down almost straight during the summer months. I had never been further south than northern Alabama and southern California before, and then only in the winter.

The next morning we went to the airport to take the plane to Panama. It was wartime, and, in spite of our diplomatic passports, we were checked very carefully before we boarded. Lefty Lewis was surprised to have his current number of the *Saturday Review of Literature* taken away from him. Thereby hangs a tale that was not completely ended for twenty-seven years but seems to be worth recording. When we returned to Miami some two weeks later, his *Saturday Review* was given back to him with no explanation. Late in 1959, I was asked to go to Gainesville by Stanley West, Director of the University of Florida Library, for consultation on plans for his new university library building. Elinor had come to Florida with me, and one evening we had dinner at Stan's home with his wife and with the Assistant Librarian, Bill Harkins, and his wife. During dinner I told the story of Lefty's *Saturday Review*. Nina Harkins smiled and said, "I was the censor at the Miami Airport at that time, and I was the one who took the *Saturday Review* away from him. I'd been directed to do it by my superior."

But the story is not yet over. Ten years later, in 1969, I went down to Meadow Lakes Village, a retirement home in Hightstown, New Jersey, to help the widow of Azariah Root's son celebrate her eightieth birthday. Francis, her husband, was a college classmate of mine at Oberlin. I remembered that she had been a censor during the war, with headquarters in New York and Baltimore. I told her the *Saturday Review* story. She nodded and said, "I was the one who gave the order, because we found that there seemed to be a good possibility that the double-crosstics in the *Review* were being used as codes with invisible ink on them." It was in the fall of 1978 that Lewis Hanke and I met with Lefty Lewis at his home in Farmington, Connecticut, to celebrate the thirty-fifth anniversary of the Peru mission, and I told them the solution of the puzzle.

The plane from Miami stopped in Cuba and then flew over Jamaica. As we approached the Canal Zone, the attendants pulled down all the window curtains so that we could not see the Canal or the surrounding country. We stayed overnight in a Panama City hotel; much to my surprise, there were no window screens and no mosquitoes. We flew on to Lima the next morning, with a stop at Guayaquil, Ecuador. Before we came down there, we could see the snow-covered Chimborazo, its top more than 20,000 feet above sea level. We were told that long streaks in the desert of northern Peru were roads that went back to the days of the Incas. The dry beds of rivers coming down from the Andes were bordered by green areas and villages.

We thought we were being given a royal welcome when we arrived in Lima, but it turned out to be the welcome for a visiting archbishop, not for the Library of Congress mission. At the Embassy, we were met by George Vaillant, our Cultural Attaché, who took us to our Ambassador, R. H. Norweb. I found that Norweb had lived in Elyria, Ohio, where I did at the turn of the century, but he was younger, and we had not known each other. Members of the mission were taken to the best hotel in the city, the Bolívar.

A very interesting ten days followed, during which we attended a series of formal receptions and cocktail parties, and visited libraries and museums. We had meetings with President Prado. We visited the ruins of the library with Dr. Basadre, who had been appointed National Librarian after the fire. He had previously been Librarian of the University of San Marcos, the oldest university on the continent, some sixty years older than Harvard. Basadre was later Librarian of the United Nations in New York for several years. He was and is a fine scholar and administrator.

At one of the formal dinners I sat with a high government official on one side and full-blooded Indian, a senior admiral of the Peruvian Navy, on the other. Neither of them spoke any English, and I had no Spanish. At one of the cocktail parties for us, Lefty Lewis and I were talking with George M. McBride, an American, who turned to Lefty and asked, "Do you speak Spanish?" "No, I'm sorry to say, not a word of it," Lefty replied. McBride then said, "I understand you went to Yale." "Yes." McBride then told him, "I taught you Spanish at Yale for two years." (I later checked McBride's record in *Who's Who in America* and found that he taught at Yale as an instructor in Spanish for only one year. He was in Lima in connection with the Ecuador-Peru Boundary Commission.)

I noted with interest at the various government receptions we attended that champagne was always served, but the Peruvians, as far as I could see, while taking the glasses to their lips when toasts were given, left their glasses full when the affairs were over. I always wondered if the wine was enjoyed by the help.

We were taken on a tour of the Parliamentary Senate Library. There were very few books, but quite a number of tables, some of them in one of the broad corridors, with each chair occupied by a man who was staring at the open volume in front of him. We were astonished when we discovered that almost exactly half of the volumes were wrong-side-up in front of the supposed readers.

One evening I learned that there was a fair going on several miles from our hotel and decided that I would like to see it in order to learn more about the country. My two colleagues decided not to go with me. Many of the taxis in Lima were worn-out American cars that had been sold to Peru when they had reached such a state of disrepair that they could no longer be used as taxis in the United States. The one that I took to the fair had, to all intents and purposes, no floor beneath my feet, and I was not too comfortable, but it got me safely to the fair. By the time I got there, I began to wonder how I was going to get back and whether a taxi would be available. I could speak no Spanish and the driver could speak no English; I took out my watch before I left him, pointed to ten o'clock, and indicated that I wanted him to call for me at that time. I am glad to say that he did, because I would have had a difficult time finding my way back to the hotel.

We had two interesting Sundays during our stay. The first was with George Vaillant. We drove up into the mountains, after stopping at the American Ambassador's home. Beside the house, which was on a fairly steep hill, were several eucalyptus trees; they were nearly ten inches in diameter, though I understood that they had been planted there only three years before as saplings and had grown in a ditch where there was ample water at all times.

In the mountains, between ten and eleven thousand feet up, we saw some of the Indians with their terraced farms. I had never seen llamas before outside of zoos, but here they were running about freely. I developed a headache, presumably because of the altitude, but we had luncheon in a restaurant nearby and, after a cup of coffee, I felt all right again.

We had visited the National Museum of Anthropology, and Dr. Tello Rojas, the Director, was our host the next Sunday. He took us some miles out of the city to a site where archaeological excavations were in progress. He was an honorary curator of the Peabody Museum at Harvard and was eager to show us the extensive ruins. He then took us to the museum, where we saw some of the wonderful textiles from the mound where digging was now taking place. He explained that these dated back hundreds of years before the Incas; they were relics of an earlier race and civilization about which little was known as yet. He added sadly that there was enough in the one mound to keep him busy the rest of his life. He was then, I judge, in his late fifties, and there were dozens of additional mounds waiting to be excavated. I might add that there had been no rain for many years in this area, but there was green grass growing on much of the land, kept alive by the heavy dews that came in with the damp air from the nearby Pacific.

On another day we were taken to a museum belonging to the family of the country's President, where his brother, Mariano Prado, greeted us. This museum contained furniture going back many years, relics of the Incas, and paintings of the Cuzco School, which, it was said, were not represented in American museums. Lefty Lewis was able to buy one of these paintings and, with permission from the authorities, to take it out of the country, which delighted him. We were told that a Mrs. Mercedes Gallagher de Parks, who was the leading socialite in Peru, must be met if our mission were to be a success. When this was arranged, Lefty, again to his delight, found that she was interested in Horace Walpole, and she gave him a Walpole letter to add to his collection.

We visited with Dr. Basadre, of course, and saw the Library of the University of San Marcos. We met an architect, Emilio Harth-Terré, who came to Cambridge a year or two later and talked with me about plans for a new national library building. I understand that this was ultimately built, though I have never seen plans or pictures of it.

Thus far I have neglected to say anything about the real object of our visit, which was to express our regret at the loss of the national library building and its contents. There was no question about the loss or about our desire to commiserate and sympathize with the officials of the Peruvian government. But the cause of the fire that had destroyed the library seemed to be a very delicate question, and we judged that there was a strong suspicion that the former librarian, who came from a prominent old Peruvian family, had sold off the most valuable books and manuscripts, and then had poured gasoline in various parts of the building and dropped a match on it before leaving. This apparently had not been officially confirmed; but the librarian had departed, leaving behind two maiden sisters, who were in an embarrassing position. At any rate, a large number of Peruvian manuscripts and early printed books turned up in the hands of dealers in England and the United States, and ultimately were acquired by individuals or libraries. The

Library of Congress did what it could to obtain photostats of the most important items and sent them to Dr. Basadre.

When our ten days came to an end, we took the plane northward, stopping at Cali, Colombia, where Hanke and I left it, but Lefty Lewis went on home, picking up his *Saturday Review* in Miami. It had been arranged before we started on the expedition that Hanke and I would visit Bogotá, where we would try to acquire the greatest collection of Colombian books that was then in private hands. After a short wait in Cali, we continued to Bogotá on a small plane with perhaps a dozen single seats, one on each side of the central aisle. We flew over the main range of the Andes, at nearly 20,000 feet, I suppose. The plane was not pressurized, and the man sitting across the aisle from me, who apparently made the trip frequently, suddenly said, "The air is getting pretty thin in here." He got up, opened the door to the pilot's cabin, and came back with a can of oxygen, which he sprayed around the cabin.

In the Bogotá airport we picked up a newspaper, and Lewis Hanke said, "Well, it's happened again. When I was here last, the university students were on strike, and they are on strike again today." We had reservations at the hotel that, we were told, was the best in Bogotá. I do not remember its name, but our rooms were on the second floor, and there were no private baths. It was a large building, built around a central court, and there were four public toilets for men, one on each side of the floor. After a considerable search, we found the only one on the floor where the toilets flushed. Aside from that, we were comfortable.

The next morning I asked Lewis if he knew the national librarian and what kind of a person he was, because we had decided to start our day with him. Lewis said: "If you go ten miles out in the country, many miles from any river or town or lake or pond, you'll see back of the house a man sitting in a boat surrounded by ten cats. That's the national librarian." Fortunately we found the librarian in his office. The library occupied a new building with modern architecture, concrete floors, and a large stack area; as far as I was concerned, the noteworthy part of it was the librarian's office. This, as I remember it, was practically a cube, forty feet in each dimension. The east side was almost all glass, through which one saw mountains that rose several thousand feet above the city. Sitting at his desk, the librarian could look out on this wonderful view.

Later we were able to go most of the way to the top of a mountain by cog railroad, and then to walk perhaps a quarter of a mile uphill to a monastery at the very top. I was pleased to find that I could walk without difficulty; Lewis found the walking hard, though he was in good shape physically. I later talked of this with Arlie Bock, the head of the Harvard Health Services. He told me that some years earlier he had been on an expedition to Peru, studying the effects of high altitudes. Indians who were born in the mountains had no difficulty with altitude, but often suffered when they came down to sea level. Arlie himself had found that he could not stand high altitudes at all and had to give up his part in the expedition. I might add that this doctor had his ninety-fourth birthday last December and is still active.

We went to the handsome cathedral, which was a tremendous contrast to sights of poor people around the city. But we had come to Bogotá to try to purchase a fine private collection of Colombian historical and literary material. To our regret, we found that we could not obtain permission to take it out of the country. We embarked on the next plane that we could get back over the high Andes to Cali, which was then the only approach by air to Bogotá.

Cali, at that time, was a comparatively small agricultural center, very hot and humid. I think the population was about 60,000 in 1943, but I understand that it is now more than one million. We had reservations on a plane that should have taken us on to Panama the same day, but, when we went back to the airport to board, we were told that, in spite of our diplomatic passports, army officers had taken our seats, and we would have to wait at least another twenty-four hours.

We wondered how to spend the time. We talked to the American Vice-Consul, and he told us of the only library in the city, which we then visited. It was very small and unimpressive, but the librarian suggested that we might be interested in visiting a private museum that had been gathered together by a man named Buenaventura. We were able to get a taxi. It was sprinkling, unpleasant, and very humid.

Mr. Buenaventura greeted us warmly and showed us through his museum, room after room of material that, I confess, did not seem very interesting. In the last room he showed us something that he thought would be a special treat — a piece of charred wood from the Cocoanut Grove fire in Boston, in which several hundred people were killed, many by fire and others by suffocation, on the night after the Boston College-Holy Cross football game of 1942. This was one of the worst catastrophes in Boston history, and I might mention two of its effects at this point. The hospitals to which many of the victims were carried learned a great deal about the proper treatment of burns, which has saved the lives of hundreds of persons since then. The second result was that there were many new rules about exits, and these rules applied to libraries and buildings of all kinds as well as to nightclubs. I do not want to seem to complain about this; but it has meant that in Widener Library, where we had only one exit door open during the evenings, we had to open a second and place a control there as well as at the front door. When the Lamont Library was built a few years later, we had to have two exits. One might say that this has meant, indirectly, that, in each university with a large library building where two controlled exits are required instead of one, there has been one less professor; the salary of three doormen to cover long library hours equals the average salary of a professor.

My Colombian story is not yet over. Half a dozen or more years later, an elderly, seedy-looking gentleman came to my office asking for work. He seemed to be a pitiful case, and I felt that I could not turn him down without at least talking with him. I found that he had been Consul of the Republic of Colombia in Boston and had lost his position because of a change in government; such changes were taking place rather frequently at that time. It was evident that I could not offer him a position; but I told him about my experience in Cali, my visit to the Buenaventura Museum, and the charred wood from the Cocoanut Grove fire. His eyes brightened for the first time, and he said, "Yes, I sent that to Mr. Buenaventura."

After the twenty-four hour delay, we flew on to Panama, where we again stayed overnight. This time we had an opportunity to visit the United States Information Library there, and I met for the first time Marietta Daniels (now Mrs. Shepard), who has done a great deal of useful work for Latin American libraries and for the American Library Association.

The rest of the trip home was uneventful. Lewis Hanke and I were disappointed at not being able to purchase the Colombian book collection. We hoped that good will from the trip helped our country's relations with Peru. I had greatly enjoyed getting acquainted with a different part of the world, and my later work on library building planning in several other Latin American countries was easier and more effective than it would have been without this experience. I particularly appreciated the opportunity to become better acquainted with two unusual men, Wilmarth Lewis and Lewis Hanke. Elinor did not complain of having been unable to make the trip.

Since 1943 I have been called on to help with plans for the national library in Buenos Aires, for two Mexico City libraries in which the

Rockefeller Foundation was interested, and a library in Chile. I have gone to Turrialba, Costa Rica, for work with the International Agricultural Organization's library, and to Caracas to consult on plans for a Venezuelan national library building.

Chapter 18

The Farmington Plan and
The Library of Congress Mission

THE PRINTED MATERIAL relating to the Farmington Plan can properly be called voluminous. Among other things, it includes the text of the original proposal that was approved by the Association of Research Libraries, a long line of letters beginning with *Farmington Plan Letter* No. 1 in 1949, two editions (1953 and 1961) of the *Farmington Plan Handbook* by Edwin E. Williams, and critical studies over the years until the plan went out of existence in 1972. As far as I know, no detailed study has been made of the plan's influence on programs of American libraries for purchasing foreign publications. The part that I took during the first decade of the plan has not been recorded in detail; as its original proponent, I know more than anyone else about some aspects of it. Since the Library of Congress Mission was influential in getting the Farmington Plan started, it, too, will be covered here.

This chapter will also tell of the three-month trip that Elinor and I made from mid-May to mid-August 1950 in behalf of the Farmington Plan. This was my first trip abroad, except for short visits to Canada, one to England in 1938 that is reported in Chapter 4, and the one to Latin America that has been the subject of Chapter 17.

I will go into some detail in writing of this expedition because it was a completely new experience for me. It was fortunate that Elinor was with me. She had been brought up almost tri-lingually with English, German, and French, and I was able to do many things that would otherwise have been difficult if not impossible for me because I had no speaking knowledge of French or German, in spite of five years of Latin, two of German, and one of French in school and college. A reading knowledge of French or German had been sufficient for the entrance examinations of the Pratt Institute Library School nearly forty years earlier. The concluding section of this chapter will deal with our 1950 trip more than with the Farmington Plan.

Origins of the Farmington Plan

Archibald MacLeish realized the importance of interlibrary cooperation soon after he became Librarian of Congress; he also learned, perhaps to his dismay, that the Library of Congress was not acquiring foreign publications on the scale that he thought desirable. Sometime in 1941, consequently, he asked a prominent historical-society librarian to prepare a report on interlibrary cooperation and foreign acquisitions, and to make proposals for future action. MacLeish expected to present the report to research librarians at a special Meeting on Cooperative Enterprises on 26 June 1942, during the annual conference of the American Library Association in Milwaukee. He hoped to receive the report at least a month before the meeting so that he would have an opportunity to go over it and prepare suggestions relating to it. But the report was delayed and did not reach him until a week before the conference. When he read it, he was so disappointed that he decided not to present it. By this time, however, arrangements had been made for Charles H. Brown, President of the American Library Association for 1941–42, to preside over the meeting, to which research librarians had been invited. It was too late to cancel the meeting.

Unfortunately for me, Brown found that he would be unable to attend the meeting because of other ALA duties, and he asked me, as Vice President and President-Elect, to take his place. I found myself presiding over a meeting of fifty of the top librarians of the country who were expecting to hear and discuss a proposal for interlibrary cooperation; but there was no agenda. I did my best to encourage discussion of the subject. A number of the leading librarians — I particularly remember M. Llewellyn Raney — spoke enthusiastically of the importance of interlibrary cooperation, and others followed. But I was in an embarrassing position. I felt that we could not let the meeting come to an end without some kind of a proposal, and I suggested that the group approve three recommendations:

> 1) That Julian Boyd, Librarian of Princeton, be asked to report on the possibility of preparing a national union subject catalog to supplement the National Union Catalog already in existence at the Library of Congress; the latter was an author or main-entry catalog, and was to be published in book form.
>
> 2) That I be authorized to try to organize a cooperative acquisition program for New England libraries.
>
> 3) That plans be made for a national cooperative acquisition program that would bring more research material from abroad to libraries in this country. (Ten years earlier, when I was Chairman of the American Library Associa-

tion's Cooperative Cataloging Committee, I had found that the Library of Congress did not acquire foreign publications on a large scale, and that American libraries as a whole lacked many items that, it seemed to me, would have been useful to research workers in the United States.)

These three proposals were welcomed by the group, and we hoped that something would be done about them.

During the months that followed, I met with a group of New England librarians, and we talked about a cooperative acquisition program to bring about what the New England Deposit Library had failed to accomplish. We were eager to bring a larger percentage of new publications into the area and to avoid needless duplication of infrequently-used material. Julian Boyd went to work on the union subject catalog proposal; but nothing was done, as far as I know, regarding the cooperative acquisition program for the country as a whole.

In Chapter 15 I have mentioned the Librarian's Council of the Library of Congress; its organization was announced by a General Order of 23 April 1942. There were twenty-four members of the Council, which planned to meet only once a year, but there was also an Executive Committee of eight, which was called together more frequently. The third meeting of this Executive Committee was held in Farmington, Connecticut, at the home of Wilmarth S. Lewis, its Chairman, on 9 October 1942. Most of the members arrived at Lefty's home on the evening before, but I came from Chicago, arriving in time for breakfast.

I found the atmosphere very tense and soon learned that during the previous evening there had been a discussion of Boyd's proposal for a national union subject catalog, and that Bernhard Knollenberg of Yale had spoken rather strongly against it. I was told that it would not be discussed, but was asked if I would be ready to talk about one of the two other proposals for interlibrary cooperation that I had made at the Milwaukee meeting in June.

I then suggested, in more detail than I had done earlier, the idea that became the Farmington Plan. The group seemed to be interested, and MacLeish appointed a committee, on which he would serve with Boyd and me, to draw up a proposal in detail. I agreed to prepare the first draft. It was prepared with the aid of Ed Williams, who was my assistant at the time.

MacLeish, Boyd, and I met at the Century Association in New York during November, worked over the draft in detail, and agreed that it should be followed up. Archie volunteered to re-word the proposal in order to make it clearer and more interesting; after doing so, he sent his version back to me. Ed and I made a few minor changes in order, we hoped, to make it more acceptable to librarians. Copies were sent to more than 120 persons, and further revisions were made in the light of their comments. At meetings during January 1943, it was approved in principle by the Council of National Library Associations, the American Library Association's Executive Board, and the Association of Research Libraries.

As printed in the March 1944 issue of *College and Research Libraries* (Vol. V, No. 2), the "Proposal for a Division of Responsibility among American Libraries in the Acquisition and Recording of Research Library Materials" called for a cooperative undertaking, limited for the time being to current foreign publications in the Latin alphabet that were in the regular book trade; but the expectation was that it would later be expanded to include additional materials such as public documents and serials.

The ultimate objective was to make sure that at least one copy of each new foreign book and pamphlet that might reasonably be expected to interest a research worker in the United States would be acquired by an American library, promptly listed in the Union Catalog at the Library of Congress, and made available by interlibrary loan or photographic reproduction.

Alternative procedures were discussed at length, and details of the plan have been described again and again in library literature. As it eventually operated, each library volunteered to take responsibility for acquiring books in one or more subjects, preferably those of particular interest to it. Harvard's responsibilities, for example, included anthropology, Celtic languages and literatures, and law.

THE LIBRARY OF CONGRESS MISSION

While discussion of the Farmington Plan continued, a more urgent question called for attention as the end of the war approached. I had been unhappy after World War I when I learned of how a good many American libraries had "ravished" the libraries of German university professors. This came to my attention when I was Acting Chief of the Order Department of the New York Public Library and later when I was working on book selection with Harry Lydenberg; I learned still more about it after coming to Harvard. Germany had been in a desperate condition because of raging inflation. Some of our larger libraries had sent representatives to Europe with sizable sums of money; when the value of the mark declined to practically nothing, they were able to buy subject collections for much less than they were worth from impov-

erished professors who had built up fine libraries in their fields. This
helped American libraries to increase their strength and catch up with
European institutions; but it seemed to me that it was unfair and
improper to take advantage of our colleagues in German universities
when they were suffering, even though I was far from sympathetic with
German behavior during World War I.

When World War II began, I made up my mind that I would do what
I could to prevent a similar situation when the Allies won, which, as a
born optimist, I felt sure they would. I brought the matter before the
Association of Research Libraries in January 1943. After a great deal
of discussion, it was agreed that no member library of the Association
would send a representative to Germany after the war to buy books,
but that we would ask the Library of Congress to sponsor a mission to
purchase for us the books that it thought desirable.

Here I must interrupt the account to report an unfortunate instance
of my ineptitude. Before a meeting of the Army Medical Library survey
committee in the fall of 1943, I learned that Yale was sending Thomas
Mendenhall, one of its professors of history, to the Balkans and Istanbul,
and I was convinced that he would break our agreement. I asked him
to meet me at the New York Public Library, and I expressed my opinion
of the whole affair as plainly and emphatically as I could. It was evident
that he was very much embarrassed, and the conversation ended with
his agreeing that he would not buy books but would try to do other
things for Yale during his visit. After the war, I found that Professor
Mendenhall had been sent to Europe as a representative of the Office
of Strategic Services, and I had almost spoiled the whole enterprise. I
should add that Reuben Peiss, who had left Harvard to work for the
OSS in Switzerland and later Portugal, was in Europe at the time, but
I knew what he was doing. I did not meet Mendenhall again until
twenty-five years later, in 1968, when I was invited to an affair in honor
of Margaret Johnson on her retirement as Librarian of Smith College.
He was then Smith's president. He greeted me with a smile, saying,
"If I remember correctly, we have met before."

In July 1945, Archibald MacLeish, Assistant Secretary of State,
agreed, in response to a request from Luther Evans, Librarian of Congress, to place government acquisition facilities at the disposal of
research libraries, provided that they agreed upon a program of cooperative buying. Robert B. Downs was chairman of the committee, on
which I served, to work out plans. The Library of Congress was to
receive the first copy of anything it wanted that was acquired; 150
libraries were invited to indicate the subjects in which they would like

to receive publications, and priorities were to be assigned. Ed Williams worked out a classification scheme for the purpose, and, to my surprise, the librarians of research libraries agreed to the allocations and priorities before it was time for the Mission to start work abroad early in 1946.

The Library of Congress Mission was led by Reuben Peiss, who had worked in the Harvard Library from 1938 until he joined the Office of Strategic Services. With him was Harry Lydenberg, the senior member of the group, who, despite his seventy-two years, had left his post as Washington representative of the American Library Association's International Relations Board to join the Mission. The Deputy Chief, and at times the administrative head of the group, was David Clift, then Associate Librarian at Yale. (I have always had a great admiration for Clift, with whom I was associated at the New York Public Library, in a survey of the University of Minnesota Library that we made in 1949, and throughout his years as Executive Secretary of the American Library Association.)

The Mission acquired more than 800,000 volumes for distribution to American research libraries at a price of one dollar per volume.

THE BEGINNING OF FARMINGTON PLAN OPERATIONS

The success of the Library of Congress Mission was such a convincing demonstration of the feasibility of cooperative acquisition that the Association of Research Libraries, at a two-day meeting in March 1947, voted to put the Farmington Plan into operation. Arrangements were made for receipt of French, Swedish, and Swiss publications of 1948. During January of that year a grant was received from the Carnegie Corporation. This enabled the Association to send John Fall to Europe during October and November 1948 to make arrangements for acquiring publications from five additional countries, Belgium, Denmark, Italy, the Netherlands, and Norway.

During 1948, all books were sent to the New York Public Library for classification and distribution to participating libraries. Thereafter they were sent directly to libraries, and each dealer had to classify each publication and send it to the library responsible for the subject it treated.

All went reasonably well during the first two years. In 1950, I was asked to go to Europe to consult with the dealers in eight countries who were supplying materials under the tentative agreements made by John Fall and to confirm more permanent arrangements with them or, if it should seem desirable, with other dealers. I was also to visit Austria and Germany in order, if possible, to arrange for inclusion of their publications, and to visit Ireland and the United Kingdom.

1950: MY FARMINGTON PLAN TRIP TO EUROPE

I had rarely, up to this time, taken the full vacation allowed to administrative officers at Harvard, to say nothing of the extra time that President Conant had encouraged me to take if there should be an opportunity to go abroad on a library mission. A foundation grant enabled the Association of Research Libraries to pay my expenses, and I provided the funds for Elinor, as well as for the extra time we took. We did not want to attempt too tight a schedule; we tried to make sure that we would arrive on time for all of our pre-arranged appointments, which called for overnight stops in thirty-four places.

As I have already indicated, this chapter will have relatively little to say of the problems discussed with Farmington Plan dealers; primarily it will be an account of the very interesting time that Elinor and I had. This was an important addition to my liberal education and proved to be most useful to me in the years following my "retirement," during which I have travelled nearly two million miles on consultation assignments — the equivalent of eighty times around the earth at the equator.

With visits to twelve countries, in each of which I would have one or more scheduled appointments, the trip was evidently going to be complicated. I put the problem of transportation and accommodations into the hands of Thomas Cook. I was also counting heavily on Elinor for help; as has been noted, I had no speaking knowledge of even French or German.

Having set off in the middle of May on the French liner *DeGrasse*, we landed at Plymouth, and spent the week-end in the Dorset moors, with headquarters at a guest house where a friend of Elinor's had stayed. It was beautiful but wild country, with prehistoric relics in the surrounding areas. On the way to London we stopped in Exeter, where we saw its handsome Cathedral — the first I had seen — and made arrangements with the Exeter University Library to send reproductions of some of its archives to Professor Wilbur K. Jordan, who later became President of Radcliffe College, for use in his research on English philanthropy.

I talked with the Harvard Library's book agents in London, though the Farmington Plan was not to include publications of the United Kingdom because members of the Association of Research Libraries believed — correctly, in my opinion — that British publications were already being covered adequately by American libraries.

Leaving London, we took the ferry from Ipswich to the Hook of Holland and proceeded at once to The Hague, where we were greeted royally by Wouter Nijhoff, whom I had known since 1919 when I was Acting Head of the Order Department at the New York Public Library. It was tulip time in the Netherlands, an ideal season to be there. After talking over the Farmington plan with Nijhoff, we went on to Amsterdam to visit booksellers there. We took a boat through the canals, and had a herring luncheon on the second day of the herring season; this delicacy is reserved for the Queen on its first day. We visited museums in Amsterdam and The Hague, and went down to the beach at Scheveningen on a Sunday morning, seeing the masses of bicyclists starting off four and five abreast on the broad streets. We went to Delft, visited the National Library, and had an Indonesian dinner with an interminable number of courses, but no side effects. We even had time to visit the University of Leiden.

The train took us to Brussels, where we saw the National Library and for the first time met Herman Liebaers, whom I have seen again and again during the past thirty years in the United States as well as in Switzerland and Italy. We conferred with the Farmington Plan dealer for Belgium, the Office International de Librairie, and an extra day made it possible to go to Gent and Bruges.

We continued to Paris, where we started out with a visit to the Bibliothèque Nationale and a call on Julien Cain, its director, whom we met again in Chicago at the American Library Association conference in 1951. We visited Montmartre, the Louvre, the Sorbonne, the Champ-de-Mars, Notre Dame, and Fontainebleau, where I ate some wild strawberries with temporarily disastrous results, the only dietary problem we had on the trip, and the only one I was to have until 1968, in the Philippines. We did not try to go to the Eiffel Tower, but saw it from the distance. We called on a number of book dealers, but a satisfactory one was more difficult to find in France than in the other countries, where the trade appeared to be better organized. The Service des Echanges Internationaux of the Bibliothèque Nationale was to continue as our source for Farmington Plan books.

As we had done in London, we used the amazing subways. We went to the Ile de la Cité, and had a delightful outdoor luncheon with Serge Elisséeff, Director of the Harvard-Yenching Institute, and his wife. It was a dull day, but the afternoon sun came out just as we were in the Sainte-Chapelle, and we saw its magnificent windows to advantage.

We took a night train from Paris to Lucerne, where, after a trip on the lake, I left Elinor, who visited an old friend while I went on to

Zurich for the night. The next morning I left, on my own, for the long train journey to Vienna, by way of Liechtenstein, Innsbruck, and Salzburg. Much of Austria was still occupied by Russia, and everyone was checked by a Soviet guard before reaching Vienna. I arrived at my hotel there a little before midnight, after a very exciting trip. The hotel was in the heart of the city. There was a large central court that I passed through to reach my room, and the effects of a bomb that had landed there were still evident. Wartime damage was also visible at the nearby St. Stephen's Cathedral and the famous State Opera House.

In Vienna, I put myself in the hands of the National Librarian, Dr. Josef Stummvoll, who was later to be Librarian of the United Nations in New York. After we had spent some time talking in his office in the Library, he took me to a four-course luncheon that cost 25 cents in American money in a local restaurant catering to government employees. Before going to lunch, he said to me, "You may want to wash your hands," and took me over to something shaped like one of today's horizontal freezers, a little higher than a dining-room table. He raised the top, and there was a pitcher and washbowl, similar to those I was brought up with in Elyria, Ohio, where we did not have a single bathroom in a large house. When I poured the water into the bowl, Dr. Stummvoll said, "This is the bowl where the Emperor Franz Josef washed his hands regularly for sixty years."

After lunch, he took me through his handsome baroque library, which went back to the time of Maria Theresa in the eighteenth century, and to the National Art Gallery, where the Director, who fled to the United States to escape Hitler's régime in the 1930s and worked at Harvard, had now returned after the war.

One evening I went with Stummvoll to the foot of the hills just outside the city. We climbed a hill into a vineyard, where we had a supper of hard rolls and cheese, washed down with a new and quite bitter wine. We listened to the music from other groups who were in the area. It was a memorable evening as we looked out over the city.

I had an opportunity to go out to the Schönbrunn Palace, with room after room filled with wonderful furniture. One day I took a bus into the Russian Zone of the city, across the Danube, and was driven past a remarkable row of horse-chestnut trees in full bloom. It was a great experience.

I took a night train back to Switzerland and was met by Elinor at Bad Ragaz the next morning. We were able to drive up into the mountains that day in an open buggy on a rough, narrow road to the Monastery of Pfäfers. We then travelled by train through one of the main ranges of the Alps, where the tracks made a complete circle in a tunnel in order to reach a lower altitude, and came down to St. Moritz, where we had another wonderful experience. Spring was far enough along so that the cattle were being herded through the main street at night and then up into the summer pastures on the mountains, which were covered with spring flowers. On the next morning we walked through the park-like forest to an aerial tramway by which we were taken up several thousand feet. Then we followed a trail for a mile or two and came back into the bright summer day. On our return to the hotel, we walked through the forest again and passed a peasant woman with a cart and a baby. She was loading the cart with dead branches from the trees to use for firewood.

We took a bus from St. Moritz down the mountain into Italy on one of the most difficult, twisting roads that we had ever encountered. We arrived at our railroad station too late to catch our train and had to wait for the next, which took us into Milan well after dark. There was no porter on the platform, so Elinor went on ahead to find help while I got the baggage off the train before it went on to Rome. She finally found a porter and came to look for me and the bags. The porter did not realize that we belonged together, and he tried to keep us apart because he supposed that I was picking up a strange lady.

Our time in Milan gave us another thrill as we attempted to speak enough Italian to make our way. We called on booksellers, including the firm of Ulrico Hoepli, which was the Farmington Plan agent. We were guided by an American librarian from Boston who was in the United States Information Service. We were able to go up on the roof of the famous opera house, the Teatro alla Scala. I had lost a tooth filling, and our friendly librarian found a dentist who took care of it. We visited the Biblioteca Nazionale Braidense, one of the three national libraries in Italy. I saw the one in Rome more than twenty years later.

Having completed our work in Italy, we turned back to Switzerland, taking a train to Airolo, where, instead of going through the St. Gothard Tunnel, we got off and rode by bus over the pass and down to Ander-matt. I slept for the first time in a feather bed with a feather bolster; for Elinor, with her German background, it was not a new experience. We walked to the Teufelsbrücke below Andermatt and had an evening in the hotel restaurant with soldiers who were spending their short yearly session in the service.

We went by bus over the Furka Pass the next day, stopping on the way to walk to the great glacier there. The bus took us on to Brig, where we changed trains to go to Zermatt. It was still comparatively early in the spring, and, when the train came into the station, we found the streets full of men, women, and children, all in gala costumes, coming to greet two newly consecrated priests just back from their training.

The next morning we took the cog railroad up to the Gornergrat, with a view of the Matterhorn and of other mountains in all directions. It was a wonderfully clear day. We took the train halfway down the mountain to Riffelberg, where we were able to get some lunch and where we saw a prospective Alpine guide with a telescope on a stand looking at the Matterhorn, watching climbers there in one of the difficult areas. We then walked down the rest of the mountain.

Next day we took the train back to Brig and then on through the tunnel under the Lötschberg Pass to Lake Thun, where we took a boat trip to Interlaken. Returning to Thun, we continued by rail to Bern, where we were greeted by the National Librarian, Pierre Bourgeois, whom I had met twelve years earlier at Oxford. (Word of his death reached me just a few days before I dictated this.)

He had reserved a hotel room for us with a balcony looking out over the mountains. His library building was fine, new, modern, and carefully planned; our visit there was a delight. We also visited several good bookselling firms in Bern, including the Farmington Plan agent, Buchhandlung Herbert Lang & Cie. Bourgeois arranged with the dealer to drive us to Lake Geneva and then along the lake to Montreux, returning by a different route near the railroad on which I travelled nearly twenty-five years later during a conference on building planning of the International Federation of Library Associations.

The fine agricultural country of the Swiss valleys was a complete surprise to me. With my farm background, I was amazed to see the houses placed over the barns, sheltering the cattle, which in turn provided some of the heat needed during cold winters. There were two varieties of cattle, one Brown Swiss, which I had been accustomed to milking in Ohio early in the century, and the other a different color. Naturally I asked about them, and was told that those of one color were Catholic cows, and the others Protestant. I am sorry that I cannot now remember which was which.

We took a train through the mountains to Basel, where we talked with book dealers and stayed overnight before going on to Wiesbaden. It was a fine trip, with the Rhine in view part of the way.

The hotel in Wiesbaden, like the one where I stayed in Vienna, had been badly damaged by bombing during the war, but we had a comfortable room. The next day we hunted up Richard W. Dorn, who was managing the firm of Otto Harrassowitz, Buchhandlung. Having realized that he could not continue the business in the Soviet-occupied East Zone, he had moved from Leipzig, where he had worked for the firm for many years, to Wiesbaden, and was just getting started in the new location.

We found that he was living on the top floors of an old German castle with his book stock in the attic. He greeted us warmly.

Although I later talked with other German book dealers in Frankfurt, we finally made arrangements with Dorn to have the Harrassowitz firm act as Farmington Plan agent for Germany.

Dorn suggested that he take us in a small power-boat across the Rhine, which was flowing fairly rapidly, and we had luncheon on the other bank, with a fine view of the hills and vineyards on both sides of the river. He and I have kept in touch through the thirty years since then. He has come to many of the American Library Association annual conferences. With encouragement from me, he went to Australia and made arrangements for supplying books to libraries there. Not many years ago he spoke at the Boston Public Library, and on another occasion he spoke at the first meeting of the Association of College and Research Libraries in Boston. His son, Knut, whom I remember as a boy in 1950, has entered the business, and I have seen him at library conferences.

In December 1982, after the foregoing account had been written, the Harvard Library invited Richard and Knut Dorn to come to Cambridge to help it celebrate one hundred years of good relations between Harvard and the Harrassowitz firm. Elinor and I were invited to the reception; until after World War II the headquarters of the firm were in Leipzig, where she was born and where she lived until 1919. I had unpacked boxes of books from the firm when I did my first library work at Oberlin in September 1902; and in 1919, when I was Acting Chief of the Order Department at the New York Public Library, I had shifted our German purchasing from Stechert to Harrassowitz.

From Wiesbaden, we took the train to Frankfurt. There, in addition to calling on book dealers, we visited the University, where we saw one of the leading German academic librarians, Dr. Eppelsheimer. At first I thought him a little unsociable, but the situation changed when he finally understood that I came from Harvard.

We took the night train to Copenhagen that evening. It was somewhat late, and, as we waited in the station, we talked with the Cook representative, who was an unrepentant Nazi. He told us that the British had intentionally bombed the residential areas in Hamburg instead of the harbor. When we asked him about Rotterdam, he said the bombing there early in the war was not by the Germans but by the English, who wanted to win favor for their side by blaming it on the Germans.

It was still night when we passed Hamburg, but daylight had come before we crossed to the island on the train ferry to reach Copenhagen. Our hotel there was adjacent to the railroad station. The double room that supposedly was reserved for us had only a narrow, single bed in it, and we were told that this was all they could provide. They finally brought in a small chaise-longue, which had to suffice for Elinor, who is considerably shorter than I, for the few days that we were there.

The next morning the Librarian of the University Science Library, Jean Anker, who was largely responsible for founding *Libri*, an international library periodical, called for us and took us around his Library and then to Denmark's great amusement park, the Tivoli Gardens. We visited the National Library, went out past the famous Little Mermaid statue, which suffered indignities twenty years later, and on to Hamlet's castle, where we were taken down into its frightening dungeons. Later we went to the King's Gardens, a forested park with fine grass growing under the trees. On Sundays, we were told, it was full of picnickers who left not a trace of paper, bottle caps, or rubbish of any kind, which made us feel ashamed of our country and jealous of theirs. After visiting the firm that was handling the Farmington Plan, Andr. Fred. Høst & Søn, we took the morning train to Stockholm, starting with the railway ferry across the sound to Malmö.

On the train we had a strange encounter with a slightly inebriated construction worker, who looked at our hands and indicated that we had never worked. Then, when we made a long stop where he was supposed to get off, he forgot to do so. When he suddenly discovered that he was at his station, he grabbed Elinor's hat, saw that it did not belong to him, and then seized the hat of the woman who was in our compartment with her husband. He finally disembarked safely.

This gave us an excuse to talk with our neighbors. We were usually careful on train trips not to speak to others, because we preferred to look out and see the country. As the train entered Sweden at Malmö and the other couple showed their passports, we saw that they were Australians. I ventured to say that I was a librarian, and that the only Australian who had ever been to our house up to that time was an Australian librarian with the same last name as mine, and that name was Metcalf (Metcalfe, in the case of my colleague). The Australian couple looked at each other, and the man said, "We had dinner with the John Metcalfes two days before we started on our trip." It turned out that our compartment-mate had been an engineer and had lost a portion of one leg in the war; he was now taking his first trip abroad following his retirement.

We reached Stockholm at a busy time of year, in the middle of their short summer. Our reservation was in a motel several miles out of town, but we had a comfortable room and, without the language, I was able to find my way into the heart of the city, go to the National Library, and visit the book dealers in whom we were interested, including Sandbergs Bokhandel, the Farmington Plan agent.

One of the dealers said he was going to Uppsala the next day on business with the University Library, and would be glad to drive us there, an invitation that we accepted with pleasure. This was a trip of nearly a hundred miles. We saw the University, where we were greeted cordially, and then the dealer said he would like to stop for a short time at his father's summer home, halfway back to Stockholm. We learned that it was customary for everyone who could afford it to get out of the city for as long as possible during the long summer days. We had a very pleasant evening, and then were driven back to Stockholm, where we arrived after midnight. It seemed to me as we went along the last few miles that it was getting lighter, and I called this to the attention of our host, who did not think it possible. But I was right; it was getting lighter, and we realized that Stockholm, on Greenwich time, was so far east that it began to get light by midnight late in June.

The dealer, by the way, had been abroad for part of his training, which was not unusual for a European book dealer, and had spent a year in America, coming back only three years before with an American wife. The long nights of winter had almost made her go back to San Francisco to stay, but fortunately she had decided to remain in Sweden.

The next day we went into the city again to visit the public library, which occupied a very modern building. The entrance had double doors, opening outward, of course. I reached for the handle, opened the door, and found Elinor laughing. She asked, "Didn't you notice the handles?" I had to admit that I had not. They represented the nude forms of Adam and Eve, and I had grasped Eve's buttocks to open the door.

We were greeted by the librarian, who had spent a year or more in America, and whom I had met. After taking us around his very interesting and modern building, he said, "I've just been invited to dinner by an old friend, as my wife is away. He has lived for many years in the United States, and asked me to bring along one or more friends if I

cared to." We accepted the librarian's invitation and had a delightful
evening with a view looking out over the harbor.

Our host, a Dr. Hoving, who had practiced medicine in the United
States, was a Finn by birth, but had retired to Stockholm. He was a
typical old-fashioned nineteenth-century gentleman with a Vandyke
beard. Toward the end of the delicious dinner he had prepared, he
turned to Elinor and asked, "Did you ever buy anything from Bonwit
Teller?" She was startled because her first experience with Bonwit
Teller had been just before we started for Europe. The store had
recently established a branch in Boston, and she had gone there in
despair after trying other stores in Boston and New York, searching for
a purse in which she could fit her passport and other things that she
wanted to have readily available on the trip. She showed him the purse,
and said, "Yes, I bought this at Bonwit Teller's in Boston." Dr. Hoving
replied, "My son is the President of Bonwit Teller. His headquarters
are in New York, and when you next go there, please.tell him that we
had a pleasant evening together."

The train ride from Stockholm to Oslo gave us an experience different
from anything that had come before, even in Switzerland. It seemed to
me that a large share of the journey was beneath snow fences that were
high enough to block the view as we went over the mountains between
Sweden and Norway, so we saw comparatively little.

Our hotel in Oslo was fairly close to the city center. We started out
by going to the library, a combination of National Library and Library
of the University of Oslo. The Librarian was Dr. Munthe, whom I had
met when he was in the United States making a study of American
libraries for the Carnegie Corporation. This resulted in his book,
*American Librarianship from a European Angle: An Attempt at an Evaluation
of Policies and Activities.* I had been greatly impressed by it; though I
could not agree with all of its criticisms, I thought it one of the most
useful books for American librarians that had ever been published. It
gave us an outsider's view of both our successes and our faults. I had
the task of reviewing it for the *Library Quarterly* in 1940. Munthe,
unfortunately, was out of the city when we visited Oslo, but I had the
pleasure of meeting him four years later in Toronto, after which he
visited us in Belmont.

We saw the Viking ships, took a streetcar up to the top of their great
ski-jump, and visited the remarkable Town Hall, where we were told
that some of the murals depicting Nazi atrocities had been painted
without the Germans realizing what was being done.

From Oslo we took the Bergen train, but left it at Voss and travelled by narrow-gauge to the head of one of the long fjords, where we stayed at a pleasant summer-resort inn and took long walks into the hills and along the fjord. We then went on by bus, following one of the fjords, with the hills rising sharply above us. After stopping overnight in another summer resort, we continued by bus to Bergen, but it was late and rain was falling; we did not have time to see anything of the city.

The ship *Venus* took us overnight to Newcastle-upon-Tyne. We were surprised to find that we had been assigned a stateroom that must have been the bridal suite; it had a telephone to the bridge and to the Captain's cabin, and both furniture and bedding were luxurious, to put it mildly. We then understood why our tickets showed that the cost for this passage was far in excess of anything else we had on our travels; it was $75 for one night, which seemed a tremendous sum in those days. We found out later that Cook had made these arrangements because nothing else had been available.

We landed the next morning in time to catch the train to Edinburgh and to visit libraries and dealers there, though we were not trying to make arrangements for acquisition of British books under the Farmington Plan. Going on to Glasgow, we caught the night boat for Belfast, steaming down the River Clyde and across the North Channel. We stayed up late through the long summer evening, watching a group of laborers on the deck below. They were on their way home, and at first were very friendly with one another; but they quarreled, one man broke a whiskey bottle over the head of another, and the First Mate broke up the fray. It looked to us almost like a planned episode in a moving picture.

We had an interesting stay in Belfast, found a satisfactory book dealer for Harvard there, and then went on by train to Dublin, where we stayed at the Royal Hibernian, one of the city's old but very pleasant hotels, with unusually good food. We went to the Trinity College Library, where the Librarian showed us the Book of Kells, which was on exhibition in the College's handsome early-eighteenth-century building, with galleries and alcoves all around the great central hall. The shelves on the main floor and the gallery go up so high that ladders were required in each alcove. I did not see the Library again until more than ten years later, when I helped to plan an addition to the fine old building.

At the National Library, Dr. Richard J. Hayes, the Librarian, greeted us warmly and invited us to his home in a distant suburb, where he had a large greenhouse that enabled him to grow tomatoes, peaches, and other things that would not ripen out of doors in the Irish climate. We learned that the expression I had heard so often as a boy — "Come in out of the rain or folks will think you're Irish" — did not, as I had supposed, ridicule our poor Irish immigrants; if you go outdoors in Ireland you must always be prepared for rain, which tends to fall almost any time.

When Dr. Hayes came to Boston later on, he and I attended the annual dinner of the Eire Society, a Boston group interested in Irish literary and educational affairs. Arrangements were made through which, with the help of the Society and of Professor Fred Robinson of Harvard, we acquired positive microfilm copies of Celtic archival records and pamphlets that Hayes was having filmed in archives and libraries all over Europe, hitch-hiking, as he told us, from city to city. This visit, with continuing assistance from Hayes and Robinson as the years went by, has brought to the Harvard Library what I suppose is the finest Celtic collection in the United States.

We embarked at Dun Laoghaire, which is quite a few miles from Dublin, and took the late evening boat for Holyhead in Wales. The dock was crowded with perhaps a thousand others who were going at the same time, and we had to inch our way along for what seemed to us about a quarter of a mile, pushing our four suitcases along with our feet. It was the most orderly crowd we had ever seen. Authorities from the ship went through it, found elderly or decrepit persons and mothers with children, and took them on the boat first. We reached Holyhead about one o'clock in the morning under a full moon. We got on the train that, we hoped, would take us to Liverpool, but no one seemed to know whether or not it would go right through because the coming day was a bank holiday. When the train stopped in Chester, the lights were turned off, and we were left in our compartment in complete darkness, not knowing how long we might be there. Eventually, however, the lights went on, and the train started up again, arriving in Liverpool after going through the tunnel under the River Mersey. We found that we had to transfer to another railroad station for the next stage of our journey. Because it was a bank holiday, there was no food or drink to be found in either station. Our train to Skipton, in Yorkshire, made a number of long stops on the way. At one of them I saw a lunch counter where I was able to get two cups of liquid. We do not know to this day whether it was coffee or tea, but the liquid was hot, and we were glad to have it.

At Skipton we were met by a car from the Racehorse Inn; this was in Kettlewell, where we had arranged to stay for several days at the suggestion of an Oxford professor whom we had met at Harvard earlier in the year. This was the only vacation we were to have this summer, except for weekends during our European travels and for a short time in the Catskills during October. Elinor very wisely had insisted that we have a week left at the end of our journeys so that if, for any reason, we were delayed somewhere along the way we would still be able to complete our work for the Farmington Plan. We arrived at Kettlewell about two o'clock in the afternoon, and asked the landlord if it would be possible to get us anything to eat. He seemed to be shocked at the idea, because his unionized help, who had come from London, were not accustomed to being asked to work between meals. He finally brought us cups of hot milk, and we went to bed until dinner time.

Our stay at Kettlewell was one of the high spots of our three-month journey. We climbed Great Whernside, slightly higher than Pen-y-ghent, which we were to see later. We walked up an almost impassably rough and stony road on which, we were told, motorcycle races were held. We wandered out on the hills, and I remember coming over the top of one, looking down on the other side, and seeing at least a hundred rabbits scurrying into their holes when we appeared. An unusually severe winter a few years earlier had destroyed most of the rabbits and an equally large percentage of the animals that live on rabbits. Then the few remaining rabbits had multiplied far more rapidly than their predators and had taken over in the area. There were so many rabbit holes that it was unsafe to walk in the fields.

The man who had driven us from Skipton was available to drive us on other trips. We were in the country where the Metcalfs originated. The first one to take Metcalf as a name had been called Adam; he received his surname early in the thirteenth century because he owned the middle one of the Pen-y-ghent hills in western Yorkshire, which were known as the Three Calves. He was called Adam "the Middle Calf," then Medecalf, which became Metcalfe in time. Finally, with my first New England ancestor, the *e* at the end was dropped.

We were driven up a very difficult, steep, and poor road through Buckden and Hubberholme at the head of Wharfedale, with part of the way over an old Roman road, and came down near the head of the Wensleydale to Hawes. There we found that five of the first nine stores in the center of town had *Metcalfe* over their doors, each with an *e* at the end. I bought a cane there made of local wood, which I still use on occasion. We were driven down the valley to Askrigg. Our driver said that he knew where a man named Metcalfe was living only a few miles away, and he took us to see him. This man, before he retired, had lived in Nappa Hall, a manor house with a castellated tower. He was about sixty years old when we saw him. Twenty years later, my daughter and her husband went to the same area and spent a pleasant evening with the same Mr. Metcalfe in an Askrigg pub. We visited Nappa Hall; this was said to have been built of stone by one of my ancestors on his return from the Battle of Agincourt in 1415 (but the *Blue Guide* says it was built in 1484). It had an interesting courtyard with a monkey tree in it, and a fine view over the Wensleydale.

Our driver, who was the postmaster in Buckden, drove us to Oxford a few days later. We stopped on the way at a small village inn some ten miles south of Northampton; I had checked large-scale British ordnance maps some years earlier and was able to find the stone manor house built in the fifteenth century in which my mother's family had lived for generations as tenant farmers, and where she had been born in 1850, almost exactly a hundred years before we were there. It was much smaller than Nappa Hall, which we had seen a few days earlier, but in its front yard we saw the only other monkey tree that we encountered in England.

In Oxford we had the pleasure of staying in one of the old Trust House hotels. We visited the great Blackwells bookstore. When he was unable to provide a copy of one of the books by Elinor's father, Mr. Blackwell referred us to the store across the street, where several copies were in stock.

We had hoped to see the new Bodleian Library building, which had not been finished when I was at Oxford in 1938, but found that it was closed for the day. Mr. Blackwell telephoned a member of the Library staff, who was good enough to take us on a guided tour of the new building. I am reminded of the story told of its dedication, when King George VI tried to open the door with a golden key given him for the purpose. It broke in the lock, and the door refused to open.

By the time we reached London, where we were booked at the Stafford Hotel near the London Library, our ship was scheduled to sail for New York the following day. It was the great French liner, the *Ile de France*. We checked at the French Line office and were assured that our reservations were in order and that we would go down to Southampton the next morning to start our voyage. Then word came that our ship had sprung a leak in her hull after striking a rock on her way to Le Havre, and the trip had been indefinitely postponed. We went to Cook's office for help, but they could provide none. It was mid-August, a busy season, and the Korean War had started.

We remembered that Douglas Bryant was then in charge of American Information Services in England. We had a chance to visit with him. As has been reported, I had first met him in California three years before; our conversation now confirmed my conviction that I wanted him to come to Harvard when he was free to do so. This was arranged two years later, with happy results for all concerned.

We finally obtained a passage by air to Boston. After we had reached the airline station in London, had checked in, and had waited a considerable time, we were told that our plane, which was coming from Hong Kong, was in need of repair, and could not fly until the next day. Fortunately we got back to the Stafford before our room had been cleaned up, and they were able to keep us for another day, which gave us a chance to go out to Kew Gardens following a trip up the Thames.

We started early again the next morning, and the plane went on time. Elinor had not flown for twenty years, and she began to feel uncomfortable before we got over Wales on the way to Shannon. She wondered whether, if she survived until we came down in Ireland, she would not be tempted to leave the plane and not return. When the stewardess came and we told her of the situation, she said, "Don't worry. The pressurizing has not been working, and we have been flying so high that the altitude has affected you." This proved to be the case, and we had no more trouble, except that the plane hit an air-pocket and dropped several thousand feet all at once while we were having a glass of sherry, part of which nearly hit the roof. It was the first long aeroplane ride for either of us.

After stops at Shannon and Gander, we reached Boston before noon on Saturday, and I called the office. Miss Powers, my secretary, was still there, and she said, "We would be very glad to see you on Monday morning, but we have an appointment and a ticket on the train Sunday for you to go to Ellsworth, Maine, and the next morning you are to go down to Mount Desert for an important library appointment, accompanied by Mr. Ames of the College's law firm." The day there was a successful one, as noted in the section of Chapter 5 on the Emily Dickinson collection, and the ultimate result now amounts to approximately $7,000,000 in Harvard's endowment.

I have emphasized how much the trip added, with Elinor's help, to my education in a way that has been extremely useful to me during the past thirty years. It helped the Farmington Plan, which, though no longer in operation, contributed to interlibrary cooperation and to the improvement of acquisition policies in libraries throughout the United States and in many other parts of the world. As a result of the Plan,

Harvard and other libraries have materials that would not otherwise have been acquired by any American library.

The trip also helped to bring Doug Bryant to Harvard in 1952. For twenty-seven years thereafter he carried much of the administrative burden in the Harvard University Library. Since his retirement as Director in 1979, Doug has headed the American Trust for the British Library, which is trying to fill the gaps in that Library's collection dealing with the United States — gaps resulting both from war-time bombing and from long periods of neglect caused by financial problems.

Chapter 19

Library Association Assignments

THE AMERICAN LIBRARY ASSOCIATION

A s REPORTED in Part II, Chapter 15 of these Recollections, I became a member of the American Library Association in 1913, as soon as I could afford what would be a mere pittance in today's terms ($2 a year, if I remember correctly); and I have continued as a member for the past seventy years. I also joined other associations as time went on but, except for the ALA and the Association of Research Libraries, was never particularly active in any of them.

I have also mentioned the fact that I was elected President of the ALA in 1941 without competition because, for one of the few times in the last half-century, only one person was nominated, and I was that one.

I had then been a member of the Executive Board for three years of a four-year term. The presidency involved one year as President-Elect, one as President, and one as Past-President, so I was very much involved in ALA for six consecutive years. The war was going on throughout most of this time, and there was no annual conference the year I was President. The duties of the President, consequently, were less time-consuming than at any other time within my memory, and I did not have to go through the ordeal of presiding at general conference sessions or at Council meetings, which have sometimes presented difficult problems. Likewise, because of the war I did not have to attend state or local conferences, as it has been customary for the ALA President to do.

At the Milwaukee conference in 1942, when I became President, I gave something that was regarded as an inaugural address, which I entitled "Three Basic Needs in War and Peace." In it, I paid tribute to the three great librarians under whom I had worked from 1905 until I came to Harvard — Azariah Smith Root, Edwin Hatfield Anderson, and Harry Miller Lydenberg. I tried to tell something of the training and the kindness for which I was so deeply indebted to each of these men. As has been explained in the first section of Chapter 18, it was also at the Milwaukee conference that, in Charley Brown's place, I presided over the meeting of research librarians that had been requested by the Librarian of Congress; and this was when I proposed what was to become the Farmington Plan five years later.

Despite the war, there were regular meetings of the Executive Board in the fall of 1942 and the spring of 1943, over which I presided, as well as a Council meeting during the Christmas holidays of 1942. At a special meeting in Chicago at ALA headquarters, I presented the annual awards for trustees who had been particularly useful to their libraries.

As a Past-President, I continued to be an *ex officio* member of the Council until some time in the early 1970s, long after I retired. Then, because there were an unusually large number of Past-Presidents still active in library work and because it seemed undemocratic to have members who had not been elected, the by-laws were changed to exclude them.

The ALA charter had been granted by the Commonwealth of Massachusetts in 1876. While I was President-Elect, I was asked, as a resident of the Commonwealth, to try to arrange to have the charter changed to authorize the Association to continue its work of promoting library interests throughout the world rather than in the United States only. In fact, the ALA had already been involved to a considerable extent with foreign libraries despite the wording of the original charter. With the help of Ammi Cutter, who has been mentioned in Chapter 6 as counsel for the New England Deposit Library, the proposed change was approved by the Great and General Court of Massachusetts without encountering any complications. No other change in the charter has been made during the 107 years of the Association's history.

I find that I have failed to report that in 1939, when I first became a member of the ALA Executive Board, I held up for some time the adoption of revised ALA rules for cataloging; I was afraid that the new rules would make cataloging more complicated. As I look back on it, I am not at all sure that I was right, but it should be remembered that I had spent a good deal of time trying to avoid the perfectionist cataloging that Minnie Sears was attempting to institute in the New York Public Library. We had to give it up because of its cost and because it had slowed up production so greatly. One of the things that had attracted me to Harvard was the fact that T. Franklin Currier was managing a much less complicated and much less expensive system of cataloging than was to be found in most other libraries at that time. I might also mention that I encouraged Andrew Osborn in the preparation of his paper, "The Crisis in Cataloguing," which continues to be an important landmark in that field.

I continued to be active in ALA after 1943, and was Chairman of its International Relations Board from 1944 to 1946. Harry Lydenberg was in charge of its Washington office until he went abroad on the Library of Congress Mission and was succeeded by Marion Milczewski, whom I had known since 1940, when Ed Williams came to Harvard and Marion took his place as Carl Milam's assistant at ALA headquarters. Subsequently, when Doug Bryant went to England, Marion succeeded him in Berkeley as Assistant Librarian at the University of California. I have always been interested in the way in which library positions develop and tie into each other; when administrators make appointments, they change the future of the person appointed and of his family.

I continued to attend ALA conferences, both annual and mid-winter; I think I did not miss one during my eighteen years at Harvard, and I have attended as many of them as possible since my retirement.

THE ASSOCIATION OF RESEARCH LIBRARIES

I have written in Part II, Chapter 15 of the decline and dissolution of the American Library Institute during the 1920s and early 1930s. The establishment of the Association of Research Libraries may be regarded, in part, as having resulted from dissatisfaction with the Institute. Some of the directors of the largest research libraries felt the need for an active discussion group; but, if I understand the situation correctly, they were not looking for an elite organization of top librarians, which had apparently been the objective of the Institute's founders. They simply wanted an opportunity to talk with colleagues about their problems.

James Thayer Gerould was the leader in starting the new organization. Charles C. Williamson and Harry Lydenberg were also interested. Gerould arranged for the first meeting in 1932, and it was decided to establish the Association of Research Libraries, or ARL, as many of us have preferred to call it. There was to be no formal office, and as little organization as possible. It was decided, at Gerould's suggestion, that Donald B. Gilchrist be made Executive Secretary, and that he would make arrangements for the meetings and keep the records. Gilchrist, who had been Librarian of the University of Rochester since 1919, had been on Gerould's staff at the University of Minnesota Library before Gerould went to Princeton.

Membership was to be institutional, not individual, and dues were only a few dollars a year, enough to pay for sending out notices and reports. Gilchrist acquired a large, blank book, in which those attending each meeting wrote their names and the names of their institutions; this, at least until recently, was still in use. Only one director or librarian from each member library was eligible to attend. Meetings were scheduled during the annual and mid-winter conferences of the ALA.

Harry Lydenberg represented the New York Public Library at most of the meetings until 1935. Then, having succeeded Anderson as Director of the Library in 1934, and finding himself even busier than before with matters such as the Joint Committee on Scientific Aids to Learning, he asked me, as Chief of the Reference Department, to take his place. I found the discussions very much worthwhile; but, since I was simply substituting for Mr. Lydenberg, I did not take an active part until after I went to Harvard.

Gilchrist's term expired at the end of 1937 (he died two years later at the age of forty-seven), and I was asked to take his place as Executive Secretary. I accepted the assignment and served from 1938 through 1941, when Paul North Rice, my successor at the New York Public Library, followed me as Secretary of ARL.

The work involved had been minimal, and I was glad that it put me in touch with the leading academic and research librarians. In 1944, ARL took over responsibility for the Farmington Plan, and I was Chairman of its Farmington Plan Committee from that date until 1953. I should call attention again to the great help that Ed Williams gave me with this and with other ARL activities.

I did not lose interest in the organization after my retirement; the Association continued to invite me to its meetings, and I was glad to attend. Rice, when he was about to become President of the ALA, was succeeded as Secretary of ARL in 1947 by Charles W. David, Librarian of the University of Pennsylvania. Charles was more systematic than his predecessors; he was also more interested in developing a formal organization, and in finding additional activities for the Association. I must confess that I was inclined to think that this was a mistake; but, as I look back on it, I am sure that he and those who agreed with him were right.

ARL has accomplished a great deal during the forty-two years since I was Secretary. The membership, originally only forty-two libraries and restricted to fifty until 1962, has grown to 111, not surprisingly, in view of the increasing number of research libraries after World War II. With the help of the Council on Library Resources, it has done more to change and improve research libraries than any other organization.

Each of the semi-annual reports of its meetings and activities now makes a good-sized volume.

THE MONTICELLO CONFERENCE

A special project of ARL in which I was involved was the conference it sponsored on financial problems of university libraries. The University of Illinois was host to the conference, which met at Allerton House, near Monticello, Illinois, from 29 to 31 October 1954; hence it has commonly been known as the Monticello Conference.

In 1952, John D. Millett, who was then a professor at Columbia University and was about to become President of Miami University in Oxford, Ohio, completed a report for the Commission on Financing Higher Education of the Association of American Universities. Financed by the Carnegie Corporation and the Rockefelller Foundation, it was published by the Columbia University Press as *Financing Higher Education in the United States.* I felt that he made too few references to libraries in it, and I was bothered by those he did make. At one point he wrote that librarians put "little emphasis on economy." In the institutions he visited, he found "dissatisfaction with and confusion about the library services of higher education." He seemed to imply that Harvard, by constructing the Lamont Library, had shown that a large institution could provide satisfactory library service with a collection of 100,000 volumes.

I felt that I must do something about these comments. Millett's report was published during the years soon after World War II, before the plush period of the later 1950s and 1960s had arrived. Librarians were finding it desperately hard to obtain adequate appropriations for books, staff salaries, and services. I felt that the Lamont Library was being used to make it even more difficult for librarians to get the funds they needed.

At the ARL meeting of June 1953, I proposed that ARL request the Association of American Universities, made up of the presidents of most universities whose libraries belonged to ARL, to appoint a committee to study research library problems. This committee should be made up of AAU members and the director of its study should be selected by the AAU, but a well-informed academic librarian should work with it, pointing out problems that were faced by ARL members.

Several of those attending the ARL meeting were inclined to deride the idea, but a special committee was appointed to consider plans for a conference on problems that arise in research libraries in connection with finance and cooperation. I was made Chairman, serving with Lewis Branscomb, Director of Libraries at Ohio State University, and Raynard Swank, Director of Stanford University Libraries. We were also to try to persuade the Association of American Universities to make the proposed study.

The President of the AAU was then President Dodds of Princeton, and I went down to see him and talk with him about it. He did not seem to be particularly interested. Julian Boyd had been Librarian of Princeton from 1940 to 1952; when he resigned in order to devote full time to editing Thomas Jefferson's papers, he had been succeeded by William Dix. Dodds, I was convinced, because of his association with these men, knew that, as the result of a study, he would be pressed even more than before to provide additional funds for his own library; consequently he hesitated to become involved.

Nevertheless, an AAU committee was appointed, with President de Kiewiet of the University of Rochester as Chairman and Chancellor Branscomb of Vanderbilt and President Dodds as members. A new ARL committee — Charles David of Pennsylvania, Robert Miller of the University of Indiana, and I — met with the AAU committee and representatives of the Association of Graduate Schools. The AAU committee then recommended that a study of research library problems should be made; that it should be sponsored by the AAU, which should solicit a grant for the purpose and appoint a Commission on Research Library Problems; and that it should deal with basic concepts and fundamental principles of librarianship rather than with the efficiency of library techniques. The meeting that led to these recommendations was held in New York on 2 October 1954.

Meanwhile, preparations for the Monticello Conference at the end of that month had gone forward. As a preliminary step, I prepared an article, "Financial Problems of University Libraries: A Proposal for a Conference," which was published in the winter 1954 issue of the *Harvard Library Bulletin* (Vol. VIII, no. 1). Offprints were distributed to AAU presidents and ARL librarians during March 1954. I worked on the program and arrangements for the conference during the spring and summer. At the suggestion of Bob Downs, President Morey of the University of Illinois invited us to meet at Allerton House.

The president of each university whose library was a member of ARL was invited, and was also asked to send a professor interested in research. All directors of ARL libraries, of course, were also invited.

The program was divided into five sessions, as follows: 1) Opportunities and Pitfalls — Robert B. Downs, Chairman 2) Library

Operation — Raynard C. Swank, Chairman   3) Cooperation and Specialization — Lewis C. Branscomb, Chairman   4) The Financial Situation — Robert A. Miller, Chairman   5) The Future — Keyes D. Metcalf, Chairman. There were sixteen talks in all — two by university presidents (I read President Millett's because he found at the last moment that he could not come), eight by professors, and six by librarians. I was very much disappointed that Millett did not appear; if he, instead of I, had read his paper, I believe that a very worthwhile discussion would have followed it. He had reported only a few days before the conference that he planned to attend, driving from Oxford, Ohio, to Monticello in the morning, speaking in the afternoon, and driving home that night.

The conference was attended by one chancellor (Ethan A. H. Shepley of Washington University, St. Louis), two presidents (Lloyd Morey of Illinois and Herman B. Wells of Indiana University), three vice-presidents, twenty professors (of whom three were also deans and three were department heads), and thirty-nine librarians. It seemed to me particularly unfortunate that so few presidents came. I am inclined to believe that many presidents feared it would be evident that their libraries were not adequately supported financially, and that they would be placed in an embarrassing position. I regretted that President Wells of Indiana had not been asked to take part in the program; during the discussion we found that he was very much interested in our problems. He had been the one midwestern university president in office when the proposal for the Midwest Inter-Library Center was first discussed who was still there through the period when it finally came into operation, and he had steadily supported it.

The Monticello Conference papers, with summaries of the discussions, were edited by Ed Williams and published for ARL by the Scarecrow Press under the title, *Problems and Prospects of the Research Library*. This turned out well; but, unfortunately, nothing come of the proposed study to be sponsored by the Association of American Universities. I believe that there was a request for foundation funds but that the foundations had shifted their interests to other activities, feeling that they had done all they should for libraries during the 1930s and 1940s, largely in response to requests from Carl Milam, Executive Secretary of the American Library Association, and a few other librarians, particularly Harry Lydenberg, Charles Williamson, William Warner Bishop, and Andrew Keogh.

At about this time, fortunately, the money available for library salaries, new library buildings, and acquisitions increased at an unprecedented rate, and financial problems of libraries did not become serious again for another twenty years. I have always hoped that the Monticello Conference had something to do with this change.

SENATOR JOSEPH McCARTHY

An account of the following episode may belong here, because it was related, at least indirectly, to one of my library association assignments, the chairmanship of the American Library Association's International Relations Board. It was this that led to my membership on a State Department committee, made up largely of publishers, that dealt with book selection for the United States Information Libraries abroad.

Very early in the 1950s, when Senator McCarthy of Wisconsin began his witch-hunt, President Conant, realizing that a number of Harvard professors had a reputation as liberals, asked Arthur Sutherland, a professor in the Law School, to be ready to give advice to any member of the faculty who was approached by Senator McCarthy and questioned about his Communist connections.

McCarthy had published a list of Harvard professors whom he suspected of Communist leanings, and I was included in the list, though I have always thought of myself as being well to the right of center on government affairs. I must confess to having voted the Republican ticket pretty steadily, though I have been registered in Belmont for forty-five years as an independent.

Soon after the arrangements had been made with Professor Sutherland, our live-in housekeeper, Barbara King, telephoned me at Widener, her voice betraying excitement, to say that a telegram had come to me addressed to the house, and she thought I ought to know about it right away. I suggested that she open it and read it to me. It was a three-page telegram from McCarthy. It might be summed up as two questions: Had I, as a member of a committee in Washington that had responsibility for selection of books for United States Information Libraries all over the world, voted in favor of one written by Howard Fast, who is a Communist? If I had voted for it, would I do so again? A prompt reply was requested.

When I got home to Belmont that evening, I read the long telegram carefully and prepared the reply that I wanted to send. In it I simply stated, first, that I had always voted in favor of including in the information libraries books that, I believed, told about the United States as it was, regardless of whether they were written by Howard Fast or by anyone else; and, second, that I would do it again.

I went to see Professor Sutherland the next morning and told him the whole story, including its background. He asked how I expected to reply to McCarthy's telegram. I showed him the telegram that I had prepared, and said that, unless he thought it would be harmful to the University, I would like to send it.

He approved and said, "Go ahead." I sent it off collect and never heard anything more from McCarthy. As far as I have been able to learn, I was the first member of the Harvard staff to be approached by the Senator. Quite a number, of course, were involved directly or indirectly later on. In his autobiography, *My Several Lives*, President Conant devotes a whole chapter to his experience with McCarthy. He was questioned both before and after his appointment as High Commissioner to Germany.

As for the information libraries, the first of them was established by Harry Lydenberg in Mexico City during the war. Since my retirement, I have had the good fortune to visit a number of them in Australia, New Zealand, India, Kenya, and South Africa. Thomas J. Wilson, while Director of the Harvard University Press, had a great deal to do with publishing American books in third-world countries and elsewhere, many of them in translation, and with placing them in the information libraries as well as selling inexpensive copies.

Chapter 20

Miscellaneous Incidents, 1939–1955

URING MY eighteen years as Director of the Harvard University Library and Librarian of Harvard College, there were a number of incidents that have not been reported elsewhere in this volume but that seem to be worth recording. They are so varied in nature that a logical sequence seems impracticable, and an attempt to arrange them chronologically was unsuccessful.

The reader, particularly the reader of this chapter and the one that follows, should remember that I am ninety-four years old and that these are Random Recollections, not the product of research and careful checking of records. A faulty memory may be responsible for some of the details; but they are all based on something that happened, and they give some indication of the variety of experiences in which the librarian of an institution like Harvard may become involved.

JOHN LANGDON SIBLEY

I had been interested since coming to Harvard in a story about John Langdon Sibley, who was Librarian of Harvard College for the twenty-one years before Justin Winsor's appointment in 1877. According to this story, Sibley was crossing the Yard one day when he was met by someone who said, "You seem to be smiling and unusually happy today." Sibley replied, "I am. All the books in the Library are back except two, and I know who has them and I'm going after them."

I spoke of this story to Samuel Atkins Eliot, a son of President Eliot, and he said, "Yes, that's a true story. It was my father who met him, and my father knew that Sibley had been unhappy for years because the College had failed to provide a new library building for him, something that he had been trying to get for a long time."

With this in mind, I checked the old records of the Visiting Committee of the Board of Overseers, and found that the rules in those days stated that all books borrowed during the academic year were to be returned at the end of the year, and that it was one of the Librarian's responsibilities to get them back. This, even in the middle of the nineteenth century, was a difficult task, and it was easy to understand why Sibley had been happy when there were only two more to be retrieved and he knew where they were.

Clarence Walton, the head of the Order Department, was interested in the Library's history and in the Archives. I asked him to go over to the Massachusetts Historical Society to check Sibley's records, which were there. Sibley, disgusted with Harvard because it had not built a new library building for him, had left his Diary and other papers to the Society, as well as funds for continuing the great series of biographies of Harvard graduates that he had started. Walton came back triumphant. He had found a record of the occasion in Sibley's Diary, with the additional information that Asa Gray had one of the books and Louis Agassiz the other.

RADCLIFFE COLLEGE

The relationship between Harvard and Radcliffe College has changed a great deal since my early years at Harvard. The Radcliffe undergraduates were then taught in separate classes by Harvard professors who were ready to give courses at Radcliffe for additional remuneration, and the students could use only one, quite small reading area in Widener. It was customary for Radcliffe to appoint Harvard officers, usually professors, as members of the Board of Trustees for three-year terms. I served for two of these terms, from 1939 to 1945.

I soon realized why I had been chosen. Radcliffe was outgrowing its library, which had been constructed with Carnegie money in 1908, wanted to add to it, and thought that I could be helpful with this. The Library was rectangular, with the entrance on the long side facing the Radcliffe Yard, and the long façade to the rear was on James Street, which bounded the Yard on its west side. The architect proposed that a wing, equal in size to the original building of 1908, be built. This would be connected with the old building, would back onto Brattle Street, and would provide a main entrance in a blunt, V-shaped area between the old building and the new. We worked on the plans in some detail, but I finally recommended strongly that the addition should not be built. I was looking forward to construction of an undergraduate library at Harvard, and thought that, with the Radcliffe graduate students having the free use of all research collections, the existing Radcliffe building would be sufficient for an undergraduate collection matching in size the one that I hoped to provide for Harvard undergraduates. I had my way, but this may have turned out to be a mistake.

As reported in Chapter 8, when the Lamont Library was planned, it was agreed that Radcliffe students would not be admitted to it. But, beginning during World War II, Radcliffe students had been admitted to undergraduate classes in the Harvard Yard, and they needed a place to study when they had an hour or two between classes; both the Radcliffe Library and the Radcliffe dormitories were a considerable distance away. Temporary accommodations were found for them in the basement of Memorial Church, where a reading room with some reserved books was installed.

In 1966, after my retirement, I should add, Lamont was opened to Radcliffe students, and during the same year a new Radcliffe library, the Susan Morse and Frederick Whiley Hilles Library, was completed; it had been constructed on one side of the Radcliffe dormitory quadrangle. Hilles and Lamont are open to both Harvard men and Radcliffe women, and the two colleges are now coeducational in almost every way.

Another mistake I made in connection with Radcliffe was when the question arose of building up a collection on the history of women. I discouraged this because Smith College, with its Sophia Smith collection, was already specializing in the field, and the New York Public Library had a number of good research collections on women. I thought it would be unwise to start another collection, competing with these, in the northeastern United States. Again, I was wrong. The Arthur and Elizabeth Schlesinger Library on the History of Women in America, which began as the Radcliffe Women's Archives, is housed in the former Radcliffe College Library building. It has grown rapidly, and is now probably the most valuable American collection in its field.

I particularly remember one other Radcliffe incident. In 1943, when I was still on its Board, Ada Comstock, who had been President of Radcliffe for twenty years and was well into her sixties, surprised the Trustees, including me, by announcing that she was resigning and was about to marry Wallace Notestein, a professor of history at Yale.

THE INSTALLATION OF PRESIDENT PUSEY IN 1953

President Conant resigned in January 1953 to become High Commissioner to Germany, but his actual retirement did not take place until after Harvard's Commencement in June of that year; and he returned to preside over the ceremonies. President Pusey took office on 1 September 1953. In accordance with a custom that went back many years, the Librarian of Harvard College had the duty of carrying the Relics of the College, as they are called, in the procession preceding the formal installation. The Relics included the College Charter of 1650, the oldest charter in this country. It is an elephant folio sheet in a red morocco binding.

The installation was held in the Faculty Room of University Hall. First, however, I was asked to go to the President's Office in Massachusetts Hall, joining the procession there. The case holding the Charter was so large that, with my comparatively long arms, I was barely able to put it under one arm while maintaining a grip on it with my hand. I doubt that any one of my successors could have done this, and I do not know how the Charter was handled when President Bok was installed.

LOCAL RESIDENTS

I could fill a long chapter with stories of my dealings with Cambridge residents and others with whom I became acquainted as a result of my position in the Harvard Library.

Bliss Perry had come to Harvard as a professor in the English Department after years of teaching at Williams College, followed by years as Editor of the *Atlantic Monthly*. He had retired some time before I arrived, but still came to the Faculty Club occasionally. I was often seated next to him, and enjoyed the stories about Cambridge residents that he liked to tell. I remember particularly one about a professor's wife who lived near Harvard Square and could not understand how one of her friends could be happy a few blocks out on Brattle Street, because "it was so far away." Anyone interested in Harvard during the first half of the twentieth century will enjoy Perry's account, as published on pages 1-20 of *The Saturday Club, A Century Completed, 1920–1956*, edited by Edward W. Forbes and John H. Finley, Jr. (Boston: Houghton Mifflin, 1958).

The widow of Arthur Kingsley Porter, one of Harvard's distinguished professors of fine arts, was still living in what was then thought of as the James Russell Lowell House; it is now occupied by President Derek Bok. Mrs. Porter and I met on an occasion involving the City of Cambridge rather than Harvard. Later on, I was invited to her home to see the great collection of pamphlets that her husband had assembled; these ultimately came to Harvard, where they have been very useful in the Fine Arts Library.

I do not remember how I happened to meet Samuel Atkins Eliot, a
son of President Eliot of Harvard; he was a highly regarded Unitarian
minister who had no formal connection with the University. He had
been President of the American Unitarian Society for many years and
then the minister of the Arlington Street Church in Boston before
retiring in 1937. In talking with him one day at the Faculty Club, where
he came occasionally, I remarked that I had been told that he resembled
his father. He replied with a smile that the official portrait of President
Eliot, which hangs in a prominent place in the Faculty Room in University Hall, was painted in the President's old age; the President had
sat for the portrait while the head was painted, but, in order to avoid
taking his time and tiring him, the model for the body had been his
son's.

THREE PROPER BOSTONIANS

The men involved in the three incidents that follow can appropriately
be classified, I think, as "proper Bostonians." At least, I cannot think
of a more suitable term.

Charles Francis Adams was a great-great-grandson of John Adams,
the second President of the United States. He was President of the
Boston Athenaeum for some years while Elinor was Librarian there,
was Treasurer of Harvard College and President of the State Street
Trust Company during much of the first third of the century, and had
been Secretary of the Navy during the Hoover Administration. One
winter evening early in my Harvard years, I found myself in Grand
Central Station in New York during a snowstorm. I was headed for the
Harvard Club, a quarter of a mile away; I met Adams, who had come
down from Boston on the same train, and I found that he too was going
to the Harvard Club. Quite properly, I thought, I asked if I could get
a taxi for us. He scoffed at the idea, and we waded through the snow
to the west forties. He was in his seventies at the time.

Allston Burr was to refuse a similar offer of mine during the winter
of 1949. This was after the dinner that was given in the Lamont Library's
Forum Room in honor of donors to that Library's endowment fund.
Burr was one of the guests. He had been interested in the architecture
of the building; some months earlier, when it had been criticized by a
few of the more conservative Harvard graduates because they thought
it too modern to fit in with Harvard's Colonial Georgian buildings, he
had asked Elinor (he was then a Trustee of the Boston Athenaeum) if
Mr. Lamont had realized what the building was going to look like.

(Lamont had died before the building began to show above ground.) Elinor was able to assure Burr that Lamont had seen the plans and a model of the building, and had told me that he approved of them. As a result of this conversation, I had taken Burr around the building, and he had been pleased with the interior arrangements.

After the dinner that has been mentioned, I found that there was fresh snow on the ground and that it was snowing heavily. I suggested to Mr. Burr that I call a taxi for him, and said I would accompany him across the fifty feet of level ground between the front door and the taxi. He refused the offer as Adams had done, saying, "I've got two good legs, and what are they for?" He was nearly eighty-two at the time. It can be imagined that I was pleased, not long after he died, to learn that he had left several million dollars as an unrestricted legacy to Harvard. A science classroom building, Burr Hall, was built with a portion of this money; now, in 1983, it is being razed to make room for an addition to the Fogg Museum.

Godfrey Lowell Cabot lived to be over one hundred. In 1951, when he was ninety, he received an honorary degree from Harvard, and I sat beside him on the platform at the Harvard Alumni Association meeting on the afternoon of Commencement Day. The alumni meetings often have a tendency to drag on, and it was getting late. Cabot looked at his watch and saw that it was nearly four o'clock. Turning to me, he said, "I'm sorry, I'm going to have to leave." There was a way out at the back of the platform, so he could depart inconspicuously. I knew that he lived in Boston some four miles away. Once more I volunteered to get a taxi. Like Adams and Burr, he would have none of it. "What are my legs for? And the subway is still running." Off he went.

Cabot was probably the wealthiest man in Boston at the time, and he left millions to Harvard. In 1973, the University's new Science Center for undergraduate instruction in the sciences was opened, and the library that it houses was named the Godfrey Lowell Cabot Science Library. This is Harvard's undergraduate science library, containing many of the books that had formerly been in science collections of Lamont and Hilles; it is also the research collection for mathematics and statistics, and its stacks house infrequently used back files of scientific periodicals transferred from more specialized science research collections. As has been noted in Chapter 13, a science library had been proposed years earlier by Edwin Cohn.

I cannot resist telling another story about Godfrey Lowell Cabot. He was a deacon at the First Unitarian Church in Boston, where my Wellesley sister was a member. His duties included helping to take up the collection. One Sunday he was unable to find his collection plate, and substituted his derby hat for it. When he took off his hat after having walked home from the service, a nickel fell out. He immediately walked back to the church to turn in the five cents because he was unwilling to have any part in "embezzling" church funds.

DISTINGUISHED VISITORS

Gustav Adolf, Crown Prince of Sweden, visited Harvard during the summer when many members of the faculty were out of town. Those of us who were in the area were asked to meet in the University Hall Faculty Room to greet him and to hear him speak. While speaking, he stood near where President Conant sat during faculty meetings, and placed the sheets from which he was reading on a lectern in front of him. It was a hot day, and the window behind him was open; a strong breeze blew in and threatened to blow them away. He tried to hold them down; then, finding this difficult, he quite naturally turned around and closed the window. It was immediately evident that the window and window-sill he touched had not been dusted; his fingers were dirty, and he did not know how to dust them off without calling attention to the problem. It was an embarrassing moment for the Crown Prince and for those who were responsible for the physical condition of the room, to say nothing of the rest of us.

At the close of his talk, Gustav Adolf suggested that he would like to see the Widener Library. I rushed on ahead and met him at the door. He came in with an attendant who handed him a large volume, which he passed on to me as a gift to the Harvard Library. It was a reprint of the first Swedish edition of the Bible. While it was not as large as an unabridged dictionary, it was heavy, and I wondered if I ought to carry it around with me as we went through the building. Fortunately I saw our Swedish cataloger nearby. I introduced her to the Prince, handed the volume to her, and began the tour of the building.

The Duke of Windsor was another member of a royal family whom I had the pleasure of escorting through Widener. He had come to Boston with the Duchess, but she was not feeling well, and the Duke came to the University alone. He asked, among other things, to be taken through the Library. Accompanied by Paul Buck, who was then Provost, I took him through the public reading rooms and the work rooms and then into the bookstack. We were going down the stairs adjacent to the elevator on the east side of the stack when the Duke suddenly turned to Buck and said, "I've seen you before somewhere." "Yes," Paul replied, "in 1922, when I was a Sheldon Fellow, I was in England and was invited to Lady Astor's for tea. You were there, and I was introduced to you." I was impressed so much by the remarkable memory of the former King of England, recalling a face he had seen some twenty-five years before, that I unintentionally took him down to the lowest (D) stack level, to which the elevator did not go, and we had to climb the stairs as the tour continued.

I think it was in December 1950, at the time when the United Nations was considering a plan for the federation of Eritrea with Ethiopia, that the Emperor Haile Selassie was in this country. It was about that time, at any rate, that he visited Harvard and asked for an opportunity to see the Harvard Library. We found that he was particularly interested in rare books, early printing, and manuscripts. I took him into the Houghton Library, where Bill Jackson showed him our Coptic manuscripts and other materials by which he seemed to be greatly impressed. It was evident that he was well informed and that his knowledge was not limited to early Ethiopian manuscripts and books. He was very agreeable and appreciative, and seemed to be in good health and spirits. I was amazed at how short in stature he was.

I never saw the Emperor again, and have never been to Ethiopia, though I flew over it in the spring of 1959 en route from Bombay via Karachi and Aden to Nairobi, and had a view of its impressive mountains and valleys. Without going to Addis Ababa, I became professionally involved with Ethiopia in planning their National and Haile Selassie University Library, which was constructed largely with American funds.

Konrad Adenauer, some time after he became Chancellor of the Federal Republic of Germany, came to the United States and stopped in the Boston area. He visited Harvard, and I had the pleasure of taking him through the Library. He was an impressive figure, but I have no definite memory of him except that he was very much impressed by our collections.

One day when the Faculty Club dining room was unusually full, I was seated at a table for two with a man whom I thought I ought to have known and recognized. He welcomed me pleasantly. I introduced myself, and he said, "I'm Charles Lindbergh." I then realized that, while the face was familiar, he no longer had the head of curly hair that showed in his pictures twenty years earlier.

HONORS AND AWARDS

I suppose it was to be expected that the Director of the Harvard University Library would receive honors and awards of one kind or

another during his term of office. More than my share of them came
my way during my eighteen years at Harvard. Most of them, I am sure,
were the direct result of my position rather than of anything I had done.

Oberlin awarded me an honorary degree in 1939, not because I had
turned down the position of librarian there twelve years earlier, but
because it gave them an opportunity to honor a graduate who had
become the head of the country's largest university library. I believe it
was also because Oberlin realized that it had failed to award an honorary
degree to Azariah Smith Root, with whom I had worked eight years in
my early career. He did a great deal for the College during his forty
years of librarianship there. He died unexpectedly and prematurely,
and I think the Oberlin administration regretted that it had not had the
opportunity to award him an honorary degree, realizing the importance
of its Library and of what he had accomplished in it with limited funds.
During his forty years there he had built the collection from one of a
few thousand volumes to the largest and most heavily used college (as
distinguished from university) library collection in the country, if we
exclude Dartmouth, which is really a university. His standing as a
librarian was demonstrated by his election as President of the American
Library Association in 1921, and by the action of the Carnegie Corporation in endowing his position after his death. Only the President
at Oberlin, incidentally, received a higher salary. William Warner
Bishop, who was widely recognized as the best of our university librarians during his time, wrote that, when he was looking for a professor
for his newly-organized library school at the University of Michigan,
Root would have been the ideal candidate for the position and better
than anyone else in the country. It should be remembered also that
when Mary Wright Plummer, Principal of the Library School at the
New York Public Library, was unable to continue in her position, Root
was chosen to serve in her place for a year and to help in finding a
successor; as a result, I spent that year, 1916-17, as Acting Librarian at
Oberlin. My only regret regarding my honorary degree from Oberlin
is that it came just a year after the death of my first wife, Martha
Gerrish Metcalf, and that she, an Oberlin graduate who had worked in
the Library, did not know about it.

In 1944, I became President of the American Documentation Institute, which is now the American Society for Information Science
(ASIS). I had been interested in the Institute from the beginning, and,
as Chairman of the American Library Association's Committee on the
Photographic Reproduction of Library Materials, I was instrumental in
persuading the Carnegie Corporation to support the Institute, during

one of its critical early years, by paying the salary of an able administrator who could keep Watson Davis, the Editor of *Science News Letter*, on the right track. Davis was a man of great imagination and initiative in the field.

In connection with this work, the Rockefeller Foundation sent me in 1938 to the meetings of the International Documentation Institute in Oxford and London, as reported in Chapter 4. This assignment brought with it an elaborate document, in some ways resembling those presented to recipients of honorary degrees, signed by Cordell Hull, the Secretary of State.

I had completely forgotten that I had ever been President of the organization that became the American Society for Information Science until a few years ago, when I was asked to send a photograph to be placed with those of other presidents from the beginning of the Society.

Another elaborate document, dated 23 December 1943, prepared for the United States Department of War and signed by Robert Patterson, Secretary of War, set forth my appointment and my patriotic work in a position of trust and responsibility for the Army Medical Library. There was a gold seal, and there were signatures of Colonel Jones, the Librarian there, and Major General Kirk, the Surgeon General, a record of my patriotism, integrity, and high accomplishments, and a statement that I was to be an honorary consultant for as long as it was my pleasure to serve. Service continued, I might add, during the time I helped to plan the new library in Bethesda, which was called the National Library of Medicine by this time.

I ran across these awards from the Government recently while going through old files in my basement. Fortunately they had not been damaged by three floods in my basement during the past forty-five years.

Yale University, with a laudable desire to call attention to its Library and special collections, arranged in the autumn of 1946 for a special convocation to honor representatives of a number of great libraries. The Librarian of Harvard could not be ignored, since Harvard had the only university library larger than Yale's. I was particularly pleased because my good friend and mentor, Harry Lydenberg, and the Librarian of Congress, Luther Evans, were also awarded honorary degrees. Elinor was pleased because her father had received an honorary degree from Yale at a special convocation in the autumn of 1901, almost exactly forty-five years earlier.

Yale treated us royally. We were watched over by Dr. Fulton, who had been at Harvard but left for New Haven at the time Dr. Cushing moved from the Harvard Medical School to the Yale Medical School, where he was permitted to teach and operate after Harvard's regular retirement age for surgeons. Both Fulton and Cushing were very much interested in libraries, and did their best to build up Yale's Medical Library, to which they brought Fred Kilgour as Librarian in 1948, after he left the Office of Strategic Services. Fred, as reported in Chapter 11, had been my first assistant at Harvard.

Harvard awarded me an LL.D. at its Commencement in 1951. I was naturally very much pleased because I regarded it as recognition of the importance of the Library to the University, and an indication that the Lamont Library, the first of its kind, was a success.

The degree from Harvard made it easier for me during the years that followed to recommend an honorary degree for Harry Lydenberg, the retired Director of the New York Public Library, whom I regarded as the greatest librarian of his generation. I was finally told that the Corporation's Committee on Honorary Degrees felt that, while he deserved one, he was now too old. He became eighty in 1954, and had graduated from Harvard in 1896. During his College days, he had worked in the Library under Justin Winsor, who hoped that he would stay after his graduation. However, John Shaw Billings, the first Director of the New York Public Library, persuaded Lydenberg to come to New York, which was to prove very fortunate for me during my years there from 1913 to 1937.

The University of Toronto, which is the largest university in Canada and has much the largest library in the country, gave me an honorary degree in 1954. I had done some consulting work on an addition to its old building and on the library school in Toronto. In 1954, the University decided to call attention to its Library by arranging for a special library convocation at which it also honored representatives of a number of Canadian and European universities.

Wilhelm Munthe of Norway's National and University Library was asked to represent the Continental universities. J. N. L. Myres of the Bodleian Library at Oxford represented the British, and W. Kaye Lamb, who had come from the University of British Columbia to Ottawa as National Archivist and who became the National Librarian, represented Canada. As Librarian of Harvard, I was chosen from the United States.

Elinor and I had hoped to see Munthe in Oslo in 1950, but we reached Norway during July, when Norwegians vacation if possible. In Chapter 18, I have mentioned the book of his that I reviewed for the *Library Quarterly*. I was delighted to find that he was coming to Boston after the Toronto convocation, and we were able to persuade him to come to our home in Belmont. Doug and Rene Bryant were with us when he arrived, and we had a delightful time together. I remember that one of us asked him if he skied. He replied that you might say he was born on skies, and had continued to use them, though he was beyond what is generally considered the age for skiing. We spoke also of the way degrees were conferred at Toronto, where those receiving the Ph.D. knelt before the President of the University while he placed his hand over their heads. Those who were given honorary degrees, fortunately for most of them, did not kneel; but Munthe dropped to his knees to show how it ought to be done, and then stood as readily as a young man.

During World War II, I had been greatly interested in what was happening to European libraries that had some of their collections destroyed and were unable in many cases to acquire current publications. Harvard put aside a great number of duplicates in the hope that they could be used after the war to help these libraries, and many of them were sent to Norway when peace came. In recognition of this, the King of Norway decided to make me a Knight of St. Olaf, First Class.

One morning Bill Jackson called Elinor at home and asked if we had champagne glasses that she could bring to the Library. When she replied that we did not, he urged that she come in anyway for a special ceremony. At the appointed time, Jackson came to my office with the Norwegian Consul in Boston, who presented a medal that I was entitled to wear as a Knight of the First Class in the Order of St. Olaf, and with appropriate ceremony attached it to the lapel of my coat. He also gave me a button that would indicate my new title less conspicuously. In the box that had contained the medal there was a document explaining that, on my death, it was to be returned to the King of Norway.

Chapter 21

Assignments Resulting from My Position at Harvard

BOSTON PUBLIC LIBRARY VISITING COMMITTEE

I T WAS DURING my second or third year at Harvard that I became a member of the Visiting Committee of the Boston Public Library. Abbott Lawrence Lowell, President *Emeritus* of Harvard, was another of the members. It was a year, like those that have occurred all too frequently in Boston, when the City was attempting to reduce library appropriations. The authorities seemed to believe that the easiest way for the Library to cut its budget would be to buy fewer books. Lowell agreed, saying that the Library had a very large number of volumes that, he was sure, none of its patrons had read; he felt sure that no one would have any difficulty in finding something to read there that would interest him.

With some hesitation, I spoke up and said that our experience in the New York Public Library had indicated that a cut of $100,000 in the book appropriation for the Circulation Department resulted in a reduction of one million volumes a year in circulation, which indicated that the Library was losing a good deal of its importance and usefulness to its patrons. It meant also that many of the important books that were not purchased when new would become unavailable later or, if available, would cost more. I won out; any substantial reductions in the budget were made in places other than acquisitions.

Naturally I feared that Lowell would take a violent dislike to me. I had been told that he had been upset at the time of the dedication of the Widener building in 1915, when the Director of the Library, Archibald Cary Coolidge, said to him as they left the ceremony, "It's time to begin planning what we will do when Widener is full." Coolidge realized that it had taken many years to replace Gore hall, Widener's predecessor, and feared that a similar problem would arise again. Lowell and

Coolidge had been close friends up to that time, but I have been told that they never were thereafter.

I am glad to be able to report that I saw Lowell from time to time until his death in 1943, and he was always friendly, as he was also with Elinor at the Boston Athenaeum. I should add that Lowell, after he retired, at no time interfered with the operation of the Harvard Library, to say nothing of the University as a whole, something that too many retired administrators have been inclined to do.

MASSACHUSETTS STATE LIBRARY TRUSTEE

When Professor Samuel Eliot Morison was appointed Historian of the Navy by President Roosevelt and began work on his great fifteen-volume *History of United States Naval Operations in World War II*, he had to give up his assignment as a trustee of the Massachusetts State Library. I was appointed to take his place and, with one minor exception, was reappointed term after term until my year-long trip around the world in 1958–59. Daniel Marsh, President and later Chancellor of Boston University, was Chairman of the Board of Trustees throughout this period. Marsh, it will be remembered, had dealt magnificently with Boston University's problems over a long period, and he made a very satisfactory Chairman when circumstances were difficult. Dennis Dooley, the State Librarian, had no previous library experience; but he had been Dean of the Law School at Boston College, and knew enough about State politics to manage amazingly well during the difficult years that followed, probably better than any professional librarian then available would have been able to do.

The other members of the board changed from time to time. I remember particularly that one of them during my first term was Charles Townsend Copeland. He was then eighty-two, and had retired fourteen years earlier as Boylston Professor of Rhetoric and Oratory at Harvard; he was one of the legendary characters in the Harvard faculty of his time. I had already had two interesting experiences with him.

Soon after I came to Harvard, Copeland called me one evening and said, "I've heard about you and I want to see you. Please come to my apartment on Concord Avenue tomorrow at 7:30 for the evening." When I told him I had already made arrangements for that evening, he said, "I'm an old man and, of course, you must come to see me at the time I suggest." I had heard about Copey, and thought I had better shift the previous appointment; I did so, and spent an interesting evening with him.

A little later he invited me to have dinner with him at the Commander Hotel in Cambridge to meet his nephew, Charles F. Dunbar, a grandson of the well-known Harvard economist whose textbook on money and banking I had used in my college days. I was glad to meet him, and next year, when my daughter Margaret was at the Katharine Gibbs business school in Boston, she found that the person in charge was Katherine Dunbar, Charles Dunbar's wife. Seven years later, when Maxwell Small, now Margaret's husband, joined the staff of the Brookhaven National Laboratory in Bellport, Long Island, they found that the Dunbars were next-door neighbors, and they were close friends for more than thirty years thereafter. Charles was Secretary and legal counsel of the Laboratory.

I had also to deal with Copey as a member of the Library Committee at the Harvard Freshman Union, where he was a problem because his ideas on book selection for that collection differed from those of the librarian there and from mine.

There were similar difficulties with Copeland at the Massachusetts State Library. He was interested only in book selection, and it seemed to me that he had little comprehension of the needs of a state library that was primarily for members of the Commonwealth's General Court and its other employees.

Copeland did not continue as a trustee very long, and I kept on working as closely as I could with President Marsh and Dennis Dooley. We were having a difficult time keeping the budget up to a level at which it could support a first-class state library, which the Massachusetts State Library had been until it became involved in politics early in the century.

My appointments as trustee were always for three-year terms. Governor Foster Furcolo did not reappoint me, selecting instead the librarian of one of the cities in Eastern Massachusetts that had appointed untrained and inexperienced librarians. This man was one of a group with whom, during my earlier days at Harvard, Andrew Osborn and I had worked informally, helping them to learn about the library problems they faced. When he discovered that I had not been reappointed in order to make a place for him, he went to the Governor, said that he was resigning, and insisted that I be reappointed. He had his way.

I might add that the head of the State Archives, like the State Librarian, had a difficult time throughout my terms as a Trustee. My acquaintance with the situation and my experience at Harvard and the New York Public Library made it possible for some of us at Harvard to learn of the theft from the State Archives of a very valuable letter written by Peter Stuyvesant, the Dutch Governor of New Amsterdam before it became New York, to officials in Massachusetts. When he found that it must have been stolen, a dealer brought it to Bill Jackson. Then, accompanied by a number of other librarians from the Boston area, I had the pleasure of going to the Governor and giving him the letter, together with a plea for better care and operation of the State's valuable archival collections.

STOCKHOLDER OF THE HARVARD COOPERATIVE SOCIETY

Another assignment resulting from the war came when one of the stockholders of the Harvard Cooperative Society resigned because he had been called for war service. If I remember correctly it was Professor Morison, and I was his replacement here as well as on the Board of Trustees of the State Library. The Harvard Coop, as it is known, was required by law to have stockholders, though they were strictly "dummies," with no financial stake in the non-profit organization. They met several times a year and had luncheon together at the Harvard Faculty Club; during the wartime period of food rationing, a roast was provided as a special treat. We had no tasks to perform except to approve or, theoretically, disapprove the actions of administrative officers of the Coop, and to vote on the size of the rebate to be given at the end of each fiscal year to members of the Society.

The assignment gave me some information about the operation of a large retail store; the Coop, with its main store at Harvard Square and branches at the Harvard Business School and MIT, was the largest business enterprise in Cambridge unless one counts educational institutions. One of the stockholders was the Treasurer (Bursar) at MIT, with whom I had worked closely when we were both members of the Council of the American Academy of Arts and Sciences. Another was Professor Andrew James Casner of the Law School, a specialist in estate planning who has been a good and useful friend to me for forty years.

THE AMERICAN ACADEMY OF ARTS AND SCIENCES
AND THE LINDA HALL LIBRARY

My membership in the Shop Club, for which I was proposed by Harlow Shapley, has been mentioned in Chapter 1. Some seven years later, when he was President of the American Academy of Arts and Sciences, Shapley asked me to look into problems presented by the Academy's Library. The Academy is the second oldest learned society in this country, preceded only by the American Philosophical Society, which was founded by Benjamin Franklin in Philadelphia in 1743. The Academy, founded in 1780, had as its first president James Bowdoin, for whom Bowdoin College was named; its second President was John Adams, who was also the second President of the United States, and he continued to preside over the Academy until 1814, serving much longer than any of his successors. While the Academy has always been national in scope, a large portion of its membership, even as late as the 1940s, was made up of residents of New England, many of them from Harvard, MIT, and other colleges and universities in the area. This has changed during the past forty years. When I first became acquainted with it, the Academy occupied a building on Newbury Street in Boston. There was no possible way of adding to it. A large percentage of the space was reserved for an auditorium in which dinners and monthly meetings were held throughout the the academic year. Practically all the rest of the building was taken up by the Academy's Library, which consisted largely of long files of learned society publications from all over the world; these had been received during the preceding 160 years in exchange for the Academy's publications.

Harlow Shapley, who was President of the Academy from 1939 to 1944, had come to realize that something needed to be done about space if the Academy were to broaden its activities as he and the Council wanted to do. He knew of my struggles with the space problem at Harvard and asked me if I would be willing to look into the situation at the Academy. As in the case of my Pennsylvania assignment, I asked him if he would approve of my arranging to have Harry Lydenberg study the problem with me. Adding Lydenberg's name to my report would add considerable weight to it. Harry came up from Washington and spent some time with me at the Newbury Street building. Our most important findings were that: (1) Fewer than twenty volumes had been used by members during the previous year; and (2) A large share of the Academy's income was spent for binding and taking care of the collection.

We reported that almost everything in the collection could be found in other libraries available to the Academy's members. We recommended that, after any volumes not already available in a library in Eastern Massachusetts had been transferred to one of these libraries, the Academy should try to dispose of the rest of its collection to a library that would purchase it *en bloc* at a reasonable price. We hoped and believed that this could be done to advantage, and the the money received would help the Academy to carry out its plans for the future.

As a reward (?) for my services, I was asked to find a way to dispose of the collection for a satisfactory price, the larger the better, of course.

The Academy assignment came to me at almost the same time that the brilliant young Director of the New England Museum of Natural History, Bradford Washburn, had decided that something needed to be done about the Museum's Library, which was made up of a more miscellaneous collection of scientific publications than the Academy's, and which was used little more than the Academy's, perhaps even less. He had decided that the Museum ought to dispose of its building on Berkeley Street, less than two blocks from the Academy, by selling it to Bonwit Teller, which was looking for space in which to establish a retail store in Boston. With returns from the sale of the building and the library, the Museum planned to build a new and much more satisfactory structure, which could be enlarged and would be located where more parking space was available. Washburn and his trustees felt that the Library, which was large and expensive to maintain, should be replaced by a much smaller but more popular collection selected with younger readers in mind.

The Museum, which is now the Museum of Science, found a site for its new building on made land facing the bridge from Boston to Cambridge where the Charles River is dammed up. Washburn also found a purchaser for the collection; it was acquired, with money from the Edward Doheny bequest, by the University of Southern California Library. When the matter was called to my attention before the contract for sale had been signed, I suggested, as in the case of the Academy, that nothing be sent from the Museum library that was not in another library in Eastern Massachusetts.

In both cases, we included as Eastern Massachusetts institutions, in addition to Harvard and MIT, the Boston Public library, Boston Athenaeum, and Marine Biological Library at Woods Hole, where there was a large collection with a good deal of material not in other libraries. Washburn readily agreed, and the libraries that have been mentioned began checking their collections with catalogs of both the Academy and the Museum. I assigned each work that was to be retained in this area to the library that had the strongest collection on that work's specific subject.

At just this time I was fortunate enough to have a visit from Malcolm Wyer, then Librarian of the Denver Public Library and Director of the University of Denver Libraries, who had been President of the American Library Association in 1936–37 and was a half-brother of James I. Wyer, the father-in-law of one of my nephews. As I remember it, he was accompanied by Carl Milam, Executive Secretary of the ALA, with whom I had become well acquainted in the course of my Association activities.

I should add, however, that Wyer, in *Books and People: Short Anecdotes From a Long Experience* (published by the Old West Publishing Company in 1964), wrote that he came with Joseph C. Shipman, not Carl Milam. Shipman, who was to be Librarian of the Linda Hall library, had previously been head of the science collection and then Associate Librarian of the Enoch Pratt Free Library in Baltimore. I must realize that I am writing at the age of ninety-four while Malcolm was only eighty-seven when his book was published.

In any case, I still think that when Wyer came to see me the first time he was with Carl Milam. They had been sent by the Trustees of the Linda Hall Foundation, which had a multi-million-dollar fund derived from the bequest of H. F. Hall of the Hall-Baker Grain Company. The trustees had decided to use the fund to finance a reference library in Kansas City, Missouri. As I remember it, Wyer and Milam had recommended that this be a science library, because at that time there was no first-class science library between Chicago and the Pacific Coast. They hoped that I would have some suggestions to make. I did, of course. It should be easy to imagine my pleasure at finding a way to dispose of the Library of the American Academy.

After discussion and consultation with the President and other officers of the Academy and with the Linda Hall trustees, it was agreed that the new library in Kansas City would take all of the Academy's library material with the exception of a comparatively small collection of the Academy's historical archives and of volumes not to be found in an Eastern Massachusetts library. Within a comparatively short time the contract for sale was agreed upon; Malcolm reports that the amount was $320,000, but I think it was $300,000. This was to be added to the Academy's endowment. It was agreed also that, in the years to come, current learned society publications received on exchange by the Academy would be sent to the Linda Hall Library in return for an annual payment of $3,000 to the Academy.

Looking back at what seemed to me and the Academy's officers to be a good price at the time, I realize that the Academy's collection could easily be sold today for something closer to $3,000,000 than $300,000, just as I realize that the duplicate set of Audubon that Harvard sold in the early 1940s, with my approval and Bill Jackson's, for $12,000 might sell today for close to $1,000,000. Times and prices do change! Receipt of $300,000 by the Academy enabled it to start on plans that ultimately resulted in publication of its quarterly, *Daedalus*.

The Museum of Science has prospered in its new location, becoming one of the most successful and most useful science museums in the country, with a tremendous number of visitors every year. A very large share of the credit belongs to Bradford Washburn, who has been an innovative director and an amazingly successful money-raiser.

The Academy also has prospered, thanks to the work of a series of capable presidents. Not long after the sale of its Library, an opportunity came to it to use the Brandegee house in Newton, where it established its headquarters for more than a generation. Then, in time for its bicentennial year, it completed a new home designed for it in Norton's Woods in Cambridge, on the site of the residence once occupied by Charles Eliot Norton and later by Paul Sachs. The membership has been enlarged, with additions from all parts of the United States and from foreign countries; in addition to monthly meeetings in Cambridge through the academic year, there are now regular meetings in the Midwest and on the Pacific Coast.

In 1945 I was elected to the Academy, and became a member of its Council a year or two later. There I had the pleasure of sitting beside George Kennan, the prominent diplomat, who was a nephew and namesake of the George Kennan with whom I was acquainted in New York. The elder Kennan, as has been mentioned in Part II, chapter 6, gave the New York Public Library his great collection of material on Russian Siberia.

While serving on the Council, I was asked to be Chairman of the committee to reclassify the membership. The old classification had remained unchanged over the years while great changes were taking place in scholarly disciplines. With the aid of a very satisfactory committee, the new classification was drawn up, and the council approved it. I should add, however, that the life of the new classification proved to be much shorter than that of the old; it has already been replaced. I now find myself in Class III (Social Arts and Sciences), Section 6 (Educational and Scientific Administration). In October 1981 there 107 active members in that section, and my election to membership in 1945 took place before that of any of the other 106. When I realized that, at the time of my election I was well along in years (fifty-six), I was a bit appalled.

Two other results of sale of the collections of the American Academy and the Museum of Science seem to be worth recording. Both libraries had used shelving of various kinds. We found that some of the shelving could be moved, and it was transferred to Harvard, where it has been used in the sub-basement of Widener and in other Harvard libraries where it could be installed for less than the cost of new shelving.

My connection with the Linda Hall Library did not end with the acquisition of its basic collection. I was asked to help in picking the site for its building and in planning that building. This was an interesting assignment because the requirements of the library were quite different from those of any library with which I had worked up to that time.

During the summer of 1953, Elinor and I drove to the American Library Association conference in Los Angeles and had a wonderful trip. On the way out, we stopped in national parks in Colorado, Arizona, and Utah. We drove across the desert from Las Vegas to Los Angeles in the night to avoid the extreme heat; but, instead of suffering from the heat, we were delighted to find a place where we could get some hot coffee to warm us up.

After the conference, we drove up the coast to Oregon and Washington, states that I had not visited before, seeing the sights along the way, stopping with a nephew in Pasco, Washington, and then going on through Idaho over the Bitterroot Mountains. We stopped at Quartz, Montana, where I had spent the summer of 1907 driving stakes where I was instructed to put them, marking the route of the Chicago, Milwaukee, St. Paul, and Pacific Railroad, our last transcontinental railroad. I like to say that I made sure that the railroad was put where I had told them to put it.

After a few delightful days in Glacier National Park, we stopped at Grand Forks to see the comparatively new, modular building of the University of North Dakota Library. There I found a message waiting for me, saying that I was wanted in Kansas City to meet, as soon as possible, with Linda Hall trustees, architects, and the Librarian. We hurried on, stopping for only a few hours with Carl Milam at the home to which he had retired after his work as Librarian of the United Nations. Leaving Elinor with my brother in Chicago, I flew to Kansas City, where I found everyone connected with the Linda Hall library easy to work with.

This was one of my first experiences with planning a library building that materialized satisfactorily. It was dedicated at the time of the Kansas City ALA conference in 1957, and a reception for members of the Association was held one evening in the new building. I was not content with seeing only the inside; a large group of librarians were waiting to go in when we arrived, so I took the opportunity to walk around the building in the dark. The next morning I was uncomfortable from chigger bites, my first and only experience with them.

Chapter 22

Other Consultation Assignments of the 1940s

I N ONE OF MY FIRST talks with President Conant, as reported in Chapter 10, I told him that I would want to continue my work with the Association of Research Libraries and the American Library Association, and would want also to spend a day or more each year in at least two other research libraries in order to keep in touch with what was going on in my profession. He readily approved. At the time I had no idea of the extent to which I would become involved in special assignments at Harvard, which would include membership on three *ad hoc* University committees, as reported in Chapter 14. I had not realized that I would be working on three new library buildings at Harvard that were constructed during the 1940s, the New England Deposit Library, Houghton, and Lamont, of which I have written in Chapters 6, 7, and 8. I had not even dreamed that I would help to start the *Harvard Library Bulletin* in 1947 and contribute eight articles to it by the end of 1949.

In addition, beginning early in the war years, there was the extensive work I did for what was then the Surgeon General's library, to say nothing of the study of some fifty Army and Navy libraries in Washington (Chapter 16). Chapter 15 has told of activities involving the Library of Congress, and my month-long assignment in Peru and Colombia is reported in Chapter 17. The Farmington Plan and related affairs are the subject of Chapter 18. All of these things were well beyond my horizon during my first years at Harvard. Moreover, I did not then realize that I would become a member of the Executive Board of the American Library Association and would then have three years as President-Elect, President, and Past-President of the Association. For several of the outside assignments that took me away from Cambridge for considerable periods, I received honoraria in amounts that would seem minuscule today, but which, as agreed, I turned over to the University.

From the foregoing account, it might seem that I was too active in work outside the Harvard Library; but there were six other non-Harvard assignments that have not been described thus far. Each, I believe, was useful to me; I hope that each was also of some value to libraries generally and not without some benefit to Harvard.

THE UNIVERSITY OF ILLINOIS LIBRARY SCHOOL

Carl White had become Director of the University of Illinois Library and head of the Library School there in 1941, following the retirement of Phineas Windsor. The next year, White decided that a study of the school by outsiders would be useful. He asked me to serve as Chairman of a three-man team to do the job. It was understood that, while our primary purpose would be to help the Illinois school plan for the future, we should also consider library schools in general. The two other surveyors were Andrew Osborn of the Harvard library staff, and John Dale Russell, a professor of education and Dean of Students at the University of Chicago. Our report was divided into two distinct parts, a theoretical one dealing with American standards and ideals for the education of librarians, and one that applied the theoretical conclusions to the Illinois school.

We worked intermittently for nearly two years before submitting a two-volume mimeographed report on 1 May 1943. No one of us was at that time directly connected with a library school, but each of us had been involved in professional training, and we knew that part of the responsibility for recruitment and training of librarians ought to be assumed by librarians in the field.

I must confess that, during the forty years that have intervened, I had forgotten all the details of the study except that most of the work was done by the other two surveyors, and that my chief problem consisted of getting them to agree on a report. Osborn and Russell gave particular attention to methods of instruction and library-school operation, while I concerned myself chiefly with administrative aspects.

Before writing this chapter, I looked over the two bound volumes of typescript. I do not have the printed version of a portion of the report that was published by the University of Illinois Press as *The Program of Instruction in Library Schools*; this ran to only 140 pages, while the two volumes of typescript in my possession include 410 pages. The first of these volumes begins with an introduction, "Fifty Years in Education for Librarianship," followed by three parts, "The First Year's Program of Instruction," "The Second Year's Program of Instruction," and "Some

Aspects of Library School Administration." This third section is divided into three chapters: "Executive and Legislative Functions," "Faculty," and "Problems of Student Personnel."

The second volume includes a summary of a program and recommendations for the University of Illinois Library School, followed by seven appendices, entitled: "The First Year Program of Instruction," "The Second Year Library School," "Some Aspects of the Administration of the Library School," "Finance and Budgetary Procedures," "Faculty," "Problems of Student Personnel," and "Looking for Effective Service."

If I am not mistaken, these volumes represented the most detailed study of library education that had been made since Charles C. Williamson's monumental report of 1923, twenty years earlier. In view of the time and thought that the surveyors devoted to it, I hope that the results were of some value to the profession; but I must admit that I have very little memory of results, except that I was given an opportunity to become acquainted with Errett McDiarmid, who was a professor in the Illinois school at the time, and later became Director of the Library and Library School at the University of Minnesota. A few years afterward, as will be reported in a later section of this chapter, he asked me to study his problems at Minnesota.

Nearly forty years later, I might add, the Illinois report was called to my attention by Professor Peter Hernon of the Simmons Library School, and, at about the same time I read Sarah K. Vann's review article, "Conant and Williamson," in the October 1981 *Library Quarterly*. This dealt with Ralph W. Conant's report, *A Study of the Education of Librarians*, published in 1980 by the MIT Press. Apparently the Illinois report was not considered important enough to be mentioned in the Conant study.

THE WISCONSIN STATE HISTORICAL SOCIETY AND THE UNIVERSITY OF WISCONSIN LIBRARY

Sometime in the first half of 1943, soon after the Illinois report had been completed, Theodore C. Blegen, Dean of the Graduate School of the University of Minnesota, and I were asked to study the problems faced by the two Wisconsin libraries that jointly occupied a building on the campus of the University of Wisconsin. The Historical Society Library was very strong in printed and manuscript material on American history; it also had collections in a number of other fields that it had neglected for ten years or more. Both libraries depended almost entirely on the State of Wisconsin for financial support to provide staff, acquisitions, and accommodations for books and readers.

The Wisconsin State Historical Society, largely thanks to the work of Reuben Gold Thwaites, had been one of the great state historical societies in earlier years. He had been its Superintendent for many years, and was President of the American Library Association in 1899-1900. The University Library, in part at least because of Professor Richard Ely, an economist who had been at the University for many years, and Professor Frederick Jackson Turner, who was in the History Department at Wisconsin until Harvard took him away in 1910, had developed until, by 1922, it was larger, if one included holdings of the Historical Society Library, than the library at Illinois, Michigan, or any of the other midwestern universities.

Since the early 1920s, however, both libraries had been steadily falling back. During the ten years from 1922 to 1933, the two libraries on the Wisconsin campus had increased in size by only thirty-five percent, while those at Illinois and Michigan had increased by ninety percent. For the twenty years ending in 1942, the figure for the Wisconsin libraries was fifty-eight percent, while their rival at Minnesota had almost tripled in size. (I might add that Cornell and the University of Pennsylvania, with both of which I became involved later, were in a situation similar to Wisconsin's, though not quite as serious.)

Inadequate growth, combined with crowded conditions in the library building and dissatisfaction of faculty and students, had prompted President Dykstra to decide that something must be done. He had been City Manager in Cincinnati and a successful administrator at the University of California. He knew that Blegen had formerly been in charge of the Minnesota Historical Society, which was one of the better state historical societies and was not connected with a university. I suppose that I was called upon because I was President of the American Library Association that year.

Blegen and I looked into the situation carefully. In our report, of which I have a typewritten copy in my files, we recommended construction of an addition to the joint library building as well as a separate undergraduate library; the latter was something I was hoping to obtain at Harvard, but Lamont was still five years in the future. We also emphasized the urgent need for more adequate book appropriations and for additional staff to catalog the new acquisitions.

Blegen had to return to Minneapolis before our report was completed, but he did much of the preparation. I found him to be an agreeable companion, and his knowledge of libraries and their problems was extraordinarily good. As I have told in the second section of Chapter 15, I thought so well of him that I urged his appointment to succeed MacLeish as Librarian of Congress.

I had an opportunity for a long talk with President Dykstra before I returned to Cambridge. I found that he knew and liked the Librarian, Gilbert Doane, and was accustomed to play golf with him on Saturday afternoons. But, when I spoke to him about the very serious deficiencies in book appropriations, he said that Doane had never said anything to him about this. Our conversation was in the spring — April, if I remember correctly — and Dykstra had a $40,000 surplus in the university budget for that academic year. He immediately turned it over to the library for the purchase of books, more than doubling the amount that had been appropriated for the full year. I was satisfied that we had accomplished something. The amount budgeted for purchases that year had been $36,500, having declined from more than $70,000 in 1930-31 and more than $62,000 in 1935–36, during the depths of the great depression.

THE COLUMBIA UNIVERSITY LIBRARY

Charles C. Williamson had become Director of the Columbia University Library and Dean of the School of Library Service that he established there in 1926. During the late 1920s and early 1930s, he was able to help plan the Butler Library, which was completed at about the same time as the Sterling Library at Yale. His report of 1923 on library schools had been a landmark in the history of education for librarianship. He was a good administrator, but inclined to perfectionism, and was perhaps a little stubborn in his dealings with faculty and students, by whom he was not always well liked. In the spring of 1938, to the surprise of many, he was defeated by Ralph Munn, a much younger man, for the presidency of the American Library Association. During his later years at Columbia, he had been handicapped by the aftermath of a serious operation. As reported in Part II, Chapter 13, I had decided in 1941 not to leave Harvard and go to Columbia as his successor.

In 1943, not long after the survey of the Illinois Library School had been completed, Carl White went from Illinois to Columbia to succeed Williamson, and decided the next year that he would like to have studies of both the library school and the Library. The technical processes departments were surveyed by Maurice F. Tauber, who was then at the University of Chicago, and L. Quincy Mumford, who was then in charge of technical processes at the New York Public Library.

White then asked Donald Coney, Librarian of the University of Texas, to serve as Chairman of a committee to study the library's other problems. The members of Coney's committee were Louis Round Wilson, who had gone back to the University of North Carolina after his ten years as Dean of the University of Chicago's Graduate Library School, and I. Each surveyor took responsibility for specific sections of the report, which was to cover ten subjects. Coney dealt with the first four, government, organization, personnel, and accounting. Wilson took two, the program for libraries and the School of Library Service. I was responsible for the remaining four sections, the libraries in the future of the building program of the University, the library budget and library costs, the privileges of the library, and library exhibits. We spent about ten days on the report in the late winter of 1944, talking with staff members in various libraries of the University and the School of Library Service, with administrative officers of the University, and with members of the faculty. We observed the operation of two units, the main University Library and the School of Library Service. We felt that we were unable, in the time available, to probe deeply into many of the problems or to gather extensive data for our study. Our purpose was to become as familiar as possible with the problems and to suggest solutions in the light of our own experience.

Reports on the various sections were written independently but were read by all three of us; data and recommendations were discussed while we were together at Columbia. The report, therefore, can properly be regarded as a joint product, for which the surveyors were jointly responsible. We had no difficulty in agreeing with each other; this was quite different from the situation at Illinois, which was the only survey reported here in which the surveyors found it hard to reach agreement.

THE UNIVERSITY OF PENNSYLVANIA LIBRARY

It was in December 1944 that Charles David, Director of the University of Pennsylvania Library, asked me to study the situation in his library. I had seen it for the first time back in the 1920s, when I had gone to Philadelphia with Charles McCombs to see it and the new Philadelphia Free Library building, with its unusual steel chairs and tables, which had been finished shortly before. I knew that the library situation at the University of Pennsylvania had been a serious one for years. The library was still occupying a building that, I had been told, was called "a symphony in brick" by H. H. Furness, who was the editor of the well-known variorum edition of Shakespeare and was also the architect's brother. By the standards of the 1940s, to say nothing of today's, it was a very unsatisfactory building. It had been constructed in the 1890s. Much of the collection was stored in the basement, in an area known locally as "the Catacombs." Other serious problems included the fact that it was not far from the Pennsylvania Railroad track, and prevailing winds blew dirt and soot into the library windows, which were open much of the time in order to provide ventilation. The roof tended to leak when there was rain.

C. Seymour Thompson had been Librarian in the 1930s, but he had been unable to improve the situation, and Charles David was appointed Director in 1940. He was to become one of the most remarkable of our country's librarians. He was born in the Midwest and received much of his education there before earning a Ph.D. at Harvard and winning a Rhodes Scholarship. He had been professor of European history at Bryn Mawr for years, and was a leading spirit in establishment of the Philadelphia Bibliographical Center, which compiled and maintained a regional union catalog, the first of its kind in the country and perhaps the most successful. As a result, while still a professor at Bryn Mawr, he was asked to serve as Librarian of the University of Pennsylvania, and he held both positions for six years, while also continuing work on the union catalog. Later in his career, in 1947, he succeeded Paul North Rice as Executive Secretary of the Association of Research Libraries. He continued at the University of Pennsylvania until he reached retirement age in the middle 1950s, but was unable to obtain a new library building. He had become interested in library building planning, however, and was co-editor, with Julian Boyd and John Burchard, of *Planning the University Library Building* (1949), a volume summarizing discussions at the first six meetings of the Cooperative Committee on Library Building Plans.

When he invited me study his library, I told him that I would like to serve as chairman of a committee for the purpose, and would like to ask Harry Lydenberg, who was still in Washington at the American Library Association's International Relations Office, and Ralph Beals, who was then at the University of Chicago Library and Graduate Library School, to serve with me. I barely knew Beals but had been impressed by him, and thought this would give me an opportunity to become better acquainted. He had been graduated from the University of California and, after earning an M.A. at Harvard, had taught at Harvard and New York University. He had been involved in work of the American Association for Adult Education, which had been sponsored by the Carnegie Corporation. Following a year at Chicago's Graduate Library School, he had been Assistant Librarian of the District of Columbia Public Library before returning to Chicago. Less than two years after our survey, he became Director of the New York Public Library, and it was good to be able to work with him before he went there.

Our survey recommended construction of a new building behind the present Library, replacing a still older structure there. We thought that satisfactory rehabilitation of the present building would be difficult if not impossible, particularly in view of its leaky roof. I was able to obtain an interview with the President of the University, but he was not particularly interested. He knew all too well that the University had inadequate funds and that an attempt at this time to raise money for a new building could not be counted on to be successful.

We also looked into the situation in the larger departmental libraries, some of which had outstanding collections.

Charles David and I disagreed on only one recommendation the surveyors made; this was that a check-out be installed at the exit. We had learned that, as at Harvard fifteen years earlier, a good many books were disappearing. He was afraid that this would discourage use; but, before I came down to his library the next time, he had changed his mind and an inspection desk had been provided.

I recall two other visits to Philadelphia before my retirement. One was during the celebration of the two hundredth anniversary of the University of Pennsylvania in 1950. It had been hoped that Winston Churchill would be able to attend and to speak. When Elinor and I agreed to come, I was told to bring my cap and gown because it was to be an academic affair. We were combining the trip with one to Greensboro, North Carolina, where we were visiting the Lydenbergs, who had settled there after he had finally retired, and where I was to speak at a North Carolina Library Association meeting, the first to which librarians from black colleges had been invited. The conference included a reception with refreshments in the library, and there was some apprehension about desegregation there; fortunately, however, no problems arose. We were very glad to see the new library building that was being occupied by Charles Adams, who had worked in the New York Public Library and at Columbia before becoming Librarian of the Women's State College in Greensboro.

We had driven down to North Carolina in our own car, and I had carried my cap and gown in and out of inns for some days before we reached Philadelphia and found that Churchill had been unable to keep his appointment and that we would not need academic garb.

Elinor was seated at dinner between Dr. A. S. W. Rosenbach, the noted rare-book dealer, and the British Consul in Philadelphia. She got along well with the latter; but Rosenbach was no longer in good shape physically and sat through most of the dinner staring at the wall in front of him. She finally got a word out of him when he asked, "Do you happen to know Bill Jackson, who is at Harvard?" She was able to respond, "Yes." And that ended their conversation.

The talks presented at the symposium celebrating the bicentennial of the University of Pennsylvania library were printed in a volume entitled *Changing Patterns of Scholarship and the Future of Research Libraries*, published by the University of Pennsylvania Press in 1951. On glancing through the volume recently, I was amazed to see how successful Charles David had been in persuading scholars and librarians to speak at the meeting, which included six sessions. Distinguished professors from Harvard, Yale, and the University of Pennsylvania took part, as well as Senator George W. Pepper, the President of the Federal Reserve Bank in Phildelphia. Librarians who gave papers included Verner Clapp, Ralph Ellsworth, Harry Lydenberg, Carl White, and Louis Round Wilson.

My own contribution was entitled "The Ever Expanding Demand for Materials and the Threatened Decline of Support: How Shall the Gap Be Filled?" This was a subject in which I had been interested ever since I went into the office at the New York Public Library in 1919 and began struggling with the library budget. In addition to the speakers, there were discussion panels for each of the sessions, and those who led them included Ralph Beals, Charles H. Brown, Donald Coney, Luther Evans, Warner Rice of Michigan, and Louis Wright of the Folger Library.

We were at the University of Pennsylvania Library again for the first week in July 1955, when the annual conference of the American Library Association was held during one of Philadelphia's hottest and most humid intervals. Elinor and I were assigned a hotel room that was not air conditioned or ventilated in any way; we were finally able to move to another room after two of the most uncomfortable nights I can remember.

Andrew Osborn and I had prepared a paper I read at this meeting in which we advocated as strongly as we could that the National Union Catalog at the Library of Congress be printed in book form. This paper was published in *College & Research Libraries* (Vol. XVII, No. 1) the following year, and I am glad to say that the catalog was finally printed.

I am glad also that the University of Pennsylvania finally constructed a new library building, though not until some years after Charles David's retirement. I was fortunate enough to have a part in its planning.

THE NEW YORK STATE LIBRARY AT ALBANY

It was in 1947 that Andrew Osborn and I were asked to make a survey of the New York State Library. Charles Gosnell, who had worked with me for years in the New York Public Library, had become Librarian of the State Library in 1945, succeeding R. W. G. Vail, who had been at the Library School of the New York Public Library and had worked in the Library on two separate occasions. He went to Albany from the American Antiquarian Society, and left the State Library to become Librarian of the New York Historical Society in New York City. He was a great collector of material on American history, and his interest was in collecting rather than administration, so Osborn and I could understand why Gosnell asked for our help.

We both knew Gosnell well from his New York Public Library days, and were glad to be able to work with him again. I was glad also to have an opportunity to look at the New York State Library building. This had been built after a disastrous fire in 1911 had completely destroyed the old building and its contents. I was interested in seeing the present state of the library in which Melvil Dewey, Edwin Hatfield Anderson, and their successors, all of whom I had known, had worked. A fine new collection had been assembled since the fire. In glancing through it, I was very much interested in finding some two thousand volumes that I had sent there from Oberlin on exchange in 1912. These were volumes that I had placed in the duplicate collection when I had charge of combining the Oberlin Union Library Association (the Library of the Student Literary Society) and the Oberlin College Library in 1908, after we had moved into the new library building.

Two other things interested me in the New York State Library building. I found there a type of carrel for individual seating that was different from any I had seen before, and quite different from what we called stalls in the Widener building. This proved to be useful to me in the late 1950s and the 1960s, when I was doing my best to provide individual seating for scholars in libraries throughout the United States and in many other countries.

The second thing that particularly interested me was the small storage room where, a few years earlier, several ranges of free-standing stacks that had not been fastened to the floor had fallen down like a house of

cards. Much greater disasters of a similar type were to happen thereafter, but I hope that no installation with which I have been involved
will have this misfortune.

THE UNIVERSITY OF MINNESOTA LIBRARY

I have mentioned the fact that I became acquainted with Errett
McDiarmid during the Illinois Survey, when he was a professor in the
Library School there. After he had gone to the University of Minnesota
as Director of the Library, he asked me to come to Minneapolis to
survey the situation. I suggested that I bring along David Clift, with
whom I had worked during my last six years at the New York Public
Library, after which he had been Williamson's assistant at Columbia.
Then, following war service and work as Deputy Head of the Library
of Congress Mission in 1946, Clift had gone to Yale as Associate
Librarian. I was always glad to be associated in a survey with a younger
man who would be able to do things that I could not do. Clift and I
worked together very well. Two years later, in 1951, he became Executive Secretary of the American Library Association, where he
remained until he retired in 1972.

I do not have a copy of the 18-page typewritten report that Clift and
I made on the University of Minnesota Library, but I remember that
the space situation was serious and that we recommended construction
of an addition to the central library building as well as an undergraduate
library adjacent to it. We also studied and reported on the University
of Minnesota Agricultural College, which is only a few miles away in
St. Paul. The proposed addition to the central Library was never built,
because it would have interfered with a main traffic corridor through a
busy part of the University.

Many years later, however, after McDiarmid had become a dean in
the University and Ned Stanford had succeeded him as Librarian, I was
called back to advise on planning. Working with Stanford and the
architect, I helped with a proposal for a completely new library building
on the other (west) side of the Mississippi River. There was also a new
bridge with two levels, one for vehicles and one below, protected from
the wind and snow of Minnesota winters, for pedestrians; this provided
easy access from the older part of the University to the new. I always
look back on this building with pleasure because it was one of the few
constructed during recent years for which the construction contract was
less than the architect's estimate. This made it possible to install an

escalator between the tunnel from the pedestrian level of the bridge and the main entrance to the Library.

I might add that, in my visits to the University in Minneapolis, I was particularly interested in the large underground garages that the University had provided, giving protection from the area's severe winters and solving, at least in part, one of the most serious problems faced by academic institutions all over the world today.

When McDiarmid left the University Library to become Dean of the College, the library profession lost one of its most promising members. He had been President of the American Library Association in 1948-49, and was the only one of our presidents I can remember who left librarianship for a different academic position, if we except Melvil Dewey, who left it after losing his position in Albany.

Chapter 23

Preparation for Retirement and Selection of a Successor

I KNEW, when I came to Harvard in 1937, that I must give up the New York Public Library's retirement plan, which had been adopted only a short time earlier. It was connected with the New York State pension plan and, unlike the TIAA plan used in many academic institutions, was not transferable. If I had continued in New York until my late sixties, I would have had a pension amounting to well over half my salary at the time of retirement — one percent for each year of service before the plan was adopted, and one and one-half percent for each year thereafter. By leaving New York and starting afresh, instead of having twenty-five years of credit for past service, I would receive a much smaller pension, but, at the age of forty-eight, this did not worry me.

I am not sure if I knew at that time just what Harvard's TIAA annuity plan would amount to, but I soon learned, if I did not know already, that I would have to retire not later than the first of September following my sixty-sixth birthday, that is, on 31 August 1955. In earlier years there had not been a definite age for retirement of Harvard administrators; but, as I understand it, President Conant believed that his two predecessors in office, Charles W. Eliot and A. Lawrence Lowell, had made a mistake by staying on until they were seventy-six. In order to make sure that he would not be tempted to continue after he reached his middle sixties, he asked the Corporation to rule that administrative officers must retire the summer after they became sixty-six. Professors might stay on longer under certain conditions.

I have always felt that this was a wise decision on Conant's part. As it turned out, he retired soon after his sixtieth birthday in order to become High Commissioner to Germany. As I have already mentioned, I was disappointed by this because, knowing that I was four years older than he, I had thought I would not have to work for another president, and I had been convinced before coming to Harvard that I could get along with him satisfactorily.

While I hoped that I would be physically and mentally able to continue work after I was sixty-six, I was sure that the Harvard rule was a good one; and I thought that an administrative officer who had deteriorated because of age or other reasons could damage his institution considerably more than a somewhat senile professor whose condition would adversely affect a smaller segment of the University. So I expected to retire in 1955, and tried to prepare for it in advance.

SELECTION OF A SUCCESSOR

I learned in January 1953 that President Conant was leaving almost immediately, though his term of service would not officially end until after Commencement that year. Nathan Pusey took over in September. Paul Buck, having resigned as Provost and Dean of the Faculty of Arts and Sciences, had gone back to teaching and research; McGeorge Bundy had replaced him as Dean, and I was to report to him as Librarian of Harvard College.

Early in September I had my first meeting with President Pusey and Dean Bundy; I had arranged the appointment in order to remind them that in two years I would reach the retirement age. I was bold enough to suggest that it was time for them to begin to look for my successor. In my opinion, I said, no man ought to be involved in the selection of his successor because, almost inevitably, he would be inclined to recommend someone with qualifications similar to his own. He would fail to realize that he had weak points, and one of the most important qualifications of his successor ought to be the ability to take care of things that he had failed to accomplish. I suggested that there were two reasons why they should look for my successor promptly. The first was that, when it became known that I would soon retire, they would be flooded with a large number of applications, and they might prefer not to struggle with applications from unqualified persons. The second was that it might be desirable to have the successor selected early enough to give him an opportunity to consult with me before I retired. I felt that I should have nothing to do with the Library after I gave up the office; I did not believe in the "dead hand."

The President and the Dean seemed to agree with me; but they asked me to give them a list of persons who, in my opinion, would be or should be the top candidates for the position, including any members of the Harvard Library staff who ought to be considered. I promised to provide such a list, and did so a few days later. It included four men then on the staff and a number of other American librarians. They then asked if I could tell them what I considered the desirable qualifications and characteristics for the Director of the University Library and Librarian of Harvard College. After hesitating a short time, I said, "The important thing is to find a good administrator who will have the confidence of the University administration and its faculty." Their next question, quite naturally, was, "Do you know anyone who has these qualifications?" I suppose I should have said, "No." Paul Buck was the only person I could think of who seemed to me to have them. I knew that he had wanted to go back to teaching and research and to get away from administration. He had told me this at the time he resigned his administrative duties. I decided that it was safe, blurted out "Paul Buck," and forgot about it for a full year.

I was disappointed when I heard nothing more about the search for a successor from either the President or the Dean as the months went by. Then, in October 1954, after plans had been completed for the Monticello Conference, of which I have written in Chapter 19, Elinor and I had gone to the Catskills, as had been my custom since the early 1920s, for our regular holiday. I received a telephone call there from President Pusey's office, saying that they had decided to announce the name of my successor some time during the next week, and asking me to come back to Cambridge to tell the staff about it before the news was released to the press.

I returned to Cambridge and went directly to the President's office, where he and Bundy told me that they were glad to be able to report that my successor would be Paul Buck. I was completely surprised, and gave a little gasp, realizing that the appointment of anyone other than a professional librarian would be criticized by many of my colleagues. I had expected the appointment of one of the top academic or research librarians of the country. Mac Bundy realized how surprised I was, and spoke gently, saying, "You remember, this was your suggestion."

I called the staff together and made the announcement. I knew that there were at least three members of the staff who hoped that they would be chosen, but no one of them ever complained to me about it. I was pleased that Paul Buck had already agreed to speak at the Monticello Conference and believed that this would be a good introduction for him to the academic librarians of the country. After the conference, Paul, who had already been assigned a study in Widener Library, came in to see me and said that he hoped we could spend a great deal of time together during the next ten months before I retired, talking over in detail the Library's problems, its staff, and their assignments. I readily agreed and spent at least an hour in his study several days a week, answering his questions and discussing Library matters.

I was not surprised that some librarians were upset because the man chosen as my successor was not a trained librarian. I particularly remember a letter expressing their point of view by Jerrold Orne, Librarian of the University of North Carolina, that appeared in a widely-read library periodical. Ten years later, after Paul had retired from the Library and gone back to teaching and research, I was greatly pleased when Jerrold wrote again to the same magazine to say that he had been mistaken in his earlier letter, and that Buck had been a very good choice.

I do not hesitate to say that Paul Buck accomplished a number of things I had been unable to do and that permanent improvements in the Library resulted. I remembered that Archibald MacLeish, who was opposed by many librarians when he was appointed Librarian of Congress, accomplished more than any trained librarian would have done during his five years in that position. I still believe in library training and think that in most cases a librarian should be appointed to head an academic or research library, but "Circumstances alter cases. No rule is so general, which admits not some exception."

REPORT ON THE HARVARD UNIVERSITY LIBRARY

Enough of these preliminaries! In the fall of 1954 it was time for me to make two major decisions. The first was to choose a special project on which to spend considerable time during my remaining months in the Library. The second was to keep in mind that I would not be content just to sit down and do nothing but read, something that I would be very happy doing, after retirement.

The first decision was that it would be desirable, with the aid of the staff, to make a rather detailed study of the present situation in the Library, and then go on from there to indicate what we believed to be the greatest needs for the future.

I have always thought that many administrators spend too much of their own time and take up too much time of their senior staff in committee work, but I knew that I needed help in preparing this report on the Library. Instead of having a formal committee, I called staff members together from time to time for discussion of specific subjects on which they were qualified to advise. For several months I met with them very frequently in my office. Ed Williams, who had been, and still is, so useful to me in many ways, kept the record, and the report was gone over word by word with the group as it was prepared.

In previous years I had known Thomas D. Morris of the firm of Cresap, McCormick and Paget, Management Consultants, which had been doing a great deal of survey work for academic institutions. I had worked with Morris in Washington on American Library Association and other library problems, and thought he could be extremely useful in this project. I would not call on him to write the report, but to edit what the staff and I had prepared in order to make it more understandable and convincing for the University administration. I knew that it would cost several thousand dollars to engage him and to publish the report. I asked the President for a small grant for the purpose. I readily understood his reluctance to arrange for a special grant; he was being approached from all parts of the University for funds, and I realized that he hesitated to face library problems that, he felt, would inevitably involve large sums of money.

Fortunately the Chairman of the Overseers' Committee to Visit the University Library was Arthur W. Page, whose father, Walter Hines Page, had been our ambassador to Britain during World War I. Arthur Page then held a responsible position as a Director and Advisor to the American Telephone and Telegraph Company. He responded without hesitation and obtained half the required amount from the Carnegie Corporation; the University provided the rest. This enabled us to pay Morris for his work, to have a useful map drawn by an expert, and to have the report printed.

The first draft of the report stated that, in order to catch up with tasks that needed to be done at that time, large sums would have to be added to the College Library's endowment, with additional amounts for the large libraries of departments and graduate professional schools. I took the draft to Edward Reynolds, Financial Vice President of the University, and Dean Bundy, suggesting $10,000,000 for the College Library. This was in spite of the fact that, during my eighteen years at Harvard, an average of $2,000,000 a year had been added to Library endowment, either by gifts directly to the Library or by assignment of unrestricted University funds. When they saw the figure of $10,000,000 for the College Library alone, Reynolds and Bundy said, "Please don't put that in." So, against my better judgment, I reduced the figure for the College Library from $10,000,000 to $5,440,000.

Only a year or two later, I am glad to be able to report, when plans were agreed upon for a campaign to raise $82,500,000 for the Faculty of Arts and Sciences, Paul Buck succeeded in having $15,000,000 of the total, not $5,440,000, designated for the Library. It was hoped that the sum designated would be contributed directly to the Library in the course of the campaign. It was not; but the campaign as a whole reached its goal of $82,500,000, and $15,000,000 of this was assigned to the Library thanks to the influence of Paul Buck.

President Pusey wrote the Foreword to the 131-page *Report on the Harvard University Library: A Study of Present and Prospective Problems*, and I was pleased when I found that he had included in it the following:

> One of Mr. Metcalf's Harvard colleagues has spoken of "the continual excitement of self-dissatisfaction" and indeed it would be a poor builder who is ever completely pleased with the job he has done and with the ability of the work of his creation to stand forever unchanged. Thus, characteristically, Harvard's Librarian on the eve of his retirement restates in unmistakable terms the ever recurring library problems of cost and selection and space — always cost, selection and space.
>
> Mr. Metcalf has set realistic and reasonable goals in his factual report of Harvard's problem. Even he, as one accustomed to turning dissatisfaction into success, would be the first to wonder whether all could be achieved. But they are there to be sought, as Mr. Metcalf has quietly and plainly indicated.

OPTIONS AFTER RETIREMENT

By the time the report was in and I was completing my last year as Director, I had become very much interested in what I was going to do in the years ahead. I knew that only about one fifth of my final salary would be provided by my TIAA annuity, half of which could now be assigned to its sister plan, CREF, where returns were not fixed but would depend on the stock market, plus $52 per month from a special plan that Harvard had arranged a few years earlier. I had been fortunate enough to make some investments that would bring in a larger sum. Elinor had done the same and had inherited some annual income. However, with continued inflation, which I feared and which has turned out to be a major factor, it would evidently be desirable for me to work unless we were to move to a less expensive area, which neither of us wanted to do. I knew I would like to continue to work in the library field; the problem was not only what I would decide on, but what opportunities I would have to find suitable assignments.

Four things appealed to me.

The first, and apparently the simplest, was to spend enough time in my vegetable garden, which was a large one, to provide, by intensive cultivation, freezing, and canning, enough produce to reduce greatly the cost of our food bills. I might have done this if I had not discovered only a year later that I had a "heart," which apparently went back to my serious attack of influenza during World War I. Beginning in 1956, this limited the hard physical labor I could do and reduced my fruit and vegetable production by more than one-half.

A second interest was administrative training for librarians and other academic officers. I had been disappointed at not being able to do anything about this. I had been wondering what could be done about the library part of this program. A statement entitled "The Proposed Training Program for Library Administrators" was included as Supplement E in the *Report on the Harvard University Library*. Lowell Martin, Dean of the Rutgers University Library School, which had begun the year before, wrote to me in the spring of 1955, asking if I would like to come to Rutgers as an adjunct (part-time) professor. He offered me a more or less free hand as to what I would teach. It would be approximately one-third time, and he said I would still have an opportunity to do other library work if I wished. The proposal interested me, and I accepted the position, beginning in the fall of 1955 after our regular vacation in the Catskills.

A third interest was interlibrary cooperation. I believed that more could be done in cooperative storage and acquisition, though I had failed to bring into existence the northeastern interlibrary center that I had struggled with five years before. I felt also that more work was needed on the Farmington Plan and on what we have now come to call consortia. I hoped that I could do work along these lines.

The fourth string to my bow was library building planning. Ever since the opening of the Lamont undergraduate library, I had been called upon from time to time for help in this field. I had been involved also, except for its first meeting, with the informal Cooperative Committee on Library Building Plans that was started by Julian Boyd of Princeton, Charles David of the University of Pennsylvania, and John Burchard of MIT. Each of the three had begun work on planning a new building before Lamont had reached that stage; but I had been fortunate enough to have Lamont completed before the MIT and Princeton buildings were finished, while the one at Pennsylvania, on which David struggled so valiantly for years, was not built until after he retired.

I ventured to talk of building planning with two friends who had been involved in construction for a good many years. The first was Irving Parkhurst, Superintendent of Buildings and Grounds at Harvard, with whom I had worked closely on four buildings, Littauer Center, the New England Deposit Library, Houghton, and Lamont. He encouraged me to go ahead and said he hoped he could work with me. The second was Patrick Murphy, with whom I had become acquainted at Beechknoll in the Catskills, on our annual vacation in Woodland Valley, near Phoenecia, New York. Pat, after completing his academic work at the University of Maine and Cornell, had been a foreman on construction of the New York subway and the Pulaski Bridge over the Hackensack River in New Jersey. During World War II, he had been in charge of some forty thousand men who were building a defense line south of Egypt when it was feared that the Germans would defeat General Montgomery's forces in that country. He was an authority on building foundations, had been called in when the Boston Post Office building started to sink, and had been a consultant on the Dew Line airstrips in northern Canada and at Thule, Greenland. He had now retired except for small construction and contracting jobs in the Catskills. He suggested that Parkhurst and I start a consulting firm on library building planning. Parkhurst and he would do the engineering, cost, and maintenance work, and I would provide the knowledge of library operations and function.

After thinking it over carefully, I decided that, while I did want to do library building consulting, I did not want to be tied down to work with others or to spend months on a single assignment. I thought I could be more useful and that it would be more interesting if I simply tried to provide basic information about the functional side of library planning and construction.

It turned out that I was able to do something in each of the four fields that interested me; but the fourth took an increasing portion of my time as the years went by.

INDEX

Acquisitions, 41-55; cooperative, xvii, 201-202; *see also* Farmington Plan
Ad hoc university committees, 151-159
Adams, Arthur S., 175
Adams, Charles Francis, 234
Adams, Charles M., 259
Adams, Randolph G., 162
Adams, Sherman, 175-176
Adenauer, Konrad, 237
Administrative training, 270
Agassiz, Louis, 231
Agriculture, US Department of, 171-172
Air conditioning, 71, 76-77, 90, 98-99
Air Force Library, 186
Air raids, 151-154
Alarm system, war-time, 154
Allen, Dudley Peter, 183
Allen, Helen B., 23, 25
Allen Memorial Library, 183
American Academy of Arts & Sciences, 245-250
American Antiquarian Society, 12-13, 21
American Board of Commissioners for Foreign Missions, 147-148
American Documentation Institute, 238-239
American Library Association: actions on appointment of Librarian of Congress, 160-165, 174-178; approval of Farmington Plan, 203; catalog rules, 222; charter, 222; International Relations Board, 228; meeting on cooperative enterprises, 201-202; offices held by KDM, 221-223; relations with Evans, 168, 172; incidental references, 1, 206, 238-239, 252
American Library Institute, 223
American Society for Information Science, 238-239
American Trust for the British Library, 220

Ames, James Barr, 52, 219
Anderson, Edwin Hatfield, 135, 221, 224, 261
Andover Theological Seminary, 147
Andover-Harvard Library, 7, 139, 146-148
Andover-Newton Theological School, 147-148
Anker, Jean, 212
Archer, John, 155
Architectural archives (of KDM), iv
Architecture collection (Harvard), 149
Archives, Harvard University, 17-18, 20-21; Massachusetts State, 244-245
Armed Forces Medical Library, 171-172, 181-186, 239
Army libraries, 186-189
Army Medical Library, 171-172, 181-186, 239
Army War College Library, 186, 188-189
Arnold, John Himes, 6
Arnold Arboretum Library, 150
Arts & Sciences, Faculty of, 4-5, 136-141; Library Committee, 138-139
Association of American Universities, 225-227
Association of Graduate Schools, 226
Association of Research Libraries: action on post-war buying, 204; approval of Farmington Plan, 200, 203, 205; grant for European trip, 206; leadership of Library of Congress in, 179; participation of KDM in, 223-225; sponsor of book on library lighting, 114, & of Monticello Conference, 225-228; incidental references, 1, 110, 221, 252
Astor, John Jacob, xvi
Atmospheric conditions, 97-99
Atomic bombs, 116-117
Audubon set, 248
Austria, 208
Awards, 237-241

Baker Library, 7, 98, 144-145
Ballard, James F., 6, 145-146
Barbour, Thomas, 106
Barrows family, 181
Basadre Grohmann, Jorge, 193, 195-196
Beals, Ralph A., 258, 260
Beckman, Margaret, iii, v-vii
Belgium, 207
Bennett, Julia D., 176
Berlin, Charles, 52
Billings, John Shaw, xvii, 182, 240
Biological Laboratories Library, 150
Bishop, William Warner, 160, 227, 238
Black Rock Forest, 150
Blackwell, Basil Henry, 218
Blake, Robert P., xvii, 2, 5, 24, 39, 104
Blegen, Theodore C., 169-170, 254-256
Bliss, Mr. & Mrs. Robert Woods, 150
Blodgett, John W., Jr., 44-46
Boas, Franz, 147
Bock, Arlie V., 197
Bok, Derek C., 233
Bolton, Herbert Eugene, 171
Bombing, 151-154
Bond, William H., 52, 78, 130
Boni, Albert, 12
Boni, William, iii, 12
Bonwit Teller, 214, 247
Book selection: by Arthur Cole, 7, 144; by
    C. T. Copeland, 244; for Lamont, 127-
    128; for US Information Libraries, 228-
    229; for Widener, 41-42
Boorstin, Daniel J., 179-180
Borgeson, Earl C., 143
Boston Athenaeum, 59, 189, 247
Boston College, 59, 64
Boston Medical Library, 5-6, 145-146
Boston Museum of Fine Arts, 152
Boston Public Library, 59, 65, 152, 242-
    243, 247
Boston University, 59, 64
Bostonians, proper, 234-236
Botanical Museum, 150
Bourgeois, Pierre, 210
Bowdoin College, 144-145
Boyd, Julian P., 162, 201-202, 226, 258,
    270
Boylston Hall: building, 80-81, 150; Library,
    8, 26, 42

Branscomb, Harvie, 226
Branscomb, Lewis C., 226-227
Bridge: Minnesota, 262-263; Widener-
    Houghton, 75
Briggs, Walter B., 15-17, 120
Brigham, Clarence S., 12
Brinkler, Bartol, 131
British (Museum) Library, 32, 220
Brown, Charles H., 201, 222, 260
Brown, Henry John, 32
Brown, Ralph, 33
Bryan, Mary M. (Mrs. Kirk), 20
Bryant, Douglas W.: career, 133; earlier
    years, 219-220, 223; Harvard years, 47,
    108-109, 134, 241
Bryant, Rene Kuhn, 241
Buck, Paul: as dean & provost, 85-86, 114,
    137, 138, 141, 265; as Director of Library,
    2, 10, 131, 266-269; *General Education in
    a Free Society*, 83; *Libraries & Universities*,
    128; policies, 79, 87; remembered by
    Edward Windsor, 236-237
Buenaventura, Manuel María, 197-198
Building planning, 270
Building upkeep, financing of, 109
Bundy, McGeorge, 265-266, 268
Bunker, Frank Nathaniel, 74
Burchard, John E., 258, 270
Burr, Allston, 234-235
Burwell, Charles Sidney, 6, 145
Business School, 7, 98, 144-145

Cabot, Godfrey Lowell, 235-236
Cabot Science Library, 139, 142-143, 235
Cadbury, Henry J., 7, 146
Cahoon, Herbert, 125
Cain, Julien, 207
Cairns, Huntington, 155
California, University of, Santa Cruz, 144
Canadiana, 53
Card duplication, 39-40
Carmichael, Leonard, 113
Carnegie Corporation of New York: grants,
    37-38, 60, 68, 128, 185, 205, 214, 225,
    238, 239, 268
Carpenter, Kenneth E., iv
Carrels, 17, 27-28, 121, 261
Case, Charles Z., 20
Casner, Andrew James, 245

Catalog: cards (LC), 172; Department (Widener), 22, 104, 133; rules (ALA) 222; use of, 27
Ceiling heights, 90
Celtic collection, 216
Censorship (World War II), 192
Center for Research Libraries, 36-37, 65, 66-69, 227
Century Publishing Co., 151-152
Cervantes collection, 53
Changing Patterns of Scholarship, 260
Charter, ALA, 222; Harvard, 233
Checkroom, 100
Chicago, Milwaukee, St. Paul, & Pacific Railroad, 250
Children's books, 137
Chiu, Alfred Kaiming, 149
Church history collections, 146-147
Churchill, Sir Winston, 118, 259
Circulation (Widener), 17, 23, 27-28, 120-121
Civilization, record of, 116-117
Claflin, William H., Jr., 57, 60, 84, 152, 156
Clapp, James F., Jr., 85, 87, 89
Clapp, Verner W., 168, 173, 174-175, 260
Clark, Donald T., 127, 132, 144
Clarke, Gilmore D., 25
Classics collection, 63
Classification, medical, 183; Widener, 131; AAAS membership, 249
Clift, David H., 205, 262
Club of Odd Volumes, 10-11, 43, 53
Coatroom, 100
Cocoanut Grove fire, 94, 197-198
Cogswell, Joseph Green, xvi, 4
Cohn, Edwin J., 142, 235
Colby, Charles C., III, 126, 145-146
Cole, Arthur H., 7, 144
College Library, Harvard: administrative status, 136, 138; endowment, 268-269; units added to, 142; *see also* names of constituent units, collections, & functions
Colombia, 196-198
Colonial Society of Massachusetts, 13
Columbia University: Butler Library, 28, 101-102; Law Library, 173; Library School, 120; Library survey, 256-257; Teachers College, 30, 148

Commission on Research Library Problems (proposed), 226
Committee on Scientific Aids to Learning, 112-113
Committees, *ad hoc* University, 151-159
Communism, 228-229
Comstock, Ada Louise, 232
Conant, Grace Thayer Richards, 116, 118-119, 142
Conant, James Bryant: advised on Nieman bequest 35, 111, 161, on preserving record of civilization, 116-117, & on space problems, 24, 30, 71, 141; appointments, 83, 112, 151; approval of extramural activities, 110-111, 206, 252; arrangements during World War II, 114; consulted on Divinity School Library, 146-147, on Lamont Library, 84-85, 87, 117-118, & on Library staff, 15, 18, 19; dinners with, 11, 111; memorial service, 119; relations with Law School, 6, 144, & with Senator McCarthy, 228-229; relationship to KDM by marriage, 114-116, 143; retirement, 118, 232, 265; views on coordinated decentralization, 10, 26, 112, on retirement rules, 264, on tuition, 112, & on University Archives, 18, 21; incidental references, 54, 61, 81, 106, 111, 116, 137, 140
Conant, Ralph W., 254
Condon, Edward U., 171
Coney, Donald, 257, 260
Congregational Library Society, 148
Congress (US): appropriations for Library of Congress, 163, 172-173, 179, & for National Library of Medicine, 182; establishment of NLM, 185-186; hearings on appointment of Librarian of Congress, 165, 176-178; relations with Librarian of Congress, 160, 167, 168, 171, 179-180; Senate action on appointments, 164, 165, 170, 178
Consultation fees, 189-190
Consulting assignments, iii-iv, 91, 110, 198-199, 252-263, 271
Cook, Thomas (firm), 206
Coolidge, Archibald Cary, xvii, 4, 6, 38, 47, 242-243
Coolidge, John Phillips, 155

Cooperation, interlibrary, 60-61, 270
Cooperative Committee on Library Building Plans, 270
Cooperative storage, 20, 56-70, 270
Coordinated decentralization, 9-10, 26, 112
Copeland, Charles Townsend, 243-244
Cordingley, Nora E., 50-51
Cork (floor covering), 89
Corning Glass Co., 74
Corporation (Harvard): approval of Houghton architect, 74, of Lamont architect & site, 84, 118, of New England Deposit Library loan, 60-61, & of space plan, 30; functions & members, 10
Cottrell, G. William, Jr., 126
Council, Library, 41, 136, 138
Council of National Library Associations, 203
Council on Library Resources, 224
Countway, Sanda, 145
Countway Library, 20, 145
Courts, light, 25
Crane, Stephen, 44
Craver, Harrison W., 160-161, 163
Cresap, McCormick, & Paget, 268
Cummings, Martin M., 185
Curley, Walter W., 132
Currier, Margaret, 16, 127, 135
Currier, T. Franklin, 16, 22, 39, 222
Cushing, Harvey W., 239-240
Cutter, Charles Ammi, 60
Cutter, Richard Ammi, 59-60, 222

Daedalus, 249
Dakin, Anna F., 17
Dana-Palmer House, 84, 118
Daniels, Marietta, 198
Dartmouth College, 55
David, Charles W., 224, 226, 257-261, 270
David, Donald K., 144
Davis, Harold Stearns, 60
Davis, Watson, 239
Davis, William Stearns, 60
Dearborn, Walter F., 113
Decentralization, 8-10, 26, 30, 112, 139
Defense Committee, 151-154
Defense, Department of, 184-185
de Kiewiet, Cornelis W., 226
Denmark, 211-212

Dental School Library, 8, 65
Design, Graduate School of, 7-8, 82, 139, 149
Desk (KDM's), 2-4
Deterioration, paper, 97-98
Dewey, Melville, 261, 263
Dickinson, Emily (collection), 52, 78, 219
Dictionary of American Biography, 146
Dioramas, 106, 153
Discarding, 137, 141
Distinguished visitors, 236-237
Divinity School, 7, 139, 146-148
Dix, William S., 226
Doane, Gilbert H., 256
Dodds, Harold W., 226
Doe, Janet, 181
Dolan, Philip H., 125
Donham, Wallace B., 7, 144
Dooley, Dennis A., 59, 243-244
Dormitory libraries, 8, 26-27, 28-29
Dorn, Knut, 211
Dorn, Richard W., 210-211
Dow, Sterling, 139
Downs, Robert B., 204, 226
Drainage, 76, 78, 94-97
Duggan, Laurence, 49
Duggan, Stephen, 49
Dumbarton Oaks, 150
Dunbar, Charles & Katherine, 244
Duplication: by Army libraries, 187; by Law Library, 143; in social sciences, 7; of cards, 39-40; of reserve books, 42-43
Durant, Aldrich, 151, 153
Dykstra, Clarence A., 255-256

Eames, Wilberforce, 18
Eastman, Linda A., 160
Eaton, Marion G., 157
Ebeling, Christoph Daniel, xvi
Economic Botany Library, 150
Education, Graduate School of, 7, 30, 139, 148
Education, (US) Office of, 189
Eggers & Higgins, 184
Eire Society, 216
Eisenhower, Dwight D., 174-176, 178, 188
Eisler, Gerhart, 45
Elevators, 4, 78, 107-108, 140
Eliot, Charles W., 29, 56, 146, 230, 234, 264

Eliot, Samuel Atkins, 230, 234
Elisséeff, Serge, 9, 207
Elliott, William Yandell, 139
Ellsworth, Ralph E., 260
Ely, Richard T., 255
Endowment, College Library, 268-269
Engineering Library, 126
England, 31-34, 206, 216-219
Entrances & exits, 94, 198
Eppelsheimer, Hanns W., 211
Erickson, Alan E., 143
Ernst, William B., 125-126
Esdaile, Arundel, 32
Esterquest, Ralph T., 68
Ethiopia, 237
Europe, trip to, 205-220
Evans, Luther H., 166-174, 179-180, 204, 239, 260
Exhibition cases, 104
Exits & entrances, 94, 198
Eye-fatigue, 113

Faber du Faur, Curt von, 54
Faculty Club, 5
Faculty Library Council, 41, 136, 138
Faculty studies, 17, 28, 121
Fairbank, John King, 9, 149
Fall, John, 67, 205
Farlow Reference Library, 150
Farmington Plan, 200-220, 224, 270
Fast, Howard, 228
Fay, Mr. & Mrs. Sidney B., 46
Fees, consultation, 189-190
Felsted, Leona, 126-127
Feng, Yen-Tsai, 134
Ferguson, Milton J., 164
Financial problems of university libraries (conference), 225-228
Financing Higher Education in the United States, 225
Fine Arts Library, 142, 149, 233
Finley, John H., 83
Fire protection, 78, 92-94
Fischer, Ruth, 45-47
Fiske, Robert F., 39-40
Flagler, Harry Harkness, 43
Fleming, Thomas P., 181
Fletcher, Robert, 182
Flooding, 76, 78, 94-97

Florence (Italy), 122-123
Florida State University, iv
Fogg Museum: directorship, 154-155; Fine Arts Library, 142, 149, 233
Forbes, Edward Waldo, 155
Forced ventilation, 97
Foreign Newspaper Project, 35-37, 69, 111, 161
Forest, Harvard, 150, 153
Four Continents Bookshop, 49
Foxwell, Herbert S., 98
France, 207
Frankfurter, Felix, 162, 163, 164
Freehafer, Edward G., 173
Freeman, Douglas S., 171
Freitag, Doris C., 134
Freitag, Wolfgang M., 134
Freshman Library, 8, 26, 42, 244
Freshman Union, 82
Friedman, Lee M., 51-52
Fulton, Marshall N., 239-240
Fund-raising, 30, 111-112, 268-269
Furcolo, Foster, 244
Furness, Horace H., 257-258
Fussler, Herman H., 32-33

Gallen, John J., 8
Garages, underground, 263
Gardening, 269-270
Garfield, Harry A., 51
Garland, Hamlin, 43-44
Garrison, Fielding H., 182
General Education in a Free Society, 83
George VI, 218
German professors after World War I, 203-204
Germany, 210-211
Gerould, James Thayer, 37, 223
Gerould, Winifred Gregory, 37-38
Gifts & exchanges (Widener), 124
Gilchrist, Donald B., 223-224
Gimbel Brothers, 48
Göttingen, xvi
Goldstein, Fanny, 51
Gookin, Edward L., 3, 22, 66
Gosnell, Charles F., 261
Grace, Charles L., 22-23
Graduate professional school libraries, 5-8; *see also* names of libraries & faculties

Graduate students, 27
Graphic Microfilm Service, 36
Gray, Asa, 231
Gray, Morris (fund), 43
Gray Herbarium Library, 150, 154
Greene, Belle da Costa, 167
Greene, Jerome D., 12, 19, 21
Gregg, Alan, 181, 183, 185
Gregg, Eleanor Barrows, 181
Gregory, Caspar René, 115-116, 239
Gregory, Elinor, *see* Metcalf, Elinor
Gregory, Lucy, 115, 146
Gregory, Winifred, 37-38
Grieder, Elmer, 20
Griswold, Erwin N., 143-144
Grossmann, Maria, 133-134
Grossmann, Walter, 133
Guelph, University of, v-vi
Gund Hall, 149
Gustav Adolf, Crown Prince, 236
Gutenberg Bible, 72-73
Gutman Library, 148

Haakon VII, 241
Hagedorn, Hermann, 50
Haile Selassie I, 237
Hall, Charles Martin, 9, 149
Hall, Herbert F., 248
Halon, 94
Halvorson, Homer, 20
Hamlin, Arthur T., 43, 122-123
Hand, Augustus Noble, 51
Hand, Learned, 51
Hanke, Lewis, 191-198
Haring, Clarence H., 41-42
Harkins, Mr. & Mrs. William G., 192
Harrassowitz, Otto (firm), 210-211
Harris, Seymour E., 137
Harth-Terré, Emilio, 195
Harvard, John, xv
Harvard Black Rock Forest, 150
Harvard College Library, *see* College Library
Harvard Cooperative Society, 245
Harvard Endowment Campaign (1919), 112
Harvard Forest, 150, 153
Harvard Library Bulletin, 126, 128, 252
Harvard Library Club, 112
Harvard LL.D., 240
Harvard men who became librarians, 120-127

Harvard priorities, post-war, 116
Harvard Union: building, 82; Freshman Library, 8, 26, 42, 244
Harvard University: *see* Corporation, Overseers, & names of activities, individual entities, etc.
Harvard University Archives, 17-18, 20-21
Harvard University Library: coordinated decentralization, 9-10, 26, 112; Council, 41, 136, 138; early history, xv; Farmington Plan responsibilities, 203; *Report on*, 267-269; Statistics of holdings, 8-9; *see also* names of collections, constituent libraries, functions, etc.
Harvard University Press, 95, 155-159
Harvard-Yenching, 9, 142, 149-150
Haskins, Susan M., 23, 135
Haviland, Morrison C., 123
Hayes, Richard J., 215-216
Haynes, Robert H., 17
Health, Education, & Welfare, (US) Department of, 189
Heart trouble, 270
Hebraica, 51-52
Heller, Clemens L., 46
Henderson, James W., 165
Henderson, Lawrence J., 115, 142-143
Henniker (N.H.), 175
Hensley, Richard G., 13
Herbarium Building, 150
Hernon, Peter, 254
Hill, Lister, 185
Hill, Sidney B., 176-177
Hilles, Mr. & Mrs. Frederick W., 53
Hilles Library, 142, 232
Ho-Chi-Minh, 46
Hoepli, Ulrico, 209
Hofer, Philip: appointment, 19; honorary degree, 22; Houghton Library planning, 75-76; incidental references, 11, 52, 78, 127
Hollis, Thomas, xv
Holmes, Henry W., 7, 63
Holt, Anna C., 6, 145
Honoraria, 110, 252
Honors, 237-241
Høst, Andr. Fred., & Søn (firm), 212
Houghton, Arthur A., Jr., 53, 73-75, 79
Houghton Library, 23, 52, 71-79, 154

House libraries, 8, 26-27, 28-29
Hoving, Johannes, 214
Howells, William Dean (collection), 12, 43-44
Howells family, 44
Hull, Cordell, 239
Humidity, 98-99
Humphry, James, III, 124-125
Humphry, John, 124, 125
Hurricanes, 94-95
Hutchins, Robert M., 66-67
Hutchins, William J., 66-67
Hyde, Donald F. & Mary, 79
Hyde Park Library, 162

IBM, 40, 121
Illinois, University of, 225, 253-254
Illuminating Engineering Society, 113
Information libraries, US, 228-229
Inspection desk, 100, 259
Institute of Geographical Exploration, 96, 150
Interlibrary cooperation, 60-61, 270
International Documentation Institute, 31-33, 239
Inventory, 28, 129
Ireland, 215-216
Ishimoto, Carol F., 132-133
Italy, 209

Jackson, William A.: acquisitions, 52, 78; appointment, 18-19; honorary degree, 22; on Hyde Park Library, 161-162; recruitment of staff, 130, 135; relations with Arthur Houghton & Houghton Library building, 73-76; war-time evacuation planning, 154; incidental references, 11, 23, 41, 82, 120, 127, 237, 241, 245, 248, 260
Jakeman, Carolyn E., 23
James, Eldon R., 6, 143
Jaszi, Oscar, 46
Jenner, William E., 172, 176
Jesus, 148
Jewett, Sarah Orne, 3
Joeckel, Carleton B., 166
Johnson, Margaret L., 204
Jones, Frank N., 123, 124, 126-127, 128
Jones, Harold W., 181-182, 185, 239

Jones, John Price, 111-112
Jones, Leona, 126-127
Jordan, Wilbur K., 206
Judaica, 51-52

Keating, John S., S.J., 62
Keats, John (collection), 53, 73, 75
Kellar, Herbert A., 201
Keller, Carl T., 11, 53
Kennan, George, 249
Kennedy, John F., 185
Keogh, Andrew, 227
Keough, Francis P., 125
Keppel, Frederick P., 38, 60-61
Kesavan, Bellary S., 99
Kilgour, Frederick G., 41, 120-122, 127, 129, 240
King, Barbara, 228
King, Ernest J., 189
Kipp, Laurence J., 132
Kirk, Norman T., 183, 239
Kirkland, John T., xvi
Kittredge, George Lyman, 11
Knollenberg, Bernhard, 167, 202

Lamb, W. Kaye, 240
Lamont, Thomas W., 53, 82-84, 88-89, 234-235
Lamont Library: architectural style, 234-235; first librarian, 130; genesis & construction, 80-91; selection of books for, 127-128, 139; site, 117-118; subsequent effects, 225, 240, 270; use by women, 86, 87, 232
Landis, James M., 143
Lane, William Coolidge, xvii, 4, 102
Lang, Herbert, & Cie (firm), 210
Langdell Hall, 96
Langer, William L., 44, 121
Langmead, Stephen, v
Latin America, 191-199
Law School Library, 6-7, 96, 98, 143-144, 154
Lawrence Hall, 148
Lee, Roger I., 145
Leland, Waldo G., 169-170, 175
Lewis, Jerome T., 130
Lewis, Wilmarth S.: at dinner on Hyde Park Library, 161-162; host for Farm-

ington meeting, 202; on Library of Congress Planning Committee, 171; Peruvian trip, 191-196, 198; sought Lippmann papers, 53-54
Librarians, administrative training for, 270
Libraries, financial problems of university (conference), 225-228
Library Council (Harvard), 41, 136, 138
Library Lighting, 114
Library of Congress: appointment of librarians, 160-165, 169-170, 174-178, 180; appropriations, 160, 163, 172-173, 179; duties & qualifications of librarians, 162-163, 168-169, 177-180; foreign acquisitions, 200-205; Librarian's Council, 167, 170, 202; Madison building, 178, 189-190; medical classification, 183; Mission to Europe, 64, 200, 203-205; Planning Committee, 170-172, 176; reorganization, 166-167; salary, 190; *see also* Boorstin, Evans, MacLeish, Mumford, Putnam
Liebaers, Herman, 207
Light courts, 25
Lighting: Baker Library, 145; cold cathode, 77, 104, 113; fluorescent *vs.* incandescent, 114; intensities, 113-114; Lamont, 90; Widener, 101-105
Linda Hall Library, 248, 250-251
Lindbergh, Charles A., 237
Lingel, Robert, 48
Lippmann, Walter, 53-54
Littauer Library, 7, 16, 20, 142
Little, David M., 118
Loeb Music Library, 142
Loring, Augustus Peabody, Sr., 11
Lovett, Robert W., 21, 122, 127
Lowell, Abbott Lawrence: as Harvard president, xvii, 10, 76, 118, 264; personal relations with KDM, 242-243
Lowell, Amy, 53, 76, 79
Lowes, John Livingston, 11
Lowes, John W., 15, 18-19
Lucas, E. Louise, 125, 149
Luxemburg, Rosa, 45
Lydenberg, Harry Miller: honorary degrees, 239, 240; Jackson recommended by, 18; Librarian of Congress appointments, 160-161, 163, 165, 169-170; on LC Mis-

sion, 205, 223; organizer of Mexico City library, 229; support for *Union List of Serials*, 38; surveys with KDM, 246, 258; tribute by KDM, 221; incidental references, xvii, 97, 155, 167, 173, 181, 203, 223, 224, 227, 259, 260

McBee-Keysort, 121
McBride, George M., 193
McCarthy, Joseph R., 228-229
McCombs, Charles F., 31, 257
McCorison, Marcus A., 12
McDiarmid, Errett W., 254, 262-263
Macdonald, Angus, 68, 108
McFarland, Carl, 171
MacLeish, Archibald: appointment by Roosevelt, 162-165; as Librarian of Congress, 165-169, 172-173, 179, 180, 190, 267; at Harvard, 33, 111, 140-141, 161; on Hyde Park Library, 162; role in Farmington Plan, 201-204; incidental references, 49, 170, 174, 191, 256
McNarney, Joseph T., 186
McNiff, Philip J., 129-130, 134
Maggs, 72
Mahady, Charles A., 102
Malone, Dumas, 155-156
Manuscripts, 43-44
Map Room, 17, 20
Marine Biological Library, 247
Marsh, Daniel L., 243-244
Marshall, John, 32
Marshall, Mary Louise, 181
Martin, Louis E., 3, 132
Martin, Lowell A., 270
Masefield, John (collection), 53
Massachusetts: Great & General Court, 222
Massachusetts Historical Society, 12, 231
Massachusetts Institute of Technology, 30, 59, 64, 247
Massachusetts State Archives, 244-245
Massachusetts State Library, 59, 65, 243-245
Mead, William R., 44
Medical classification, 183
Medical School Library, 5-6, 8, 20, 145-146, 154
Memorial Church, 232

Memorial Hall, 24-25
Mendenhall, Thomas C., II, 204
Men's Library Club, 13
Metcalf, Antoinette Brigham Putman, 17, 235
Metcalf, Elinor (Gregory): courted & married by KDM, 44, 62, 114-116; family, 115-116, 143, 146, 239; first acquaintance with KDM, 13; inheritance & investments, 269; purchase of sweater, 175-176; social life (luncheons & dinners), 44, 46, 111, 115, 118, 157, 192, 240-241, 260; travel to Europe, 200, 206-219, to North Carolina, 259, to western states, 250; vacations, 154, 266; incidental references, iv, 95, 97, 119, 189, 191, 198, 234-235, 243
Metcalf, Harry, 126
Metcalf, Isaac Stevens (brother of KDM), 181, 183; (father of KDM), 144, 175
Metcalf, Margaret, *see* Small, Margaret
Metcalf, Marion, 66, 152
Metcalf, Martha Gerrish: Belmont & Cambridge months, 1, 13, 111; death, 14, 31, 33, 114, 238
Metcalf, Nelson, 66-67
Metcalf, William Gerrish, 14, 32
Metcalf (name), 217-218
Metcalfe, John, 212
Microfilm: eye-fatigue from, 113; for newspapers, 35-37, 69, 111, 161; for saving space, 24; reading machine, 112-113; to preserve record of civilization, 116-117
Midwest Inter-Library Center, 36-37, 65, 66-69, 227
Mier, Kathryn P., 171
Milam, Carl H.: assistants, 127, 223; on MacLeish appointment, 164; visit to, 250; incidental references, 181, 227, 248
Milczewski, Marion A., 223
Miller, Robert A., 226-227
Millet, John D., 225, 227
Minnesota, University of, 262-263
Minot, George R., 6
Mohrhardt, Foster E., 189
Montague, Gilbert H., 52
Montgomery, Hugh, 123
Monticello Conference, 225-228, 266
Moody, Roland H., 129

Morey, Lloyd, 226-227
Morgan, Edmund M., 143
Morgan, Henry S., 82
Morison, Samuel Eliot, 4, 137, 162, 243, 245
Morris, Thomas D., 268
Morse, William Inglis, 53
Mumford, L. Quincy: appointment & service as Librarian of Congress, 172, 173-179, 189; earlier work at LC, 166-167; surveys, 181, 256
Munich crisis, 33
Munn, Ralph, 165, 256
Munthe, Wilhelm, 214, 240-241
Murphy, Patrick, 271
Museum of Comparative Zoology: glass flowers, 152; Library, 150, 154
Museum of Science (Boston), 247, 249
Myres, John Nowell Linton, 240

National Agricultural Library, 171-172
National Institutes of Health, 184
National Library of Medicine, 171-172, 181-186, 239
National Union Catalog, 201-202, 203, 260
Navy libraries, 189
Netherlands, 207
New England College, 175
New England Deposit Library, 56-66, 114, 153, 202
New England Museum of Natural History, 247, 249
New York Public Library: American Board collection, 147; book appropriations, 242; cataloging, 222; Circulation Center, 99; Farmington Plan Office, 205; guards, 100; history, xvi; lighting, 101; retirement plan, 264; staff, 134-135; storage, 56; women's studies collection, 232; work (by KDM) at, 1, 2
New York State Library, 261-262
Newhall, Jannette E., 7, 146
Newspapers, filming of, 35-37, 69, 111, 161
Nieman, Agnes Elizabeth Guenther Wahl, 161
Nieman Fund, 35-36, 111, 161
Nijhoff, Wouter, 207
Nordbeck, Theodore, 122
North Carolina, University of, 156-157

North Carolina Library Association, 259
North Carolina Women's College, 99
Northeastern Regional Library, 69-70, 270
Northeastern University, 59
Norway, 214-215, 241
Norweb, Raymond H., 193-194
Notestein, Wallace, 232
Noyes, Penelope, 157

Oberlin College: honorary degree, 164, 238; Library, 1, 94, 100, 101, 238, 261
Oberlin high school class, 148
O'Connell, Thomas F., 133
O'Connor & Kilham, 184
Office (in Widener), 2-4
Office International de Librairie, 207
Office of Strategic Services, 38, 46, 121, 122, 204
Ohio College Library Center, 121-122
On-Line Computer Library Center, 121-122
Open-shelf policy, 79
Order Department (Widener), 22
Orne, Jerrold, 267
Osborn, Andrew D.: "The Crisis in Cataloging," 222-223; paper on National Union Catalog, 260; recruited by KDM, 19; staff members recommended by, 19, 38; selection for Deposit Library, 64; surveys, 144, 145, 166, 181, 183, 253, 261; incidental references, 23, 40, 41, 104, 120, 131, 244
Overseers: Library Visiting Committee, 18-19, 73-74, 230

Packard, Frederick C., 43
Pacl, Florence, iv
Page, Arthur W., 268
Palmer, Foster M., 19-20, 41, 121, 127
Panama, 192-193
Paper deterioration, 97-98
Parker, Franklin E., Jr., 82
Parkhurst, Irving, 151, 153, 270-271
Parks, Mercedes Gallagher de, 195
Parsons, Maisie E., 65
Patterson, Edwin F., 33
Patterson, Robert P., 239
Pautzsch, Richard O., 131
Peabody Museum: Tozzer Library, 142

Peiss, Reuben, 38-39, 41, 120, 204, 205
Pennsylvania, University of, 26, 257-261
Pension, 264, 269
Pentagon, 186-189
Pepper, George W., 260
Perlstein, Israel, 47-49
Perry, Bliss, 233
Perry, William G., 74, 76-77
Perry, Shaw, & Hepburn, 74
Peru, 191-198
Petersham, 153
Pforzheimer, Carl H., 18
Phillips, James Duncan & Stephen W., 11
Photostat, 39
Planning Academic and Research Library Buildings, v, 114, 134, 159
Plummer, Mary Wright, 238
Poole, Frazer G., 190
Porter, Lucy Bryant Wallace, 233
Potter, Alfred Claghorn, xvii, 3
Powell, Benjamin E., 178-179
Powers, Helen, 2, 82, 134, 219
Prado Heudebert, Mariano I., 195
Prado Ugarteche, Manuel, 193
Presidential libraries, 162
President's house (Harvard), 82, 118
Press, Harvard University, 95, 155-159
Priorities, post-war, 116
Problems and Prospects of the Research Library, 227
Program of Instruction in Library Schools, 253-254
Proper Bostonians, 234-236
Public Administration, School of, 7, 16, 20, 142
Public services (Widener), 16-17, 23, 140-141
Pulling, Arthur C., 6-7, 129, 143
Pusey, Nathan Marsh, vii, 133, 232-233, 265-266, 268-269
Pusey Library, 21, 51, 79, 139
Putnam, Herbert: appraisal of, 168-169; on qualifications of Librarian of Congress, 179-180; retirement, 160, 162, 165-166; salary, 190

Radcliffe College, 86-87, 231-232
Random Recollections of an Anachronism, iii
Raney, M. Llewellyn, 201

Rare Books Department (Widener), 18-19, 23, 26, 29, 73-74, 79; *see also* Houghton Library

Readex, iii, 21

Reading and Visual Fatigue, 113

Reading machines, microfilm, 112-113

Record of civilization, 116-117

Recordak Corporation, 36

Reference desk & services, 16-17, 106

Regional libraries, copyright-deposit, 70

Reischauer, Edwin, 9, 149

Relics of the College, 233

Report on the Harvard University Library, vii, 267-269

Republican Party, 228

Reserve books, 28, 42-43

Retirement, 264-271

Reynolds, Alice, 17

Reynolds, Edward, 158, 268

Rice, Paul North, 166-167, 173, 224, 258

Rice, Warner G., 260

Richards, Grace Stuart (Thayer), 115, 116

Richards, Theodore W., 81, 115, 142-143

Richardson, Elliot L., 174

Richardson, William King, 11, 52-53, 75

Roback, Abraham A., 51

Robinson, Fred Norris, 216

Robinson Hall, 149

Rockefeller Foundation: grants, 31, 35, 68, 161, 182-183, 225, 239

Rogers, Frank B., 185

Rogers, Rutherford D., 132

Rohlf, Robert H., 189-190

Roosevelt, Franklin D., 160-164, 167, 169-170, 243

Roosevelt, Theodore, 49-51

Roosevelt Memorial Association, 50-51

Root, Azariah Smith, 1, 124, 221, 238

Root, Mrs. Francis, 192

Rosenbach, A. S. W., 260

Rosenwald, Lessing J., 47-48, 171

Rush, Charles E., 157

Russell, John Dale, 253

Russian Research Center, 47

Rutgers University, 270

Sachs, Paul J., 30, 155, 249

St. John, Francis R., 166, 185

Salaries, 135, 189-190

Saltonstall, Leverett, 174-175

Sandbergs Bokhandel, 213

Saturday Review of Literature, 192

Scaife, Roger L., 156

Schlesinger Library, 232

Science library, 139, 142-143, 235

Scotland, 215

Scott, Donald, 151-154, 156

Sears, Minnie E., 222

Seating, 91, 261; *see also* Stalls

Selection, book, *see* Book selection

Shapley, Harlow, 11, 245-246

Shattuck, Henry Lee, 10, 114

Shaw, Gertrude M., 22, 42, 135

Shaw, Ralph R., 171, 189

Shea, John E., 2, 27-28

Sheldon, Edward Brewster, 53

Sheldon, Edward Wright, 53

Shelving, compact, 68, 99, 108; second-hand, 250

Shepard, Marietta Daniels, 198

Shepley, Ethan A. H., 227

Shepley, Henry R.: Lamont Library, 81-85, 87-90; New England Deposit Library, 57-58; Widener lighting, 103; Widener replacement, 25

Shipman, Joseph C., 248

Shipton, Clifford K., 12, 20-22, 41, 127

Shop Club, 11-12, 43, 113

Shores, Louis, 164

Sibley, John Langdon, xvi, 4, 17-18, 20, 230-231

Slavic collection, 47-49

Small, Margaret (Metcalf), 14, 34-35, 114, 132, 218, 244

Small, Maxwell, 34, 145, 218, 244

Smith, Hiawatha H., 130, 131

Smith College, 232

Smoking, 86

Snead Stack Corporation, 68, 93, 108

Southern California, University of, 247

Soviet publications, 47-49

Space problems, 24-30, 118, 139; *see also* Storage

Spencer Lens Reading Machine, 112-113

Sperry, Willard L., 146

Stacks: dimensions & lighting, 104-105, 108; falling, 261-262; fire protection, 92-94; "reading" or inventory, 28, 129; underground, 30

Staff, 4, 15-23, 120-135
Stagg, Amos Alonzo, 66
Stairs (Widener), 107
Stairways, circular, 77
Stalin, 44-45
Stalls, 17, 27-28, 121, 261
Stanford, Edward B., 262
Starck, Taylor, 42
Statutes (Harvard), 136, 138
Stefansson, Vihjalmur, 54-55
Stevens, David H., 35
Stevens & Brown, 32-33
Stillman, Ernest G., 150, 153
Stoddard, Solomon, 134
Storage, cooperative, 29, 56-70, 270 (*see also* New England Deposit Library); underground, 118, 139
Storm drain, 95
Students, service to, 26-27; separate library for, 28-29, 255; *see also* Lamont Library
Studies, faculty, 17, 28, 121
Stummvoll, Josef, 208
Stuyvesant, Peter, 245
Successor, selection of, 265-267
Sullivan, Gertrude M., 22, 41-42, 135
Sullivan, Margaret A., 161
Surgeon General's Library, 171-172, 181-186, 239
Sutherland, Arthur E., 228-229
Swank, Raynard C., 226-227
Sweden, 212-214
Sweeney, John L., 129
Switzerland, 207-210

Tauber, Maurice F., 256
Tello Rojas, Julio César, 194-195
Temperature, 77, 97-99
Textbook collection, 30, 63, 148
Thayer, Joseph Henry, 115-116, 146, 176
Thayer, Lucy, 115, 146
Thefts, 72-73, 100-101, 244-245
Thompson, C. Seymour, 258
Thompson, Willard, 103
Thorndike, Israel, xvi
Thursday Evening Club, 11-12, 43
Thwaites, Reuben Gold, 255
Ticknor, George, xv-xvi
Toilets, 140
Tonkery, Thomas Daniel, 185

Toronto, University of, 240
Tozzer, Alfred Marston, 136
Tozzer Library, 142
Training for librarians, 270
Travel, 14, 111, 175, 250, 259; *see also* names of countries
Trotsky, Leon, 44-45
Truman, Harry S, 170
Tucker, Mildred M., 22
Tufts University, 59, 64
Tuition, 112
Turner, Frederick Jackson, 255
Turnstiles, 100
Twain, Mark, 43

Ulveling, Ralph A., 177
Umbrellas, 100
Undergraduates, *see* Students
UNESCO, 172-173
Union, *see* Harvard Union
Union Catalog, Harvard, 37; National, 201; 202, 203, 260
Union List of Serials, 37-38
United States, *see* Congress, Information libraries, & names of libraries & other entities
University Archives, 17-18, 20-21
University committees, 151-159
University libraries, financial problems of, 225-228
University Library, *see* Harvard University Library
University Press, 95, 155-159

Vacations, 154, 191, 206, 217, 266
Vail, Robert W. G., 50, 72, 261
Vaillant, George C., 193-194
Vandalism, 100-101
van Heijenoort, Jean, 45
Van Lennep, William B., 125
Vann, Sarah K., 254
Ventilation, forced, 97
Victory Book Campaign, 61-62
Vicuña, 175-176
Viets, Henry R., 6, 145
Visitors, distinguished, 236-237
Vitz, Carl, 169-170
Vollbehr, Otto Heinrich Friedrich, 47-48

Walpole, Horace, 161-162, 195
Walsh, James E., 63, 131
Walton, Clarence E., 3-4, 7, 15, 20, 42, 43, 72, 231
War Defense Committee, 151-154
Ward, Samuel, xvi
Warehouses, 57
Warren, Charles, 18-19, 73-74
Warren Hastings Manor, 99
Washburn, Bradford, 247, 249
Water hazards, 76, 78, 94-97
Weber, David C., 131-132
Weeding, 137, 141
Wellesley College, 59
Wells, Herman B., 227
West, Stanley L., 192
White, Carl M., 253, 256, 260
Whitehead, Alfred North, 5, 137
Whitehill, Walter Muir, 189
Widener, Eleanor Elkins, 25
Widener collection & Memorial Rooms, 71, 72, 73
Widener family, 72, 75
Widener Library: building problems & changes, 92-109, 139-141; dedication, 242; replacement (possibility), 25-26; transfer of books from, 30; *see also* names of collections, departments, facilities, & functions
Williams, Edwin E.: career, 127-128; classification for LC Mission, 205; *Farmington Plan Handbook*, 200; Preface, iii-iv; selection for Lamont, 126, 127-128;

work for ARL on Farmington Plan, 224; work on *Report on the Harvard University Library*, 267-268; works edited, 172, 202, 227; incidental references, 138, 165, 223
Williams, Gordon R., 68-69
Williamsburg blue, 77
Williamson, Charles C., 123, 173, 223, 227, 254, 256, 262
Wilson, Louis Round, 157, 160, 257, 260
Wilson, Thomas J., 156-159, 229
Windsor, Edward, 236-237
Winship, George Parker, 15, 52
Winsor, Justin, xvi-xvii, 3, 4, 157, 240
Wisconsin: State Historical Society & University Library, 254-256
Wolfson, Harry A., 51
Women: in librarianship, 135; use of Harvard libraries, 86, 87, 232
Women's studies, 232
Woodberry Poetry Room, 43, 129
Woods Hole, 247
Work, Robert L., 65, 129
Wright, Benjamin F., 87
Wright, Louis, 260
Wright, Walter L., 171
Wright, Walter W., 123-124
Wright, Wyllis E., 185
Writing, 110, 252
Wyer, James I., 247
Wyer, Malcolm G., 247-248

Yale University, 54, 121, 132, 204, 239-240